HANG FIRE
COOKBOOK

RECIPES & ADVENTURES IN AMERICAN BBQ

SAMANTHA EVANS & SHAUNA GUINN

PHOTOGRAPHY BY
PAUL WINCH-FURNESS

Hardie Grant
QUADRILLE

This book is a huge thank you to each and every person that's supported us by coming to our events and eaten our barbecue. Quite simply, this book wouldn't exist without your support and loyalty. We even invented a word to describe you, 'Custo-friends', customers who invariably become our pals by the time they've placed their order. It always feels like feeding a big, extended family. Now, hand us your plate, who's for seconds?

#BBQlove

Sam & Shauna

CONTENTS

INTRODUCTION	6
ROAD TRIP: MAP	8
GETTING STARTED	11
YOUR FIRST SMOKER	12
GRILLING GUIDE	18
HOW TO USE SMOKING WOOD & CHARCOAL	20
RUBS, SAUCES & EXTRA FLAVOURS	24
MEAT	52
SIDES, PICKLES & BUNS	142
DRINKS & DESSERTS	198
INDEX	220
ACKNOWLEDGEMENTS	223

BLOOD, SWEAT AND BBQ SAUCE

We didn't grow up slathering whole hogs with vinegar or operating a pulley pit in the Texas wilds. We ate burnt burgers from disposable grills and our idea of saucing meals was solely reserved to ketchup. So what can a couple of Celtic girls tell you about American-style slow and low barbecue that you haven't already read or watched on TV? Three years ago, we made a dramatic decision to quit our long-standing careers in London and embark on a six-month road trip of a lifetime across America, eating at every BBQ joint we could afford, and becoming increasingly possessed by the spirit of smoke and fire with every meaty mouthful. This is the story of our metamorphosis from occasional backyard barbecuers to an award-winning, smokin' duo with an obsession with fire and meat.

We fell in love with the Southern States and their attitude to food and gatherings. Southern hospitality really is the ninth wonder of the world. And as we travelled around we learnt that there is so much more to barbecue than just the grill. Barbecue is a serious business.

We witnessed a heated argument about 'the best' barbecue between a Texan and North Carolinian – where the Texan had his hand on his holster the whole time. In the US, barbecue is defined by its State variations and we wanted it all: mustard and vinegar whole hog in the Carolinas, sweet and saucy burnt ends in Missouri, long horn beef in Texas, and dry rub ribs in Tennessee. As a guy from Arkansas at one BBQ competition said to us, 'So you're one of these bar-bee-cue fence-sitters, huh?'. And I guess we are.

We were so inspired by that taste of the South that we couldn't go back to our old lives when we returned to the UK. For us, and for so many others, barbecue has become a lifestyle choice. Our recipes may not be 100 per cent faithful to how the BBQ legends smoke a hunk of meat, but they are our take on what those inspirational pit masters taught us (and often the result of our own trial and error!).

The Southern States may be the birthplace of 'slow and low' but at last this style of barbecue has drifted across the Atlantic, smoldering into life in British back gardens and beyond. BBQ is now so popular that thousands of us eat at chains of barbecue restaurants up and down the country and we even hold KCBS (Kansas City Barbeque Society) sanctioned BBQ competitions. US-style barbecue is flooding the UK like a 'meatwave'.

After arriving home in the UK we knew we had to share what we had discovered immediately. In fact, we'd decided on the name 'Hang Fire' and had even designed the logo while in Nashville – we weren't messing around. Our first kitchen takeover was a weekly pop-up in a back-street pub, The Canadian, in Cardiff. We fed 10 people the first week, 40 the following week, and by the next month we were averaging 100 a night. Our dream was coming true – but that's not to say it was all a breeze. Within our first couple of months, we dealt with grease fires in the smoker, badly smoked meat, burns up and down our arms and a trip or two to A&E. Sounds like hell? It was… but we loved every minute of it.

That was back in 2013. Since then we've sold over 22,000 plates of barbecue in 2 years with just 2 people (2 is the magic number here!). We are on first-name terms with almost all the people who visit us, and many of our customer/friends have been eating our barbecue since The Canadian days. They are truly amazing.

As with any cookbook, our recipes are simply suggestions: this is not the gospel according to Hang Fire, and so you have our blessing to tweak any recipe you like to your own finger-lickin' satisfaction. There will be grilling, plenty of smoking, and we may even suggest you cook a dish or two in the oven.

So enjoy our book, build your own smoker, have fun with the recipes and create your unique style of slow and low barbecue.

INTRODUCTION 7

CALIFORNIA TO THE CAROLINAS
& A BIT IN BETWEEN

START

1. LOS ANGELES CALIFORNIA
2. SAN FRANCISCO CALIFORNIA
3. PFEIFFER BIG SUR STATE PARK CALIFORNIA & JULIA PFEIFFER BURNS STATE PARK CALIFORNIA
4. BIG BASIN REDWOODS STATE PARK CALIFORNIA
5. JACKSON STATE FOREST CALIFORNIA
6. REDWOOD NATIONAL AND STATE PARK CALIFORNIA
7. WHISKEYTOWN NATIONAL RECREATIONAL AREA CALIFORNIA
8. LAKE TAHOE CALIFORNIA
9. YOSEMITE NATIONAL PARK CALIFORNIA
10. SEQUOIA STATE PARK CALIFORNIA
11. SAN BERNADINO STATE PARK CALIFORNIA
12. VALLEY OF FIRE STATE PARK NEVADA
13. ZION NATIONAL PARK UTAH
14. BRYCE CANYON NATIONAL PARK UTAH
15. CANYON LANDS NATIONAL PARK UTAH
16. GOBLIN VALLEY STATE PARK UTAH
17. ROCKY MOUNTAIN NATIONAL PARK COLORADO
18. ROOSEVELT NATIONAL FOREST COLORADO
19. LORY STATE PARK COLORADO
20. WHITE RIVER NATIONAL FOREST COLORADO
21. NASHVILLE TENNESSEE
22. FRANKLIN TENNESSEE
23. HENDERSONVILLE SOUTH CAROLINA BACK TO FRANKLIN TENNESSEE
24. ASHEVILLE NORTH CAROLINA VIA NORTH GEORGIA
25. CHATTANOOGA VIA HIGHWAY 24 AND CHATTAHOOCHEE PARK TENNESSEE
26. ELLIJAY GEORGIA THEN BACK AND FORTH BETWEEN HENDERSONVILLE AND ASHEVILLE, THEN BACK TO FRANKLIN TENNESSEE
27. COVINGTON TENNESSEE BACK TO FRANKLIN TENNESSEE
28. MEMPHIS TENNESSEE
29. PONCHATOULA LOUISIANA
30. NEW ORLEANS LOUISIANA
31. BIRMINGHAM ALABAMA
32. DECATUR ALABAMA BACK TO FRANKLIN TENNESSEE
33. OWENSBORO KENTUCKY BACK TO FRANKLIN TENNESSEE
34. ST LOUIS MISSOURI
35. KANSAS CITY KANSAS
36. DALLAS TEXAS
37. TEMPLE TEXAS
38. TAYLOR TEXAS
39. ELGIN TEXAS
40. AUSTIN TEXAS
41. DRIFTWOOD TEXAS
42. LOCKHART TEXAS
43. LUVING TEXAS
44. HOUSTON TEXAS
45. LITTLE ROCK ARKANSAS THEN BACK TO MEMPHIS TENNESSEE THEN BACK TO FRANKLIN TENNESSEE

FINISH

8 ROAD MAP

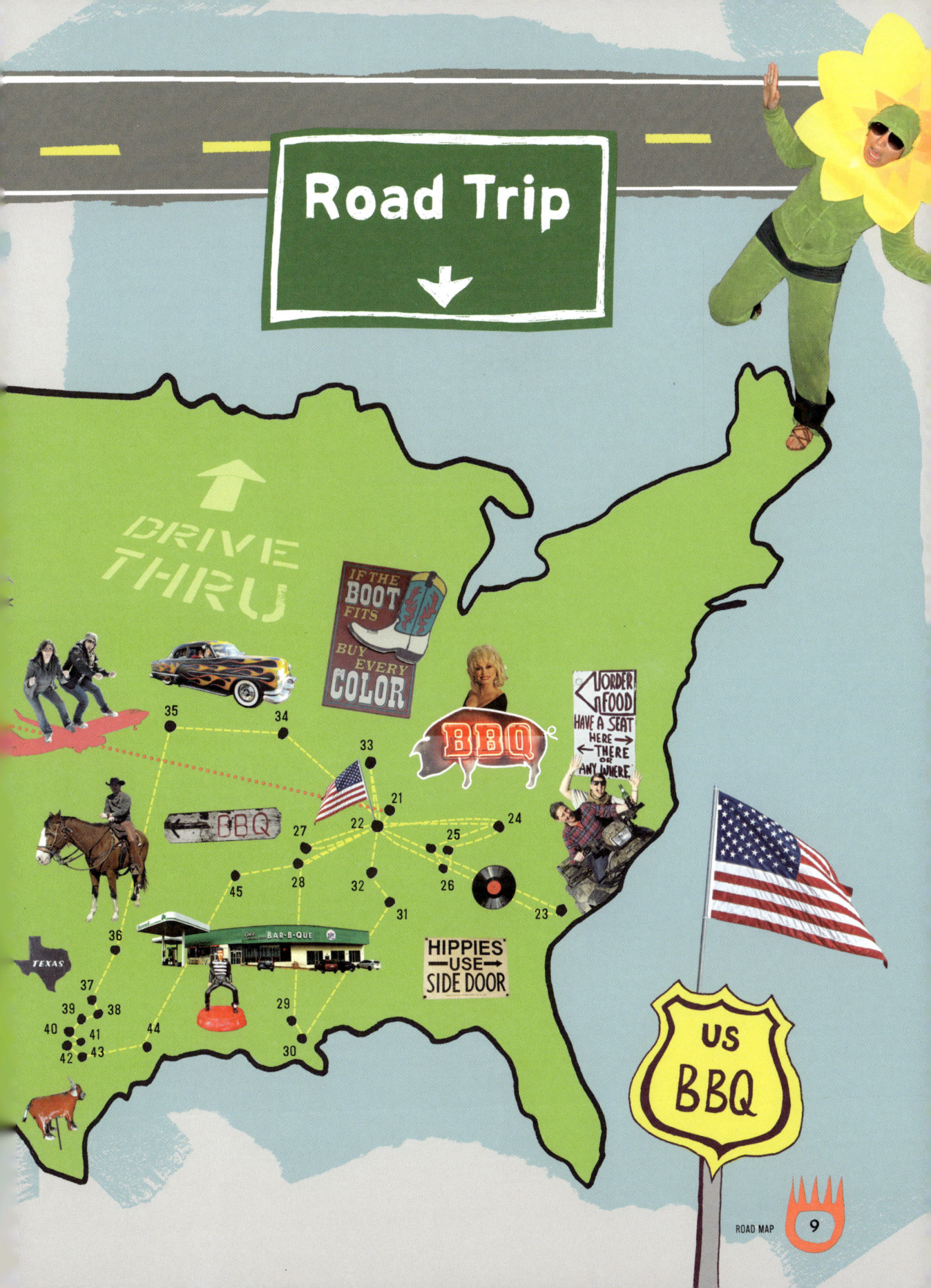

GETTING STARTED

Like any other obsessive hobby, you can totally 'geek out' and go to town buying all sorts of gadgets, from airflow control systems to high-end thermometers that record both meat, pit and outside air temperatures, and specialised wire racking to cleaning tools. The prices range from affordable to top dollar. All of these gadgets will probably improve the outcome of your barbecue if used correctly, but none of these gadgets will actually teach you the art of slow and low smoking. This, my friends, comes with practice.

But getting back to basics, you can create amazing barbecue with a simple grill as long as it has a lid. You'll also need some essential tools, a great piece of meat, quality wood and charcoal, and a little patience.

 Heat proof gloves

 Instant-read thermometer

 Chimney starter

 Flexible boning knife

 'Flamers' fire lighters

 Shaker for rubs

 Hardwood lumpwood charcoal

 Silicone basting brush

 Hardwood logs

 Bear claws

 Cook's knife

 Long-handled tongs

 Knife sharpener

YOUR FIRST SMOKER

As slow and low cooking gains popularity in the UK, you can now easily buy a grill or smoker online or even at some supermarkets. You can pretty much turn any regular grill with a lid into a smoker. But what if you want to customise or make a cooker that fits your style?

WHY BUILD YOUR OWN SMOKER

We have always thought of buying your first smoker as similar to a learner buying a new guitar. You can either buy any old thing as cheap as possible, practise loads and if you like playing (smoking) buy a decent one, or you could just go out and buy the most expensive one you can afford, which will generally be much more rewarding to use. However, unlike guitars, it's relatively easy to build your own smoker – so it makes sense to give it a go.

We have modified and reengineered quite a few different smokers, ranging from upright drum smokers to fashioning a cold smoker out of an old filing cabinet. We have bought smokers from America and the UK. But we thought it was about time we took inspiration from our barbecue heroes and built our own from scratch. There's nothing quite like the feeling of accomplishment when you build your own pit. Building a smoker may take a little bit longer than buying one, but chances are you will learn new skills along the way, save yourself a bunch of money and you'll be able to tailor the pit exactly to your own requirements.

First things first: you'll need to decide what the right smoker is for you. How often will you use it? How much meat do you want to smoke? How transportable does it need to be? Where will you store it when it's not being used? How much money do you have to spend? Are you a backyard barbecuer or do you fancy yourself as a competition team? Once you've answered these questions, you'll probably get a feel for which type of smoker is best for you.

DIFFERENT TYPES OF SMOKER

In America these are what you might call a UDS – Ugly Drum Smoker. You can easily make a smoker out of a 45-gallon drum and the components are reasonably cheap and easy to get hold of. The walls are usually only 1–2mm thick so may struggle to hold temperature over a long period of time.

MOST IMPORTANT THING TO CONSIDER WHEN BUILDING A SMOKER:

AIRFLOW – how quickly and easily the smoke moves around the chamber. It's also important to understand how airflow changes depending on the temperature. Smokers generally draw cold air in: it passes through a very hot fire, and then moves around the meat before eventually disappearing into the cooler air. Hot air rises. Making sure that hot air flows through the cooking chamber is the key. The hot air needs to be kept moving and circulating around the meat so it will smoke evenly and faster than just warm air hanging around the chamber. Vents play a crucial role in maintaining airflow.

BUILDING BB KING

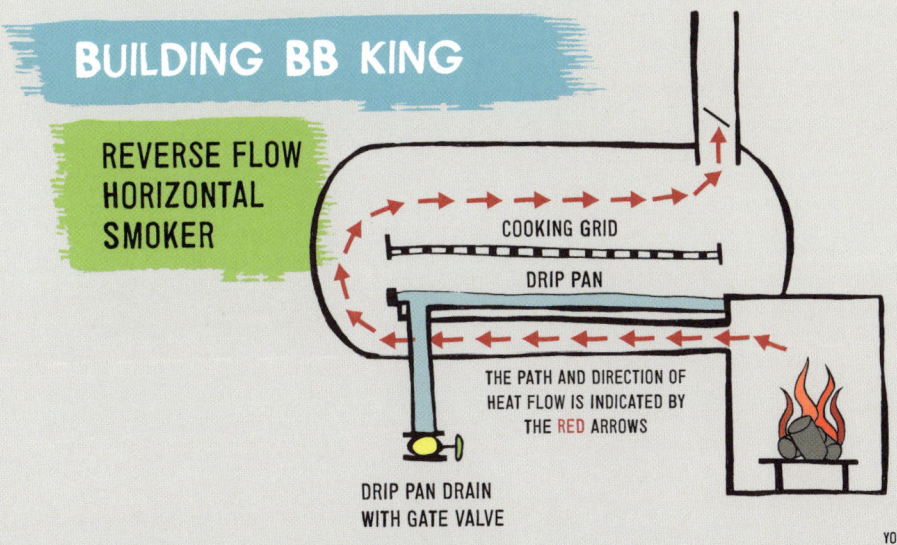

After extensive research we decided to build a reverse flow horizontal smoker.

A reverse flow horizontal smoker has the smokestack situated on the same side of the chamber as the firebox. The idea being that smoke travels across the chamber underneath the grates and meat, then gets pulled back and reverses across the meat and then out of the chimney.

We used a local metal goods supplier to purchase a whole range of steel mesh, angle iron and flat bar. You'll be able to buy sheets of metal, then cut and weld to fit the dimensions of your build. Always ask if they have any offcuts – you'll save yourself a fortune!

 COOKING CHAMBER Sourcing the cooker chamber was the number one priority. We wanted the walls to be at least 0.5cm thick so that it would hold temperature over a long period of time and all year round. We picked up a 1968, 250-litre compressor tank from a local scrap yard. Tanks like this don't come along every day, so it was a lucky find.

 DOORS After some initial cutting and tidying of the tank, we marked out the doors using masking tape. This was a nerve-wracking part of the build – you only get to cut the doors once. If you make a mistake, it could be new tank time. We agonized over whether to have two small doors or one large door. Two small doors seemed more sensible. On reflection we didn't quite get this right. We cut the doors too high, which made it more difficult to slide the bottom cooking grates in and out – but hey, it's all a learning curve.

 HINGES You can buy them, but we decided to make them ourselves. We bought a 2cm round tube and a 1cm round bar, cut them to size, slotted them together and welded them to the tank. We knew we needed strong, reliable and hard-wearing hinges to take the weight of the heavy doors. We found it much easier to weld the hinges onto the cooking chamber before cutting the doors, that way we could be more accurate with positioning.

 We used a mid-range disc-cutter to cut the doors. It's worth buying a decent disc-cutter and cutting discs. We probably went through way too many packs of discs during the build, which can become costly. We found it was best to buy thin discs (1mm) as they tended to be more accurate and seemed to last longer than thicker discs.

5 **THE FIREBOX** We bought a sheet of 4mm-thick steel, measured, cut and welded the sheet into a box shape. Components like the firebox and the chimney were mainly judged by eye, logically working out how much fuel we could get into the basket. We reinforced the firebox with another 4mm sheet to stop any warping and prevent heat loss. Using a MIG welder was a steep learning curve. If it's your first time, make sure you have supervision and practise on as many offcuts as you can before welding the final article. It was a very useful skill to learn if you want to build your own smoker. When we had the final box we cut three vents: in the door and both left and right sides, to control air intake to the firebox, plus a hole at the top where the firebox would meet the cooking chamber.

6 **FIRE BASKET** We fabricated the fire basket from lengths of 4mm flat bar and steel mesh. The basket fits neatly into the firebox, although it can be tricky to get it in and out when hot. The basket needs to be lower at the front so you can easily add more fuel when you open the firebox door. The basket slides into the firebox on runners so there is airflow between the fire basket and the bottom of the firebox.

7 It took us a long time to decide how big the smoke hole in the tank should be (the hole takes smoke from the firebox to the cooking chamber). We knew this needed to be at approximately the level of the baffle plate. We cut a hole a fifth of the size of the width of the tank/cooking chamber.

8 **THE BAFFLE PLATE** is the key to a reverse flow horizontal smoker. It's a sheet of metal the width and length of the chamber, allowing a gap on the opposite end of the firebox for smoke to pass up and over the meat. It ensures the smoke entering from the firebox moves around the chamber in a reverse flow motion (see the illustration on page 13). Without this plate, smoke would come into the cooker, rise up vertically and out of the chimney and not touch the meat. As the baffle plate was built a little like a shallow trough, when we smoke, we fill it with water and apple juice. This gives both a little sweet flavour and helps control the overall temperature. It also catches the fat from the cooking meats – hence why you need the grease tap to drain the liquid after your cook.

9 Welding the firebox to the cooking chamber was quite tricky given how heavy it was. The firebox had become super heavy since reinforcing it with double 4mm steel. We propped it up with an old car jack and pallets to get it at exactly the right level before starting the weld.

10 We cut the hole for the chimney by roughly measuring and drawing around the diameter of the 10cm-diameter pipe we had bought. We drilled loads of small holes inside the circle and knocked it through with hammer. This method isn't gonna win any beauty pageants, but it's a fast and easy way to make the chimney hole. The smokestack length is crucial for airflow, but the ability to adjust the smokestack is even more important. Too much pull, shorten the stack; not enough pull, lengthen it.

11 Being able to modify the length of the smokestack is important – we bought a 1.5 metre length of pipe, knowing we could shorten it ourselves to suit our smoker. You'll only work out what is right for your smoker when you've fired it up a few times. The vents in the firebox helped increase and decrease airflow, giving total control of the airflow and subsequent temperature within the cooking chamber.

12 **FINAL DETAILS** Fabricating the grates was relatively easy compared with other parts of the build. It's important to have stainless steel for anything that food will be cooked on. It's more expensive than regular steel, but it's easier to clean and longer lasting. Almost every detail of B.B. King is fabricated with or makes use of recycled materials. The only new components were two heavy duty thermometers for the doors and some fire rope that we used to line the doors to the firebox and cooking chamber. Before the first smoke we did a 'burn out' – which involved ramming the smoker full of wood and burning it at a very high temperature for a couple of hours. After the burn out, you'll then need to season the pit just as you would a wok. You can rub regular vegetable oil on a rag on this inside of the cooking chamber, or like us, we smoked a load of fatty pork scraps which spat and smouldered on the inside, giving a nice grease lining.

TAKING CARE OF YOUR SMOKER

Once you've put all that hard work into building a smoker, you'll need to take care of it. Forget any romantic notions of letting the grease build up over time (like some of the pits we saw in Texas) and believing that it adds to the flavour; the grates need to be cleaned out after each cook. We keep our grates clean and constantly remove meaty debris from the chamber.

We are constantly making minor adjustments and keeping on top of repairs and general TLC. We have needed to maintain different part of the smoker regularly – for example, the hinges regularly need repainting with heat-resistant paint. Obviously, the more you use it, the more work you will need to do to look after it. It took almost three months to build B.B. King, so we want him to last as long as possible.

PRACTICE MAKES PERFECT

You'll need to get as much practice in as you can. There are many reasons why barbecue is so popular in the Southern States of America – the main one being the weather! It's generally hot, dry and sunny all year round in the South. It's hard to get practice in all year round in the UK – but don't let a little rain and cold get in your way! In order to be the master or mistress of your pit, you'll need to practise. Also, it's worth remembering that no two smokers are the same and no two pieces of meat are the same. Having now smoked over 1,000 briskets, 3,000 pork shoulders and more racks of ribs that we've had hot dinners, you learn something new about the art and science of smoking meat with every cook. No two pits are the same either: there will be hot spots and cold spots, and you'll start to get a feel for how the air moves through the chamber. Even the wind speed and direction will alter the cooking time and temperature – so practice really does make perfect.

GRILLING GUIDE

DIRECT VS INDIRECT HEAT

Direct and indirect are the two ways you can deliver heat to your food when grilling.

Direct heat is when the food is grilled directly over the coals. This delivers heat to the food in two different ways. The main contender is radiant heat, which will quickly cook the fire-exposed side of whatever you are grilling, creating a nice crusty sear. The second is conductive heat, created from the super-heated grill grate, leaving those ubiquitous grill marks that proudly say to the world, 'This food has been grilled!'

Alternatively, indirect heat is when food is placed away from the coals and, when the lid is closed, hits your food with some convection heat action, much like an oven. Unlike direct heat, which blasts your food with some extreme temperatures, indirect heat delivers a more gentle heat. And even though radiant and conductive heat are in play a little, it will not create the sear and grill marks to the extent direct-heat grilling does.

So, having that down, it's time to put these methods into action with coal arrangements.

DIRECT HIGH HEAT **DIRECT MEDIUM HEAT** **INDIRECT HEAT**

 TWO-ZONE DIRECT FIRE

Sometimes you need a direct fire, but without all of that searing heat – that's where the two-zone direct fire comes into play. Two levels of direct heat are created by piling up a large concentration of coals on one side, and a smaller scattering on the other side. For foods like steak, which often needs a nice sear and then a bit of gentle heat to finish it off, this option would be good. We often like this arrangement because it affords us the ability to move food between the two zones, ensuring that whatever we are grilling has a nice crust, yet at the same time, we have more control over cooking to achieve perfect doneness.

 TWO-ZONE INDIRECT FIRE

When cooking 'hot and fast' isn't what you need, you'll most likely be turning to a two-zone indirect fire. The best way to get this going is to pile all of the coals on one side of the grill and leaving the other side completely empty; this creates both direct and indirect heat zones. A two-zone will be handling your roasts, whole birds, ribs. Basically anything that requires longer cooking times with a more gentle heat. Be a little cautious though with this arrangement, since one side of what's cooking will ultimately be closer to the coals than the other, meaning that it's important to rotate the food. We like to rotate the food a few times during cooking, at regular intervals, based on the total cooking time to ensure even cooking.

THREE-ZONE SPLIT FIRE

A lot like the two-zone fire, but instead of piling the coals on one side, two equal piles are made on either side of the charcoal grate. You'll lose a little indirect space in this arrangement, but for smaller items like chickens and pork loins, the food can be placed in the middle of the grill, giving it even heat on either side and eliminating the need for rotating during cooking. Since rotating requires opening the lid (and opening the lid allows heat to escape), the three-zone split will also cook those smaller indirect items a bit faster.

THE RING OF FIRE

Putting the same principle into practice as the three-zone split, but with an even ring of coals encircling the sides of the charcoal grate. We've only used this method once, seeing as it takes longer to arrange than the three-zone and didn't seem to benefit the final product, but it totally has the coolest naming of all the coal arrangements, so we thought it worth mentioning pretty much just for that reason.

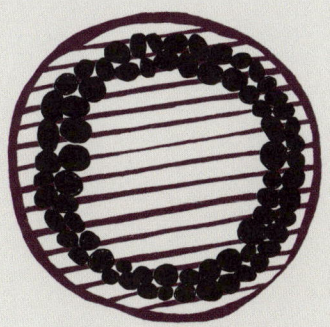

THE BULLSEYE

The bullseye is simply a reversed ring of fire. Place your charcoal in the centre, creating a great source of direct heat and the edges are obviously much cooler spots where the heat is indirect. Compared to the ring, the area full of burning coals is much smaller, so the grill is cooler overall. This should allow you greater control over cooking temperatures when cooking smaller items placed around the outside, with the lid on.

Armed with this information, it's time to put it into practice. Since each grill is a little different, it's best to play around with the different methods and placements of the coals to see what will work best.

HOW TO USE SMOKING WOOD & CHARCOAL

Smoke produced from charcoal will only offer a very slight smokiness to food – that's why wood is intrinsically important to get that full, classic barbecue taste.

Grilling and smoking with wood affords you the opportunity to add flavour that just can't be accomplished to the same degree inside a kitchen – messing around with liquid smoke is a slippery slope in terms of giving an authentic tasting smoky flavour. Knowing which woods to use and when will require a bit more experimenting on your part as different woods vary in intensity of flavour, and overall colour. That being said, here are some suggestions based on what we use. Every pit boss will have a different take, but here's ours.

CHIPS, CHUNKS, LOGS & PELLETS

Let's start by choosing the right size of wood from four basic options: chips, chunks, logs and pellets.

Chips are scraps and shavings of wood that ignite quickly, but also burn out pretty fast. The biggest advantage being that they're available in a wide variety of places, from your supermarket to garden centres. We used to use chips. But the fact that many people believe you need to soak them (see box opposite), and their burnout rate, saw us move on to chunks.

Chunks are usually about fist-sized pieces of wood that are our choice for a long, slower hit of smoke. They take longer to fully ignite than chips, but can burn for a good hour in a grill, and hours in a smoker. For city dwellers, who may not have a natural supply of wood to forage from, chunks are sold pretty inexpensively all over the internet.

Logs are full pieces of wood, like you would use in a fireplace, or to build a campfire. These are best reserved for barbecuing in a pit or with an offset smoker. They take a long time to get to the point where you cook with them and produce more smoke than you'll probably ever need when grilling. If you're smoking with logs, it's fine to leave the bark on, but make sure they're dry and well seasoned.

If you fancy trying your hand at 'stick burning' (a technique using only wood to smoke, usually with an offset smoker), then logs are the fuel for you. Ideally, you'll want uniform-sized logs to make it easier to gauge burn time and temperature control.

Smoking with logs is all about getting a really hot ember bed. First, you'll want to burn down several logs to achieve a good start bed. When it's all glowing, spread the coals out. Arrange the wood as if they are pieces midway through a game of Jenga, allowing oxygen to move freely between each piece. When these have turned black and wonderfully charred, close the door and let that fragrant wood smoke really start to work its magic. Keep an eye on your temperature. Need the temperature higher? Open the door and vents. Need to maintain and regulate the heat? Close the door and work the vents to control the temperature. Try to stack your wood near the firebox to get them warm – a warm log will catch quicker than a cold log. And don't put wood on top of your firebox and walk away as it will ignite. Take that from people who know!

Pellets are a processed wood made from highly compressed sawdust, our friend tells us they look like cattle feed. You can't use any pellets for smoking, they need to be classed as 'food grade'. They come in several wood varieties and are mostly imported from the US. Pellets are used mainly, but not exclusively with pellet-style smokers. Here, they are poured into a pellet hopper, fed down a moving auger into a little firebox, which ignites them, in turn creating fragrant wood smoke. Though pellet-style smokers are undoubtedly pricier than your other fuel sources, they are relatively economical and are built for both ease and efficiency. We've also spoken to people that have both pellet-style and offset smokers who use a handful of pellets the same way you would use chips.

2. CHARCOAL: LUMPWOOD & BRIQUETTES

There is a time and a place for using both lumpwood and briquettes when making barbecue. Perhaps one of the main points to consider is what's available to you and what you can afford.

The principal difference between briquettes and lumpwood is processing. Lumpwood is raw, burned wood and briquettes are processed forms of lumpwood and coal dust compacted into uniform shapes.

Natural lumpwood charcoal is faster to light, therefore reducing the time it takes to preheat your smoker. So if you are in hurry, in some ways, lumpwood charcoal lets you barbecue in an instant. If you are planning on cooking some chicken, burgers, steaks or anything else that cooks relatively quickly, then lumpwood charcoal will be an ideal choice. We smoke and grill over lumpwood as opposed to briquettes just because it suits what we do. However, pound for pound, we use more lumpwood than we would if we used briquettes, impacting on the costs: we add more fuel more frequently to our grill cooker. The benefit of using lumpwood is that it's less smoky than briquettes.

Some folks feel that charcoal briquettes are more versatile, and, as they're mainly uniform in size, it's easier to use them for coal-stacking techniques like 'the snake' or 'minion method' in bullet- and kettle-style barbecues. Charcoal briquettes take longer to burn down, but less is required. They can hold their heat longer, negating the need to top up as frequently as with lumpwood.

There are also a multitude of charcoal-based products on the market that will help your fuel burn more efficiently or even hotter for longer, from heat beads to hexagonal charcoal sticks. These seem expensive compared to regular charcoal barbecue fuel, but the cost is outweighed by their burn efficiency. In our opinion, a few bags of these could pay for themselves over a few bags of lumpwood or briquettes.

TO SOAK OR NOT TO SOAK?

This is only a relevant question for chips. Never soak chunks and logs.

To soak or not to soak is usually a split decision in the barbecue community. Argument for: they take longer to burn and release smoke flavour, apparently, at a lower rate, negating the need to top up every 15 minutes. Argument against: it'll lower the temperature of your pit and smoulder as opposed to burn.

We've never soaked chips, simply because it doesn't make much sense to us. We simply throw handfuls on as and when they burn out or every 45 minutes to an hour. It's your call: do whatever gives you the result you're looking for, try both techniques and see which one you like best.

 TYPES OF WOOD

When picking a wood to grill or smoke with, you always want hardwoods. Softwoods like evergreens create a sooty smoke that have the potential to be dangerous to your health and can make your barbecue taste like an air-freshener. Choose your wood based on the level of smokiness and colour it will impart on your barbecue. We break smoking woods down to three general categories: mild, medium, and heavy. Also see our wood variety recommendations below.

MILD WOODS

These include alder and fruitwoods like apple and cherry. The smokiness in these woods tends to be mild, with hints of fruit or sweetness. The mild woods pair best with more delicate meats like chicken and fish.

MEDIUM WOODS

Oak and hickory are the workhorses of medium woods. These are our go-to wood for almost anything, imparting that distinct smoke flavour without being overpowering. Hickory is heavier than oak, with a stronger flavour that's great for larger cuts of meat and long smokes. Both hickory and oak work really well with bacon, pork, beef and lamb – these are meats that can withstand stronger smokes.

HEAVY WOODS

Mesquite is like the Muhammad Ali of woods; it punches hard smoke flavour into your barbecue and is the strongest in flavour intensity of all the smoke woods. Beef and lamb are really the only meats that can hold their own against the heavyweight smoke flavour. Done right, it's amazing.

These examples are only the tip of the iceberg, and there are many more woods to mess around with. With any wood, especially ones falling into the medium and heavy categories, take care not to use too much. Smoke can quickly overpower all other flavours so if you're just getting started we recommend using one chunk in the first instance and increasing the amount as you find the right balance of smokiness.

WOOD TYPE	FLAVOUR	BURN CHARACTERISTIC	PROFILE	MEAT
Apple	Mild	Hot and slow	Sweet, fruity smoky. Strongest of the fruitwoods	Beef, pork, lamb, ham, poultry, veal, game, sausage
Cherry	Mild	Medium heat, medium length	Sweet and fruity, giving a rosy tint to light meats	Beef, pork, lamb, poultry, fish, game birds, sausage
Pear	Mild	Medium heat, medium length	Sweet and light in flavour, fruity and smoky	Poultry, pork, game, veal
Oak	Medium	Hot and slow	Rich in flavour	Lamb, ribs, beef, sausages
Hickory	Medium	Hot and slow	Rich, intense smoky flavour	Pork, beef, ham
Maple	Mild	Hot and slow	Sweet and light, mildly smoky flavour	Poultry, pork, game birds, bacon
Mesquite	Strong	Hot and slow	Strong, intense smoky flavour	Any red meat
Wine barrel chunks	Medium	Medium heat, medium length	Sweet and light, mildly smoky flavour	Lamb, ribs, beef, veal
Alder	Mild	Medium heat, medium length	Mild to medium flavour	Fish, poultry
Whisky barrel chunks	Medium	Medium heat, medium length	Mild to medium with a punchier flavour than wine chunks	Lamb, ribs, beef, veal
Beech	Mild	Quick burn, medium heat	A light, flavourful smoke	Sausage, fish, chicken, game, poultry
Pecan	Medium	Hot and slow	Medium, nutty flavour	Pork, beef, ham

 ## HOW TO ADD SMOKE TO THE FIRE

SIDE NOTE: THE SMOKE RING

A smoke ring is a pink discolouration of meat just under the dark surface crust (called bark). A good smoke ring is around 5–10mm in thickness, but this can vary between meats. Beef shows a great smoke ring, whereas chicken and turkey the least. Plus it can freak people out seeing a pink tinge to their poultry. The smoke ring is caused by nitric acid build-up on the surface of meat, which is then absorbed inwards. This nitric acid is formed when nitrogen dioxide from wood combustion in smoke mixes with the water in the meat. A smoke ring is a sure-fire way to tell if something has been properly smoked, and when you achieve it, it's definitely something to brag about. However, it's a little bit of vanity, too. We went through a stage of obsessing over achieving perfect smoke rings. Now we're only focused on flavour and technique, the smoke ring being a by-product of those two things working out for us.

Here are some of the ways that people add smoke wood to the fire:

1. Place the smoke wood on top of hot coals. Our preferred approach is to distribute the wood chunks evenly before putting the meat in the smoker. If using the minion or the snake method make sure some of your wood touches the hot coals in order to generate smoke immediately.

2. Bury smoke wood in unlit charcoal. This method is only possible when firing the cooker using the minion or snake method. You'll want to bury wood chunks through the unlit fuel, with a few chunks on top. Distribute the hot coals evenly over the unlit fuel, making sure some wood touches the hot coals to start generating smoke right away.

 ## IGNITION, TAKE OFF!

Like charcoal, hardwood needs to be ignited and properly burning before food is introduced. To do this, place the wood on top of hot coals and let it burn until the flames die down, make sure you're getting clean smoke. Meaning: watch your smokestack. Is a light blue smoke gently releasing or are thick white plumes billowing out? You want the former. If you're getting the white smoke every time you add wood, check that it's seasoned well and super-dry, otherwise it may be that your fire bed isn't hot enough, causing the wood to smoulder rather than ignite. It'll take practice. That's why, when starting out, using smaller pieces of wood reduces the margin for error.

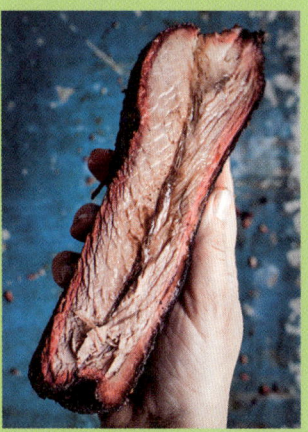

RUBS & SEASONINGS

If you have any spare, small jars handy, it's good to make a few of these in advance if you plan to do a few different smokes. Some may stick together when stored over time due to the sugar, so just loosen them with a fork, or rub together with your hands. As with all spices, keep the rubs and seasonings in a cool, dark place until you need them, where they will keep for a month.

HANG FIRE ALMOST ALL-PURPOSE RUB

We use this rub a lot at our smokehouse, having tinkered with it almost constantly since we started Hang Fire. But we're pretty settled on this version now. We like it on ribs, pork shoulders, chicken or as a seasoning for meatballs and pretty much on almost anything.

4 tbsp fine sea salt
4 tbsp paprika
3 tbsp soft light brown sugar
3 tbsp garlic granules
2 tbsp onion powder
2 tbsp coarsely ground black pepper
2 tbsp chipotle chilli powder
1 tbsp celery salt
2 tbsp ground allspice
2 tbsp toasted cumin seeds, ground
2 tbsp toasted fennel seeds, ground

In a bowl, mix all the ingredients well. Optionally, put through a blender for an extra fine powder. Transfer the rub to a jar, or shaker if using immediately.

TEXAS GRINDHOUSE RUB

We use this on our Texas-style brisket, beef ribs and as a kind of Montreal steak seasoning.

4 tbsp sea salt flakes (make sure they're not too coarse)
60g coarsely ground black pepper
4 tbsp garlic granules
3 tbsp onion granules
1 tbsp chipotle chilli powder
1 tbsp red pepper flakes

In a bowl, mix all the ingredients well. Optionally, put through a blender for an extra fine powder. Transfer the rub to a jar, or shaker if using immediately.

SMOKED PAPRIKA

Sea Salt

LIGHT BROWN SUGAR

COARSE BLACK PEPPER

ONION POWDER

CHILLI FLAKES

ONION GRANULES

Mixed spice

fennel seeds

GARLIC POWDER

CHILLI POWDER

GARDEN RUB

This one is particularly great on lamb leg, shoulder, breast and ribs and on any poultry.

4 tbsp fine sea salt
2 tbsp coarsely ground black pepper
4 tbsp garlic powder
4 tbsp onion powder
2 tbsp soft light brown sugar
1 tbsp English mustard powder
2 tbsp dried rosemary
2 tbsp dried thyme
2 tbsp dried oregano

In a bowl, mix all the ingredients well. Transfer to a jar, or a shaker if using immediately.

MOCHA RUB

We use espresso in our rub for brisket, the grinds giving a jet-black, thick bark, while the cocoa and cinnamon add a wonderfully aromatic flavour profile.

100g espresso coffee beans, freshly ground
2 tbsp sea salt flakes
3 tbsp cocoa powder
2 tbsp dark brown sugar
1 tbsp paprika
1 tbsp ground cinnamon
1 tbsp chipotle chilli powder

In a bowl, mix all the spices well. Transfer the rub to a jar, or a shaker if using immediately.

YARDBIRD RUB

This simple, herby rub will give our feathered friends a tasty bark as well as complementing their delicate flavour.

3 tbsp fine sea salt
3 tbsp garlic granules
3 tbsp paprika
2 tbsp white sugar
2 tbsp dried rosemary
2 tbsp dried oregano
2 tbsp English mustard powder
2 tbsp coarsely ground black pepper
2 tbsp celery salt
2 tbsp fennel seeds
1 tsp turmeric

In a bowl, mix all the ingredients well. Optionally, put through a blender for an extra fine powder. Transfer the rub to a jar, or a shaker if using immediately.

GET EXPERIMENTAL

One of the rites of passage for any budding pit boss is making your own rubs. It's great to use tried and tested recipes, or supporting your local barbecue community by buying championship rubs from the pros. But it is also important to find that flavour profile that really does it for you. Mix and match your favourite seasonings with a salt and sugar base. It's a great way to discover how spices change and interact over short or long smokes and how the flavours develop with various wood types.

MEMPHIS DRY SHAKE

We've been serving our ribs with this dry shake since we started this business. It has a gazillion ingredients and it's a bit time consuming rummaging through your cupboards finding them, but trust us when we say they all work together. Something magical happens when the dry shake hits the slick of warm barbecue sauce painted on the pork ribs. As it sets, it forms another depth of flavour that will see your guests 'oooh' and 'mmmm' with every bite. Apply with gusto to your slab of ribs.

4 tbsp paprika
1 tbsp fine sea salt
1 tbsp celery salt
1 tbsp chipotle chilli powder
1 tbsp toasted coriander seeds, crushed
1 tbsp ground mixed spice
1 tsp celery seeds
1 tsp toasted black mustard seeds, crushed
1 tsp toasted cumin seeds, crushed
1 tsp freshly cracked black pepper
1 tsp English mustard powder
1 tsp garlic granules
1 tsp onion granules
2 tsp dried oregano, 1 tsp ground
1 tsp dried thyme, ground
1 tsp ground coriander

In a bowl, mix all the ingredients well. Optionally, put through a blender for an extra fine powder. Transfer the rub to a jar, or a shaker if using immediately.

LOUISIANA SEASONINGS

These two seasonings are essential to all Louisiana cooking. These are our favourite blends to use and we always have these jars to hand in our smokehouse.

CAJUN

5 tbsp paprika
2 tbsp onion powder
2 tbsp garlic powder
2 tbsp dried oregano
1 tbsp sea salt flakes
1 tbsp dried thyme
1 tsp freshly cracked black pepper
1 tsp cayenne pepper
1 tsp chilli flakes

In a bowl, mix all the ingredients well. Optionally, put through a blender for an extra fine powder. Transfer the rub to a jar, or a shaker if using immediately.

CREOLE

5 tbsp paprika
2 tbsp onion powder
2 tbsp garlic powder
2 tbsp dried oregano
1 tbsp dried thyme
1 tbsp sea salt flakes
1 tsp freshly cracked black pepper
1 tsp dried basil
1 tsp ground white pepper

In a bowl, mix all the ingredients well. Optionally, put through a blender for an extra fine powder. Transfer the rub to a jar, or a shaker if using immediately.

BACON JAM

We first heard about this delicious little condiment from a food truck in Seattle. Since then, we've seen many iterations in supermarkets and restaurants, and from streetfood vendors. Here's our version with a little smoky kick from the bacon and paprika, and a savoury edge from a cup of coffee.

- 1 tsp cumin seeds
- 1 tsp coriander seeds
- ½ tsp fennel seeds
- 500g smoked streaky bacon (pages 80–81)
- 400g red onions, sliced
- 4 garlic cloves, finely chopped
- 1 tsp smoked paprika
- 3 tbsp soft light brown sugar
- 1 tsp sea salt flakes
- 1 tsp freshly cracked black pepper
- ½ tsp chilli powder
- 3 tbsp maple syrup
- 80ml brewed medium coffee of your choice
- 80ml balsamic vinegar

Take a small pan and dry fry your cumin, coriander and fennel seeds over high heat. When they start to look toasty and smell great too, transfer to a pestle and mortar (or spice grinder) and give them a good pounding until they're finely ground to a powder. Set aside.

Heat a large frying pan over medium heat. Now start frying off your bacon in batches, making sure there's enough room in the pan for the bacon to crisp up nicely, about 8–10 minutes. Transfer the bacon to some kitchen towels to absorb the excess bacon fat, keeping back about 2 tablespoons fat in the pan.

Add your red onions and garlic to the pan and cook over a medium-low heat, for 10–12 minutes, until softened. Put in the toasted and ground spices, along with the paprika, sugar, salt, pepper, chilli, and stir over medium heat for 1–2 minutes. Now add the maple syrup, coffee and vinegar, and keep stirring until well combined for a few more minutes.

Chop your bacon into small pieces, making sure there's not too much fat – you really want the meaty bits. Add the bacon to the pan, simmer and stir for about 10 minutes over low heat, until the mixture starts to thicken. Finally, transfer the mixture to a food processor and pulse a few times until you have a spreadable consistency. Serve warm, or keep in an airtight jar, in the fridge, for up to 2 weeks.

MAKE MINE A BOURBON

Bourbon bacon jam is also a proven hit around our house. Adapt the recipe above by omitting the fennel and cumin, and replacing the coffee with 80ml of your favourite bourbon.

MAKES ABOUT 500G

CHILLI JAM

This fairly simple chilli jam is an essential condiment with year-round appeal. We slather it in cheese sandwiches, glaze ham and stuff chicken breasts with it. We stir it through a beef chilli; you name it, we can find a use for it. We tend to stockpile red chillies and freeze them so we can make large batches a couple of times a year.

- 8 red bell peppers
- 10–12 fresh or frozen red chillies
- 1 tbsp groundnut oil
- 2 red onions, chopped
- 1 fresh bay leaf
- 1 cinnamon stick
- 3 garlic cloves, chopped
- 1 tsp sea salt flakes
- 1 tsp freshly cracked black pepper
- 100g soft light brown sugar
- 100ml balsamic vinegar
- 50ml sherry vinegar

First we need to get the skin off the peppers and chillies. Start with the bell peppers while you get the hang of it – the chillies will catch pretty quickly on an open flame so work fast. You can blacken the skins in a number of ways; we favour a hot barbecue either on the grill or directly on the coals, turning frequently. You can also put the peppers directly over medium-high flame on a gas hob, using long tongs to turn them as they blacken. Or use a griddle pan or blacken them under a hot domestic grill.

As soon as the peppers and chillies are pretty much black all over, transfer to a ziplock bag and seal, or to a plate and cover tightly with cling film to make them sweat. Allow to cool for 10 minutes, then remove all the skin (you might want to wear disposable gloves for the chillies).

Next, trim off all the stalks and deseed the bell peppers. If you like your jam hot and spicy, leave the seeds in the chillies. If you like it milder, remove them and the membranes. Pulse the peppers in a food processor to a rough paste – not mush – or finely chop by hand.

ONE FOR THE HOT HEADS...

If you're chilli addicts like us, you might want to experiment with the variety of chillies you use. We've made batches with added scotch bonnets as they have that perfect West Indian fruitiness and also habanero chillies that usually have us hankering for pollo mole and tequila shots (and a glass of milk in some cases). You can even add a Thai twist with very hot Thai chillies, a little lemongrass and a dash of fish sauce. Have fun with this and make it your own.

Add a splash of groundnut oil to a medium-sized pan set over low heat. Cook the onions for 10–15 minutes, until they begin to caramelise. Add the bay leaf, cinnamon stick, garlic and ½ teaspoon each salt and pepper. Cook, stirring constantly, for a further 10 minutes, until the onions look rich, golden and sticky. Stir in the chopped peppers and chillies, sugar and vinegars, and continue to cook for 15–20 minutes, until the mixture thickens and is sticky and reduced. Make sure you have a window open as the vapour from the chillies can burn your eyes and nose. Add the remaining salt and pepper, and adjust to taste (this will be tricky as the mixture will be spicy and hot!).

When you're happy with the consistency, remove the bay leaf and cinnamon stick. While hot, transfer to sterilised jars (page 33). We like to leave it for 24 hours to allow the flavours to meld together. It will keep for 2–3 months in the fridge.

RUBS, SAUCES & EXTRA FLAVOURS

SERVES 3-4

CHIMICHURRI

At our pop-ups, we serve this delicious Argentinian pesto (of sorts) in our burnt-end sandwiches and it goes down a storm. It's so good with pretty much anything from pasta to salad dressing, but steaks are where it's at in terms of perfect partners. Those asado barbecue-loving Argentinians know how to flavour their beef, and chimichurri sure packs a punch and looks beautiful, too. The key to this is to chop everything by hand – blenders tend to make the texture a little too fine.

- 4 tbsp finely chopped flat-leaf parsley
- 4 tbsp finely chopped coriander
- 2 tbsp roughly chopped oregano
- 2 garlic cloves, finely chopped
- 1 shallot, finely chopped
- 1 tsp chilli flakes
- 1 tsp finely grated lemon zest
- ¼ tsp fine sea salt
- ¼ tsp freshly cracked black pepper, to taste
- 4 tbsp olive oil
- 2 tbsp red wine vinegar
- juice of ½ lemon

Combine all the ingredients, except the oil, lemon juice and vinegar, in a bowl. Add the oil, stir through, then add the vinegar and lemon juice. Allow the ingredients to marinate for an hour before use. Just before serving, taste for seasoning. Keep in the fridge until you want to use it and allow the chimichurri to come to room temperature before using. This will keep in the fridge for 2–3 days.

RUBS, SAUCES & EXTRA FLAVOURS

MAKES ABOUT 600G

MAKES 2 X 500G JARS

CHILLI & SMOKED GARLIC BUTTER

We keep a log of this in our freezer and cut off chunks as and when we need it for corn cobs, steak, and smoked and roasted potatoes. Adjust the chilli to your liking. Rehydrate dried chillies fully so they incorporate into the butter well.

2 ancho chillies, destemmed, deseeded and deveined
2 chipotle chillies
2 tbsp smoked garlic purée (see below)
500g softened unsalted butter
2 tbsp chopped coriander
3 spring onions, finely chopped
grated zest of 2 limes
½ tbsp fresh lime juice
1 tbsp sea salt flakes
1 tsp smoked paprika

Bring a small saucepan of water to the boil, add the chillies and simmer over low heat until softened. Drain. Place the softened chillies and smoked garlic purée in a food processor and blitz until smooth. Add the butter, coriander, spring onions, lime zest and juice, salt and paprika, and pulse until completely combined. Transfer the chilli and smoked garlic butter onto a sheet of cling film. Shape into a log, wrap and chill or freeze. The butter will keep for 3–4 days in the fridge and 1 month in the freezer.

ON MAKING SMOKED GARLIC

While your smoker or grill is on, why not slip in a few whole heads of garlic? They will need about 2 hours at 110–121°C/225–250°F. Oak is preferable, but it's pretty marginal in terms of flavour. Once smoked, the garlic will keep for several weeks in the fridge. Store them in a plastic tub with a tight-fitting lid.

CRAB APPLE BUTTER

This an American classic. Someone always has a jar of this in their fridge or cupboard in the States. It's used for everything from pie fillings to a smoked pork condiment. We've used ours as a glaze, on the bun of a pulled pork sandwich and even eaten it with smoked cheese.

2.5kg crab apples
750g white sugar
2 tbsp ground cinnamon
1 tsp ground nutmeg
1 tsp ground allspice
½ tsp ground cloves

Rinse the crab apples, remove the stems and blossom ends. Place in a large heavy pan over medium heat and pour in 1 litre of water. Bring to the boil and reduce the heat to medium-low. Cover and cook, stirring occasionally to prevent it from sticking, for 45 minutes until the apples are soft.

Put through a coarse sieve over a clean bowl and use a spatula to press out the apple purée.

Return the purée to the pan, add the sugar and spices, and cook over low heat for about 2 hours, until thick. Meanwhile, sterilise your jars. Preheat the oven to 140°C/275°F/gas mark 1. Wash the jars in hot soapy water and rinse them well. Place them upside down in the oven for 30 minutes. Remove carefully and turn them the right way up, being careful not to touch the insides.

When done, immediately pour the crab aple butter into the sterilised jars, top with little rounds of baking parchment, and seal at once. It should keep for at least a year in a cool, dark cupboard.

RUBS, SAUCES & EXTRA FLAVOURS

HANG FIRE'S HOMESTYLE KETCHUP

'Making my own ketchup? Ain't nobody got time for that!' But let me tell you my friends, it's a great basis for making your own barbecue sauce and gives it an authentic taste with none of those artificial sweetener flavours so often found in shop-bought brands. This is also an awesome use of that tomato glut you may have from an overzealous planting earlier in the year – or an excuse to grow toms to make your own amazing ketchup. This versatile sauce can be used in almost any dish calling for ketchup.

2 tbsp olive oil

1 large onion, roughly chopped

5cm piece fresh ginger, peeled and roughly chopped

2 garlic cloves, sliced

½ red jalapeño, deseeded and finely chopped

½ tsp celery salt

1 tbsp coriander seeds

3 cloves

a few cracks of fresh black pepper

1 tsp sea salt flakes

500g ripe vine Roma, cherry or pomodorino tomatoes, halved

500g good-quality tinned tomatoes

50g good-quality tomato purée

70g soft light brown sugar

200ml sherry vinegar

In a heavy-based pan, add the olive oil, onion, ginger, garlic, chilli, celery salt, coriander seeds and cloves. Season with a few twists of black pepper and salt. Gently cook for 10–12 minutes, until the onions have softened. Add both types of tomatoes and the tomato purée, and 300ml water, and simmer for 30 minutes until the mixture reduces by half.

Next, transfer the mixture to a food processor or blender and blitz until smooth. Give the pan you cooked the onions in a quick rinse, then return the puréed mixture back to the pan along with the sugar and vinegar. Gently simmer over low heat for 20 minutes, until reduced to the consistency of ketchup. Adjust the seasoning to taste.

Pour the ketchup through a funnel into a sterilised jar or bottle (see page 33).

It will keep for up to 6 months in the fridge, though it rarely lasts that long with us!

SWEET CHIPOTLE BARBECUE SAUCE

A chipotle barbecue sauce is a storecupboard staple in the Hang Fire house. When you want a sauce with a sweet, spicy and smoky kick, this is the one to reach for.

- 1 tbsp olive oil
- ½ small onion, roughly chopped
- 2–3 garlic cloves, very finely chopped
- 185g ketchup
- 60ml pineapple juice
- 90g honey
- 45g dark brown sugar
- 2 tbsp blackstrap molasses
- 3 dried chipotle peppers, soaked in warm water until softened
- 1 tbsp Worcestershire sauce
- 1 tsp smoked paprika
- 1 tsp English mustard powder
- 1 tsp chilli powder
- splash of bourbon or whisky (optional)

Heat the olive oil in a large pan over medium heat, add the onions and garlic, and cook for about 10 minutes until soft and golden. Reduce the heat to low and add all the remaining ingredients. Cook, stirring occasionally, for 8–10 minutes to give the flavours a chance to combine.

Pour everything into a food processor and blitz until smooth. (It's a good idea to cover the top of the food processor with a tea towel and pulse one or two times before blending to avoid splattering.) If you want the sauce extra-smooth, press it through a fine-mesh sieve using the back of a spoon or a rubber spatula. Store in an airtight container in the fridge for up to a few weeks. Slather on everything and anything.

KEY TO SAUCES

 Blackberry & Chipotle BBQ Sauce

 Alabama White BBQ Sauce

 South Carolina Mustard

 Sweet Chipotle BBQ Sauce

 Louisiana Hot Sauce

 Maple Bourbon BBQ Sauce

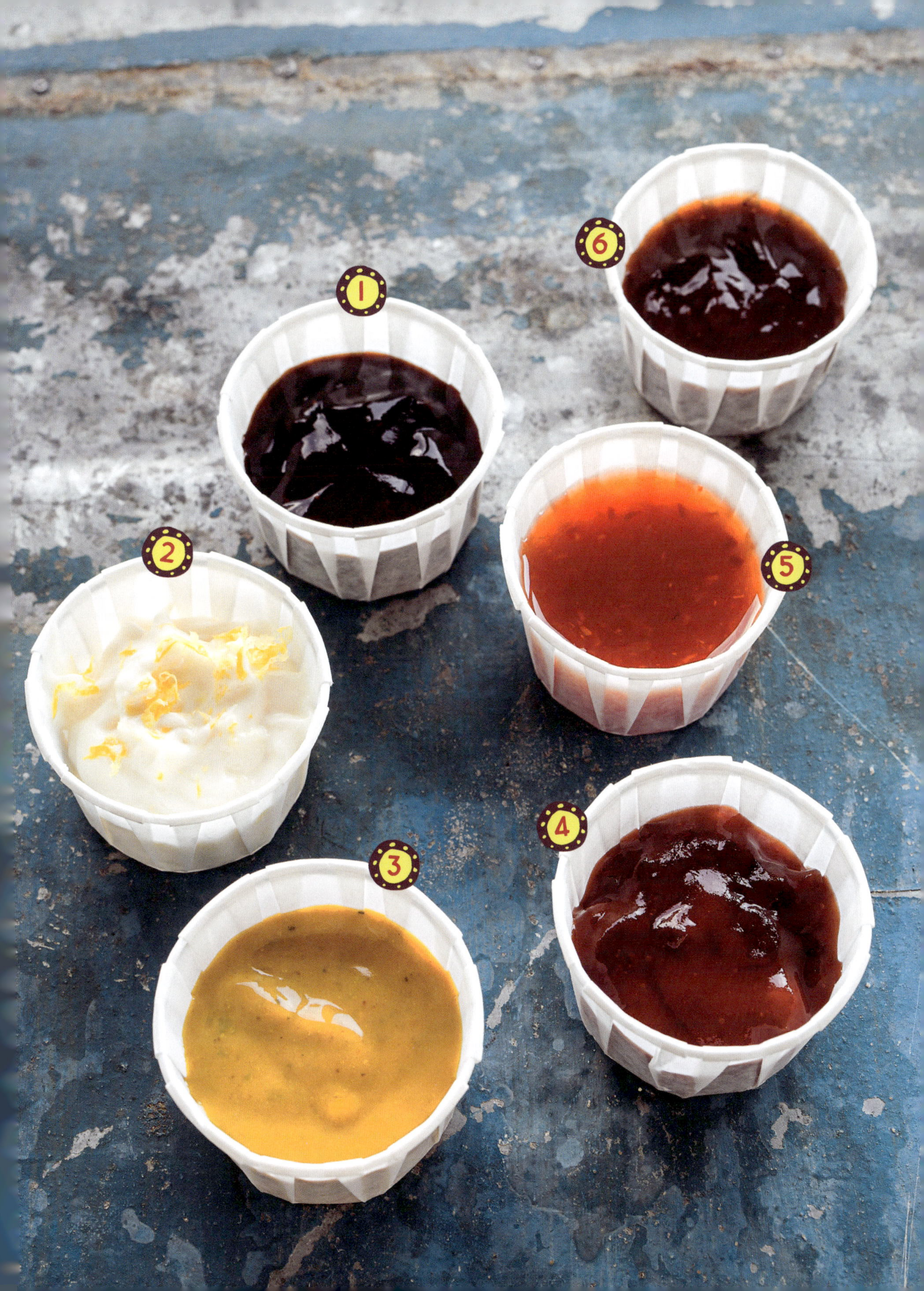
1
2
3
4
5
6

MAKES ABOUT 375G

ALABAMA WHITE BARBECUE SAUCE

This recipe was made popular by Big Bob Gibson Bar-B-Q joint in Decatur, AL. Head Pit Boss, Chris Lilly, came up with this unusual sauce that totally works with their smoked chicken. Dipping a whole spatchcock chicken in this creamy white sauce and holding it aloft will literally make you feel like a boss (and it looks amazing). We've tinkered with the recipe to give it a little extra lift with fresh herbs. See also our yardbird recipe on page 119.

200g good-quality mayonnaise
50ml good-quality apple juice
50ml apple cider vinegar
50ml fresh lemon juice
1 tbsp creamed horseradish
1 tbsp garlic powder
1 tsp onion powder
1 tsp English mustard powder
1 tsp freshly cracked black pepper
1 tsp finely grated lemon zest
½ tsp cayenne pepper
½ tsp sea salt flakes
2 tbsp finely chopped flat-leaf parsley

Combine all the ingredients apart from the parsley, in a bowl, and whisk vigorously until well mixed. Stir through the parsley and transfer the mixture to a jar. Before using, refrigerate the sauce for 1–2 hours to allow the flavours to mingle. Keeps for 2–3 days in the fridge.

MAKES ABOUT 500G

SOUTH CAROLINA MUSTARD SAUCE

Here's a recipe for South Carolina mustard sauce. This has proven to be a real hit at our kitchen takeovers and we don't serve our pork barbecue without it. It's simple to make and keeps well in the fridge for a week – omit the butter if you want to keep it for longer.

250g American mustard
125g white sugar
3 tbsp soft light brown sugar
2 tbsp tomato purée
200ml cider vinegar
1 tbsp chilli powder
1 tsp freshly cracked black pepper
1 tsp dried rosemary
2 tbsp unsalted butter
1 tsp soy sauce
1–2 tsp hot sauce (or make your own, pages 41–42), to taste

Put all the ingredients except the butter, soy sauce and hot sauce in a large saucepan set over low heat. Bring to a simmer and cook for about 15 minutes. Stir in the remaining ingredients and continue to simmer for 10 minutes. Transfer to a sterilised jar (page 33) and allow the sauce to cool before putting it in the fridge for 24 hours before using. This will allow the flavours to come together. Taste for seasoning, and if it needs a little more zip, add your hot sauce to taste.

MAKES ABOUT 500G

Blackberry Chipotle Barbecue Sauce

As a homage to the mighty 12 Bones Smokehouse in Asheville, NC, this is our version of their signature baby back rib barbecue sauce. It's fruity, spicy and sticky and one of the most delicious glazes we've tried on ribs. This a real show-stopper of a sauce, but we've given it a bit of 'hedgerow' chic by using British blackberries instead of blueberries. Slather this rich sauce on baby backs, St Louis spare ribs, or just about anything that needs a decadent barbecue sauce.

- 1 tbsp olive oil
- 1 red onion, finely diced
- 2 garlic cloves, finely chopped
- 3 dried chipotle peppers, soaked in water overnight and drained
- 180g tomato purée
- 230ml cider vinegar
- 125ml balsamic vinegar
- 500g fresh blackberries
- 250g soft light brown sugar
- 2 tbsp Worcestershire sauce
- 3 tbsp blackstrap molasses
- 1 tbsp ground cumin
- 1 tbsp chilli powder
- 1 tbsp cayenne pepper
- 1 tbsp garlic powder
- ½ tbsp ground allspice
- ½ tbsp sea salt flakes
- ½ tbsp freshly cracked black pepper

In a large saucepan, heat the oil over medium-high heat, add the onion and cook for 10 minutes, until softened. Add the garlic and continue to cook for a further 1 minute. Stir in the chipotle peppers and tomato purée, and cook for 20–25 minutes until the onions begin to caramelise and turn a deep burgundy hue. Add both vinegars and use a wooden spoon to scrape the bottom of the pan to encourage any brown bits back into the mix.

Stir in the remaining ingredients and cook over medium-low heat for 15 minutes, until the berries break down and the sauce begins to thicken. Turn off the heat and allow the sauce to cool to room temperature.

Transfer the sauce to a blender and blitz until smooth. Pass through a sieve into a bowl, to get rid of the blackberry pips, then pour the sauce into an airtight container. It will keep in the fridge for up to 7 days.

RUBS, SAUCES & EXTRA FLAVOURS

MAKES ABOUT 150G

MAPLE BOURBON BARBECUE SAUCE

This is one of our favourite, late-night barbecue sauces. The boozy kick and the natural, sappy sweetness from the maple syrup really elevates your barbecue to something wickedly decadent.

80g diced pancetta
1 small red onion, finely diced
2 medium garlic cloves, finely chopped
100g ketchup
40ml cider vinegar
40g molasses sugar
40ml Worcestershire sauce
4 tbsp your favourite bourbon
100ml Canadian maple syrup
1 tsp chilli powder
2 tsp smoked paprika
1 tsp English mustard powder
1 tsp sea salt flakes, plus extra to taste
a few cracks of fresh black pepper, to taste

Put the pancetta in a small saucepan over medium heat and fry, stirring occasionally, for about 8 minutes, until crisp. Using a slotted spoon, transfer the pancetta to a small bowl and set aside. Reduce the heat to medium-low, add the onion to the pan, and cook in the pancetta fat for about 3 minutes, stirring occasionally, until softened. Add the garlic and cook for 30–60 seconds until fragrant.

Whisk in the remaining ingredients and season with salt and pepper. Stir in the reserved pancetta and bring the mixture to the boil over medium-high heat. Reduce the heat to low and simmer for about 25 minutes, stirring occasionally, until the sauce has thickened slightly and holds a line on the back of a wooden spoon when you drag a finger through it. Season with extra salt and pepper as needed. Blitz in a food processor until smooth. Store in an airtight jar and refrigerate for up to 1 week.

MAKES JUST OVER **1 LITRE**

LOUISIANA HOT SAUCE PART 1: THE MONSTER PEPPER MASH

As huge fans of hot sauces, we decided to make our own fermented-style sauce. In 2014, we bottled and sold so much of this stuff we couldn't keep up with the demands of our main job, which was making barbecue. But we found that having a big batch of pepper mash on the go acted like a 'starter' that could be topped up week on week with more salt and more peppers.

Making a fermented hot sauce is a bit of a process, so we recommend making a fairly large batch. It keeps really well and you can use the hot pepper mash as a base for many styles of hot sauce, salsas, bastes and even curries. As we'll ultimately be making a Louisiana-style mash, we'll be using serrano and cayenne peppers for that classic bayou pepper flavour. You want your chillies to be very ripe for this recipe. If they're firm and fresh, try putting them in some brown paper bags or lay them out on a baking tray and leave them somewhere warm for a day or so. The fruit should start to look a little soft and wrinkly.

1kg very ripe red serrano chillies

1kg very ripe red cayenne chillies

70g fine sea salt

300ml sweet white wine (such as Riesling, Sauternes, Moscato)

STAGE 1: START THE MASH

When handling raw chillies, always wear gloves (disposables) otherwise you'll regret not wearing them in so many painful ways! Slice off the green tops of the chillies and split them lengthways. Put them in a large, non-reactive bowl and cover with the salt and wine. Using a potato masher, push down on the mixture, bruising the fruit a little, then cover and leave to macerate overnight. The wine, with its high sugar content, will aid the fermentation process.

STAGE 2: FERMENTATION

The next day, sterilise a 2-litre jar that has a tight-fitting lid according to the instructions on page 33. Make sure that there is enough room in the jar for the mash to rise by about double its original size during fermentation. Carefully pour the pepper mash in, using a spoon to push the mixture down well.

Seal the jar and leave for 2 weeks in a dark and cool place. You should, during this time, start to see the fermentation process happen as little bubbles form on the surface of the mash; good bacteria going to work helping you on your way to hot sauce heaven. Once a day, use a clean spoon to

Hey cowboy, the recipe continues on the next page...

RUBS, SAUCES & EXTRA FLAVOURS

push down the rising pulp and give it a stir. By the end of week 2, the rate of fermentation should have died down so the fermentation process won't appear to be so vigorous.

STAGE 3: MASHING THE MASH

You can now make your hot sauce in either of the following ways:

1. Purée in a food processor and push through a metal sieve into a clean bowl. Transfer the liquid to a sterilised glass jar.

2. Using a mouli placed over a bowl, add ladlefuls of the pepper mash, turning the handle so the juice is extracted, leaving behind the pulped chillies (which you can pass through the mouli a few times). Transfer to a sterilised glass jar.

Store the mash in your fridge, where it will keep for about 3 months. The longer your mash matures the better the flavour. You might notice some bubbling fermentation – this is perfectly normal – just give it a stir every now and then. You're now ready to make your Louisiana Hot Sauce (page 44).

SHARING IS CARING

There are lots of online places that grow chillies and will deliver them to your door. Better still, grow them yourself, or persuade a green-fingered friend to grow a few plants for you in exchange for a couple of bottles of your hot sauce.

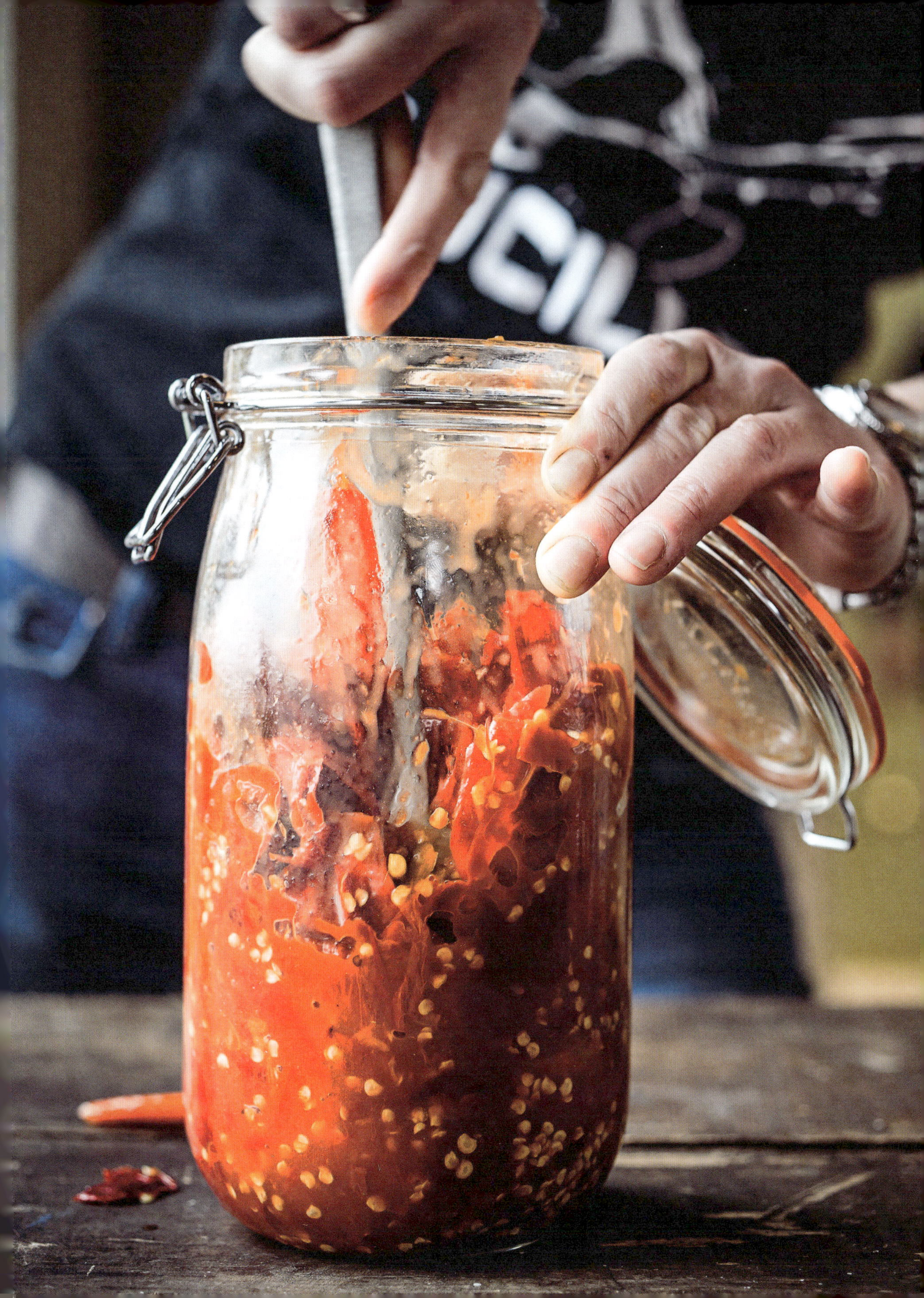

MAKES ABOUT **500G**

MAKES **240G**

LOUISIANA HOT SAUCE PART II: THE SAUCE

This is a storecupboard essential for us at Hang Fire. We figured that since we were going through so much hot sauce that we may as well make our own. This way, we could make a sauce to fit the flavour profile we were trying to create, not only in our Louisiana dishes, but through our other sauces and side dishes. And if you always have a hot pepper mash in your fridge that you top up, there's really no excuse not to make this.

300g Monster Pepper Mash (pages 41–42)
8 garlic cloves, roughly chopped
1 tbsp celery salt
juice of 1 lemon
200ml distilled white vinegar

You've done all the hard work with your pepper mash. By comparison, making your hot sauce is a simple case of combining the above ingredients. Blitz all the ingredients in a blender into a purée. Pass through a fine sieve and store in sterilised bottles (see page 33). We like to leave the sauce in the fridge overnight or for 24 hours before we use it. And it will keep for several months if stored in the fridge.

CHERMOULA

This recipe is great slathered over lamb but it also works well with other meats. Swap the mint for fresh thyme or rosemary leaves if serving with pork, beef or chicken. We love chermoula on any grilled meats.

1 tsp cumin seeds
1 tsp fennel seeds
50g fresh coriander, with stalks
100g curly parsley, remove larger stalks
30g fresh mint leaves
3 garlic cloves, roughly chopped
150ml olive oil
3 tsp paprika
¼ tsp cayenne pepper
¼ freshly cracked black pepper
½ tsp fine sea salt

Put the cumin and fennel seeds in a frying pan and dry fry over medium heat, until the spices are lightly toasted and fragrant. Pound in a mortar and pestle (or use a spice grinder) and set aside.

In a food processor, blitz the fresh herbs and garlic until they form a green paste, add the rest of the ingredients, including the toasted spices, and pulse-blend until you have a thick paste. Transfer to a sterilised jar (see page 33) ready for use. If you refrigerate, allow the mix to come to room temperature first. It will keep in the fridge for up to 1 week.

RUBS, SAUCES & EXTRA FLAVOURS

MAKES 500G

HANG FIRE SMOKEHOUSE BARBECUE SAUCE

This Kansas City-style barbecue sauce is a must for your barbecue arsenal. In our opinion, a homemade barbecue sauce always tastes better than shop-bought and you can adjust the balance of any of the ingredients to suit your tastes. Some like it sweeter, some sharper, some add a little hickory powder for an extra smoky kick.

400g ketchup (page 35)
150ml cider vinegar
100ml Worcestershire sauce
100g dark brown molasses sugar
3 tbsp fresh lemon juice
3 tbsp blackstrap molasses
3 tbsp Dijon mustard
3 tbsp smoked paprika
2 tbsp onion powder
2 tbsp garlic powder
1 tbsp sea salt flakes
1 tbsp cracked black pepper
1 tsp chilli powder

Put all the ingredients in a pan and use a whisk or electric stick blender to blend. Put the pan over medium-low heat and bring the sauce to a gentle simmer, stirring occasionally for 15 minutes, until the sauce has reduced. Transfer to a sterilised jar with a lid (see page 33) and allow to cool. When the sauce has cooled to room temperature, pop on the lid and refrigerate to allow the ingredients to bind together for 24 hours before using. It will keep for 2 weeks in the fridge.

MAKES ABOUT 220G

LOUISIANA-STYLE REMOULADE

Remoulade is the key ingredient in most Louisiana sandwiches, shrimp dips, oyster and crab cocktails. We think it goes with everything from steaks to fish to salads. Here's how to make a version like they serve with their shrimp Po'Boys in the famous Central Market in New Orleans.

200g good-quality mayonnaise
2 tbsp Dijon mustard
1 tbsp fresh lemon juice
1 tbsp finely chopped flat-leaf parsley
1 tbsp Louisiana Hot Sauce (opposite) or your favourite hot sauce
2 tsp wholegrain mustard
1 large garlic clove, finely chopped
2 tsp capers, rinsed and chopped
1 tsp Worcestershire sauce
1 tsp paprika
1 spring onion, finely chopped
¼ tsp sea salt flakes
⅛ tsp cayenne pepper

Mix all the ingredients together thoroughly in a bowl, and let the remoulade sit in the fridge for an hour before serving. This should last about 3–4 days in the fridge. Slather the remoulade on sandwiches or serve as a dip for shellfish. It's like the best seafood sauce you've ever tasted.

RUBS, SAUCES & EXTRA FLAVOURS

RUSTIC HARISSA

SERVES 3–4

You've probably heard about harissa due to its popularity over the past few years, or perhaps seen it on supermarket shelves as an ingredient for making North African cuisine. This adaptation, with its warm spices and hit of garlic, will go down brilliantly served as a steak topper or a condiment to any of your barbecued meats.

½ tsp coriander seeds
½ tsp cumin seeds
½ tsp caraway seeds
2 red bell peppers, deseeded and quartered
3 tbsp groundnut oil, plus extra for the peppers
2 dried chipotle chillies, soaked in water overnight and drained
2 garlic cloves, roughly chopped
1½ tsp cider vinegar
½ tsp fine sea salt
½ tsp freshly cracked black pepper

Preheat the oven to 220°C/425°F/gas mark 7.

Put the coriander, cumin and caraway seeds in a frying pan and dry fry over medium heat until lightly toasted and fragrant. Take off the heat, lightly crush the spices in a mortar and pestle, and set aside.

Arrange the peppers, skin side up, on a roasting tray and rub their skins with a little oil. Roast in the oven for 20–30 minutes, until blistered and blackened. Take out of the oven and pop them in a sandwich bag for a few minutes to cool down. The steam should loosen the skin. When cool enough to handle, give the peppers a rub to remove the skin; make sure all the black bits of skin are discarded.

Put all the remaining ingredients in a blender or food processor with the peppers and blitz to a smooth paste. Transfer to a sterilised jar (see page 33) and keep in the fridge for up to a week.

RUBS, SAUCES & EXTRA FLAVOURS

SERVES 4-6

BONE MARROW BUTTER
AKA "BUTTER OF THE GODS"

Bone marrow butter is decadent, easy to make, freezes well and you can create whatever flavour profile suits you, from herby to spicy. This tasty spread can add extra creaminess as a steak topper, be enjoyed on its own scooped straight from the bone, mixed through mashed potatoes, slathered on corn on the cob or used instead of regular butter. We usually make this when we have something else going in the smoker. Because it'll take time for the fat to render, it's worth popping the bone canoes around whatever meat you're cooking at the beginning of the smoke.

- 4–6 beef marrow bones, cut lengthways into canoes, about 15–20cm in length (ask your butcher to do this for you)
- 4 garlic cloves, unpeeled
- 250g unsalted good-quality butter, at room temperature
- 2 tbsp finely chopped flat-leaf parsley
- ¼ tsp fine sea salt
- ¼ tsp freshly cracked black pepper
- pinch of chilli flakes
- squeeze of fresh lemon juice

Set up your grill for indirect heat, regulate to 120°C/250°F. Because you're only smoking the bones for about 1 hour, you can use a pretty strongly flavoured wood. Oak, hickory or mesquite are good options. Throw your woodchips or chunks onto the coals and pop your bones, marrow side up, on the opposite side of the heat. Make a little foil boat and pop your unpeeled garlic cloves in then put near the bones. Allow the bones about 1 hour to smoke, or until the marrow is almost transparent and rendered. The garlic cloves will take about 30 minutes, until they are soft to the touch. Take the bones and garlic out as and when they're ready and let them cool for 15 minutes.

In a bowl, cut the butter up into smaller pieces, squeeze the soft garlic cloves from their skins into the butter and mash with a fork. Use a small spoon to add the marrow, pushing the entire contents of the bone into the butter. Now add the remaining ingredients and use an electric whisk (or a strong whisk with some elbow grease) to combine well. If you're using an electric whisk, use a medium speed and whip up until the butter is light and fluffy. If you're doing it by hand, mix very vigorously. The end result should look a lot paler than regular butter due to the incorporated air.

Lay out some cling film and spoon the butter out into the middle, shaping it into a sausage. Wrap tightly and refrigerate for 1 hour before using, or freeze until you need it. The butter will last 3–4 days in the fridge and 1 month in the freezer.

TENNESSEE & THE CAROLINAS
NASHVILLE AND MEMPHIS

"Touched down in Nashville and it's bursting at the seams with country boys and country girls following their dreams."

Roadtrip Song, by Sam & Shauna

After 8 years of living the London rat race, we felt like we wanted to run for the hills. So that's what we did. With limited cash and time, we dumped our day jobs and our old lives and headed for the United States, on a bid to discover the bounties of the American Deep South.

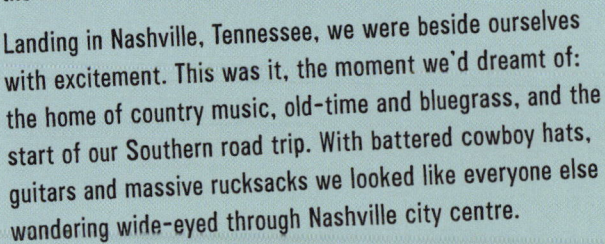

Landing in Nashville, Tennessee, we were beside ourselves with excitement. This was it, the moment we'd dreamt of: the home of country music, old-time and bluegrass, and the start of our Southern road trip. With battered cowboy hats, guitars and massive rucksacks we looked like everyone else wandering wide-eyed through Nashville city centre.

We are massive fans of Dolly Parton and were thrilled and fortunate enough to be staying with a wonderful guy called Steve who is Dolly's drummer. Steve and his partner Elizabeth introduced us to everyone and anyone in Nashville who was remotely involved in the restaurant business, had a food truck or owned a smoker. Together we sought out barbecue joints throughout Georgia and Tennessee. This trip taught us so much, not least that you have to bowl up early if you're to have any hope of sampling the best barbecue:

> "IN MY MIND I'M GOING TO CAROLINA CAN'T YOU SEE THE SUNSHINE CAN'T YOU JUST FEEL THE MOONSHINE?"
>
> Carolina In My Mind, James Taylor

many neighbourhood joints were closed or sold out by the time we arrived. ('Sold out' is a concept that Hang Fire is now all too familiar with!)

From Tennessee up to the Carolinas via Georgia, on this trip, we stopped at any number of little neighbourhood barbecue joints. One of the best was Walkers Fried Pies & BBQ in Ellijay, Georgia. Delicious deep-fried, hot pockets of blueberry filling served with creamy ice cream that are to die for, and yes they're 101% sinful (see page 212 for our version of the famous Walkers fried pie recipe).

For the next few weeks, we travelled between North and South Carolina, seeking out restaurants creating distinctive, modern flavours as well as proponents of traditional, regional Carolinian barbecue. One of the stand-out places was 12 Bones Smokehouse near Asheville, where the Obamas are apparently regulars. We were lucky enough to grab a rack of their blueberry chipotle sauce (see our version on page 39) baby-backs, plus a 'Hogzilla' sandwich which contained slices of brown-sugar bacon, a bratwurst, pulled pork, melted pepperjack cheese on a hoagie that was trying its best to hold it together. Needless to say it was regrettably enormous but as damn tasty as it sounds.

49

Road Trip

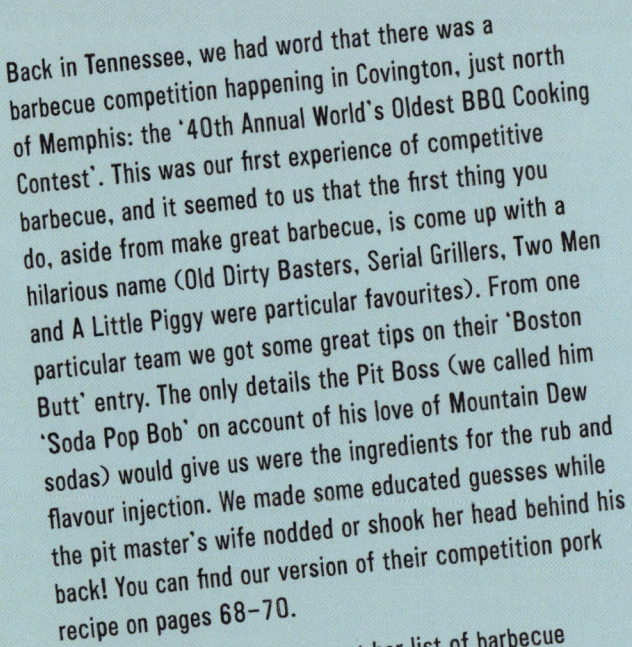

TENNESSEE & THE CAROLINAS
CONTINUED

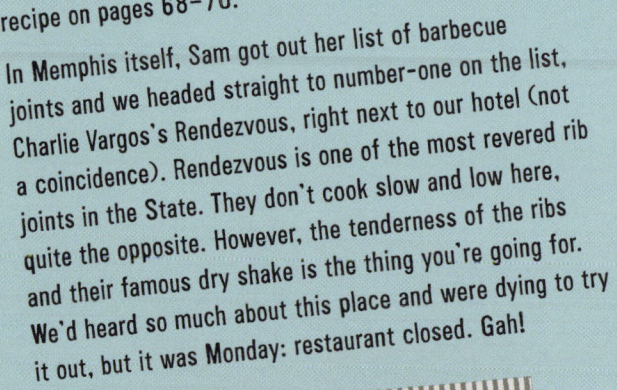

Back in Tennessee, we had word that there was a barbecue competition happening in Covington, just north of Memphis: the '40th Annual World's Oldest BBQ Cooking Contest'. This was our first experience of competitive barbecue, and it seemed to us that the first thing you do, aside from make great barbecue, is come up with a hilarious name (Old Dirty Basters, Serial Grillers, Two Men and A Little Piggy were particular favourites). From one particular team we got some great tips on their 'Boston Butt' entry. The only details the Pit Boss (we called him 'Soda Pop Bob' on account of his love of Mountain Dew sodas) would give us were the ingredients for the rub and flavour injection. We made some educated guesses while the pit master's wife nodded or shook her head behind his back! You can find our version of their competition pork recipe on pages 68–70.

In Memphis itself, Sam got out her list of barbecue joints and we headed straight to number-one on the list, Charlie Vargos's Rendezvous, right next to our hotel (not a coincidence). Rendezvous is one of the most revered rib joints in the State. They don't cook slow and low here, quite the opposite. However, the tenderness of the ribs and their famous dry shake is the thing you're going for. We'd heard so much about this place and were dying to try it out, but it was Monday: restaurant closed. Gah!

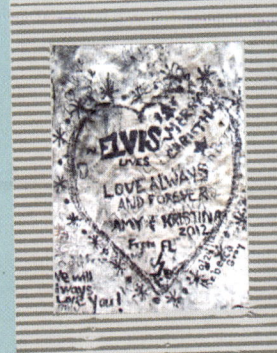

Number 2 was the ever-popular 'Central BBQ'. Central BBQ has put itself on the map by topping the 'best BBQ restaurant' chart for a while. And you can see why folks go. The counter service is slick and behind the till, you could see their pits working, racks and racks of ribs piled high, wrestled from the smoky abyss like small gators on pitch forks. Back on Beale Street there are a fair few places with barbecue competition trophies in their windows. After partying at BB King's blues club for an hour or three, we'd crossed off almost every entry on our 'must-eat' list in this barbecue town.

Memphis, the 'spiritual home of barbecue' and 'spiritual home of the blues' – that's an awful lot of reverence happening all in one place. Amen to that.

51

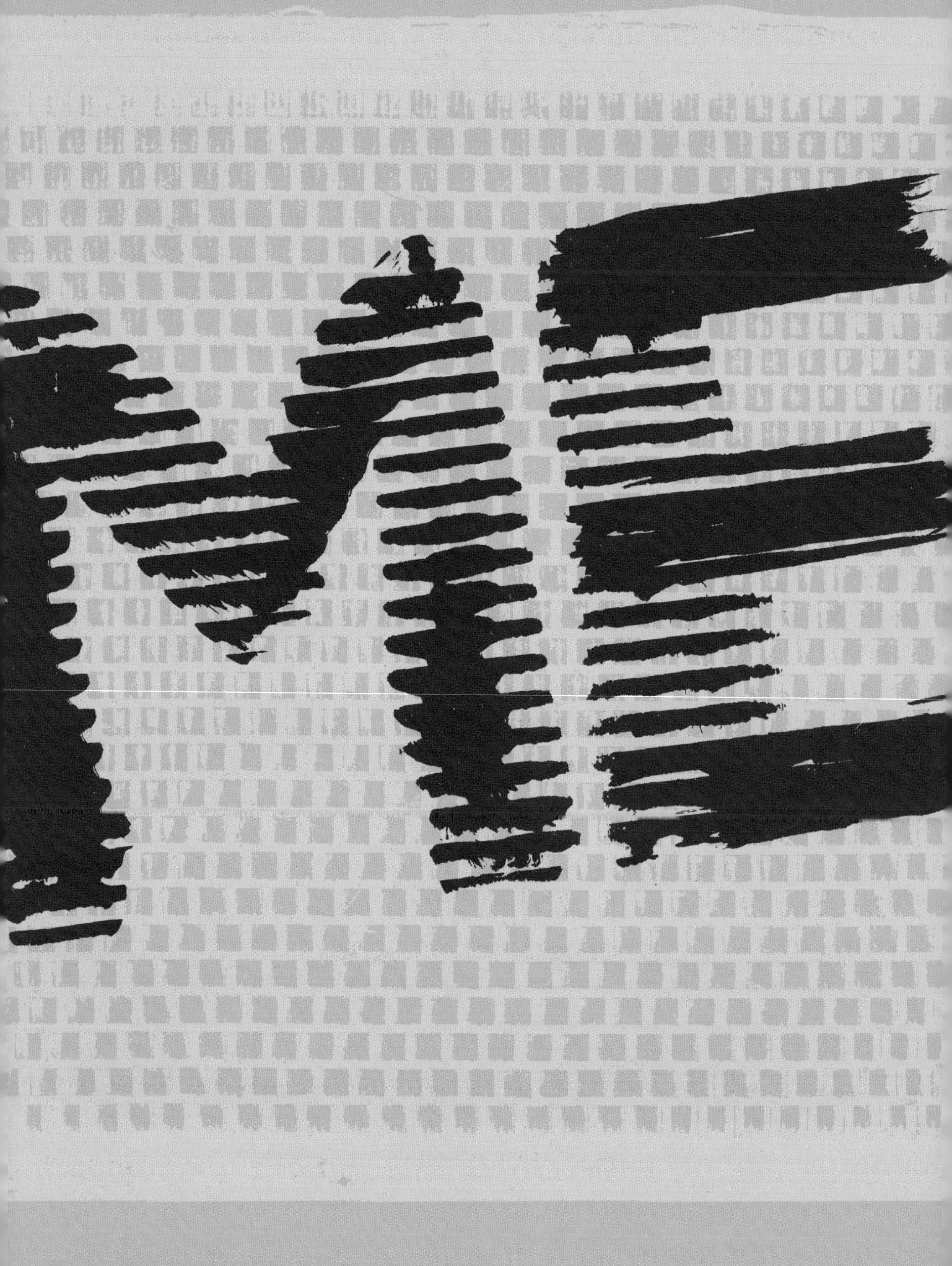

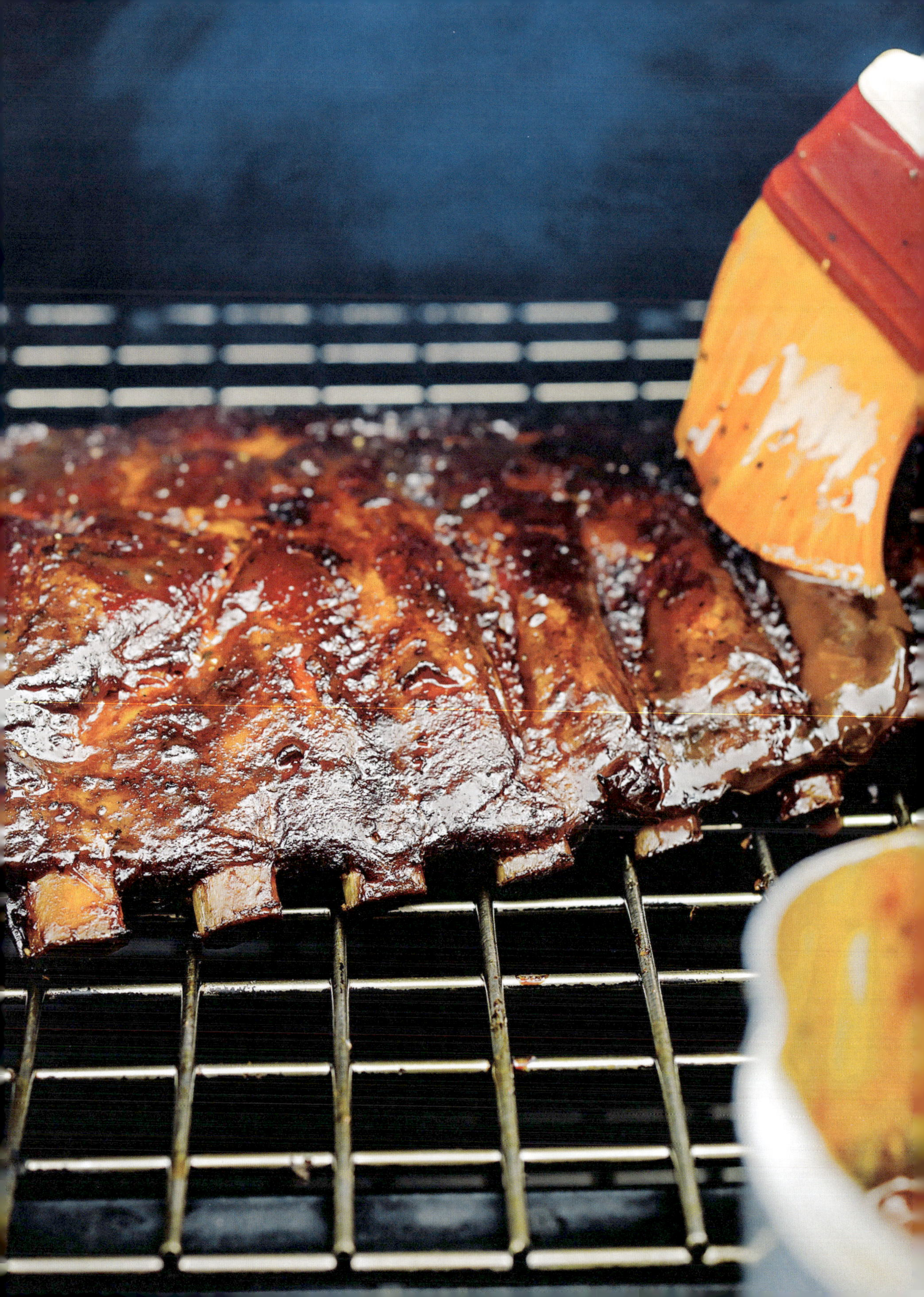

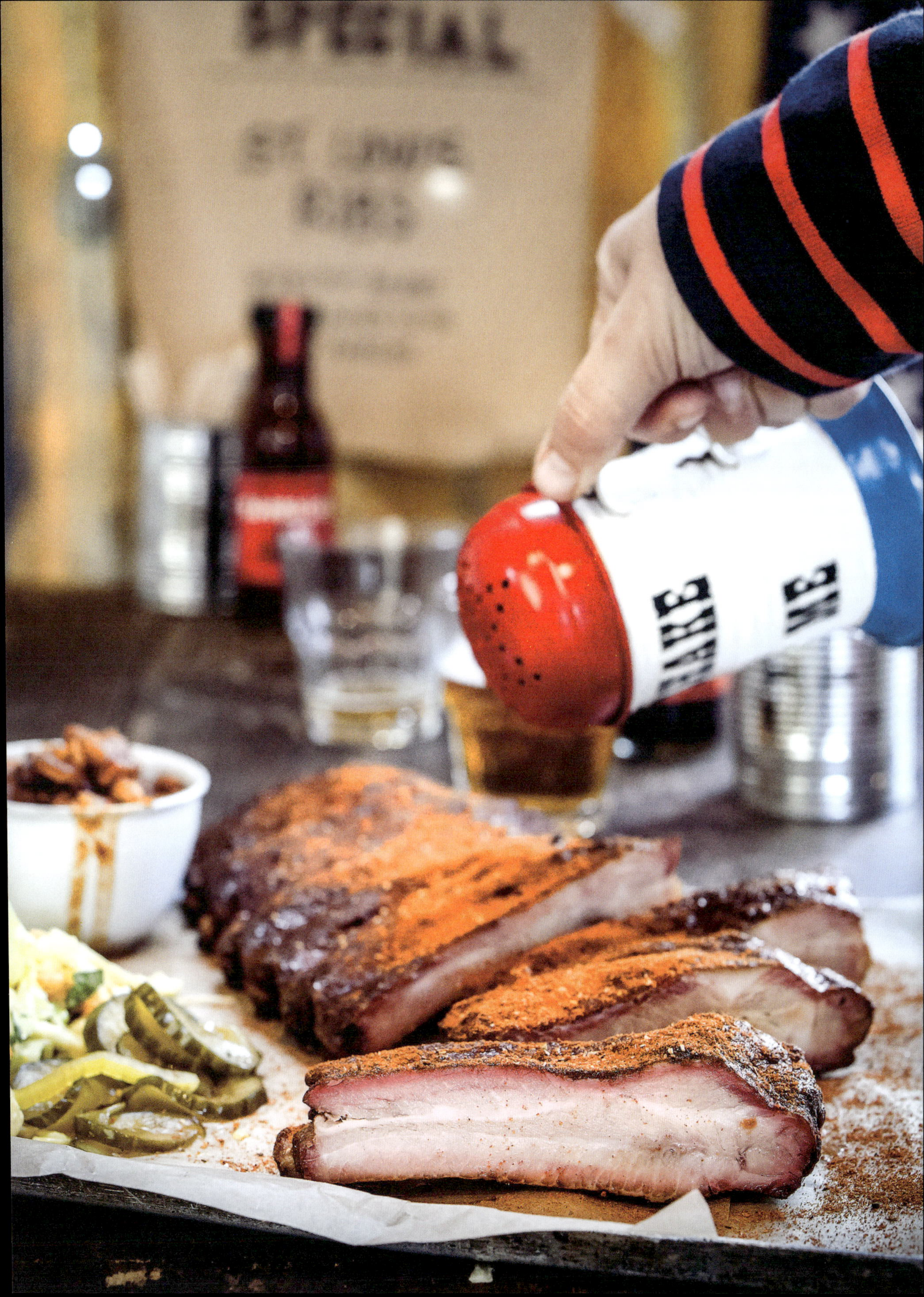
SPECIAL

①

②

③

ST LOUIS-STYLE SPARE RIBS

SERVES 8

PORK

This wouldn't be a book about barbecue if we didn't include a rib recipe or two, right? And frankly, if we sold nothing else at our HF pop-ups but pork spares, we'd make a lot of people happy! People cannot get enough of meat that comes with its own handle. And it seems to span generations. We've seen grandmas with their grandkids perched on their knee, both tucking into a pile of ribs as quickly as each other. They're a crowd-pleaser for sure.

COOKING METHODS Indirect Grilling/Smoking

WOOD Hickory, Oak

- 4 whole racks of pork spare ribs, about 1.2kg each
- 160ml olive oil or American mustard
- 12 tbsp Hang Fire Almost All-purpose Rub (page 26)
- 300g Hang Fire Smokehouse Barbecue Sauce (page 45), warmed
- 50g unsalted butter

For the Basting Mixture
- 200ml fresh apple juice
- 200ml cider vinegar

1. Trim the top and sides
2. Remove the membrane
3. Dust

Trim your ribs St Louis-style as per the pictures opposite. Drizzle 1 tablespoon of oil or a squirt of American mustard on each side of the ribs and rub in. Dust the rub onto the surface and underneath on the bone side of the ribs, coating the edges, too. Be careful not to rub it into the meat too vigorously otherwise you'll clog the pores we need open to absorb smoke. Pop in the fridge for 1 hour.

Set up your grill for indirect heat and maintain a consistent temperature around 108°C/225°F. Add your wood and when it's smoking, place your ribs in the smoker, with the curve of the bone facing down. (If you're using a rib rack, see the note on the next page.) You're looking at a 6-hour smoke time.

After 3 hours, a decent bark should have formed and you can wrap the ribs up in individual foil boats. Place a rack of ribs in the centre of two sheets of foil large enough to wrap over the top (the double layer preventing the bones from poking through). Make a little lip all round, turning the foil up at the edges. Mix together the basting ingredients, wrap each individual rib in a foil boat and pour 100ml into each packet. Wrap up and crimp the edges, making sure the foil is tightly wrapped around the rib. Return to the smoker and let them cook for about 2 hours.

After 2 hours, take the ribs out of the foil packets, discard the foil and the liquid, and return the ribs to the smoker for another hour. You should notice that the steaming stage has tenderised the meat and caused it to shrink back from the bones. The end bones should show through nicely – that's exactly what you want. The bark should have now reformed too and at the 5 hour mark, it's time to glaze these beauties.

Hey cowboy, the recipe continues on the next page...

In a saucepan, warm your Hang Fire Smokehouse Barbecue Sauce with the butter, mixing over low heat until the butter has melted. Don't let the sauce boil or bubble, simply warm through gently. Before you get glazing, test the ribs for doneness. Just after the 5-hour mark, pick them up with your tongs and do the 'bend test'. If the ribs do not crack at the ends when you pick them up with tongs, they need a little longer (you're looking at 90°C/195°F on your instant-read thermometer). At the 5 hour 15 minute mark, liberally paint the ribs all over with the warmed sauce, close the lid of the grill and let the glaze set for 15 minutes. Repeat again for the final 15 minutes of the cook.

When the ribs come out of the smoker, give them a liberal brushing with the remaining sauce. Let them rest for 10 minutes, then carve evenly between the bones to serve.

ON USING RIB RACKS

When using rib racks, we like to leave one space empty between the slabs so that the smoke and heat can flow evenly over the surfaces. If you don't have the luxury of space, make sure the ribs aren't touching each other – the slabs will take far longer to smoke.

Remove the ribs from the rib rack and lay them on top of each other in a large roasting tray. Pour in 200ml of the apple juice and cider vinegar mix then cover tightly with foil. Smoke for 2 hours, then remove and put them carefully back into the rib rack with the newly exposed bones facing upwards.

Unfortunately you may have to skip the glazing stage as it's pretty tricky to do for racks. You can, however, spritz them lightly with the basting mixture every 20 minutes starting at the 5 hour mark to help produce a good bark.

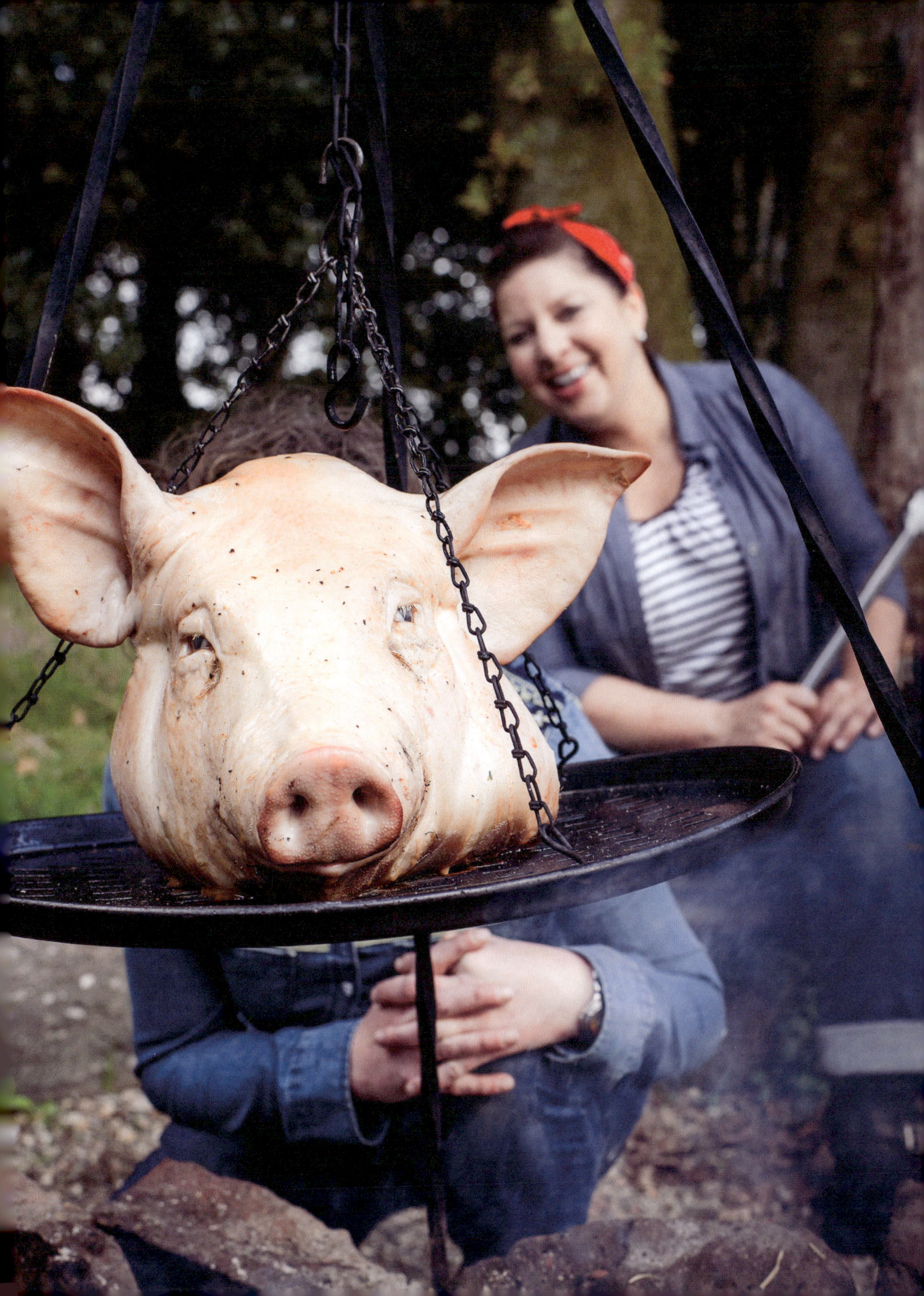

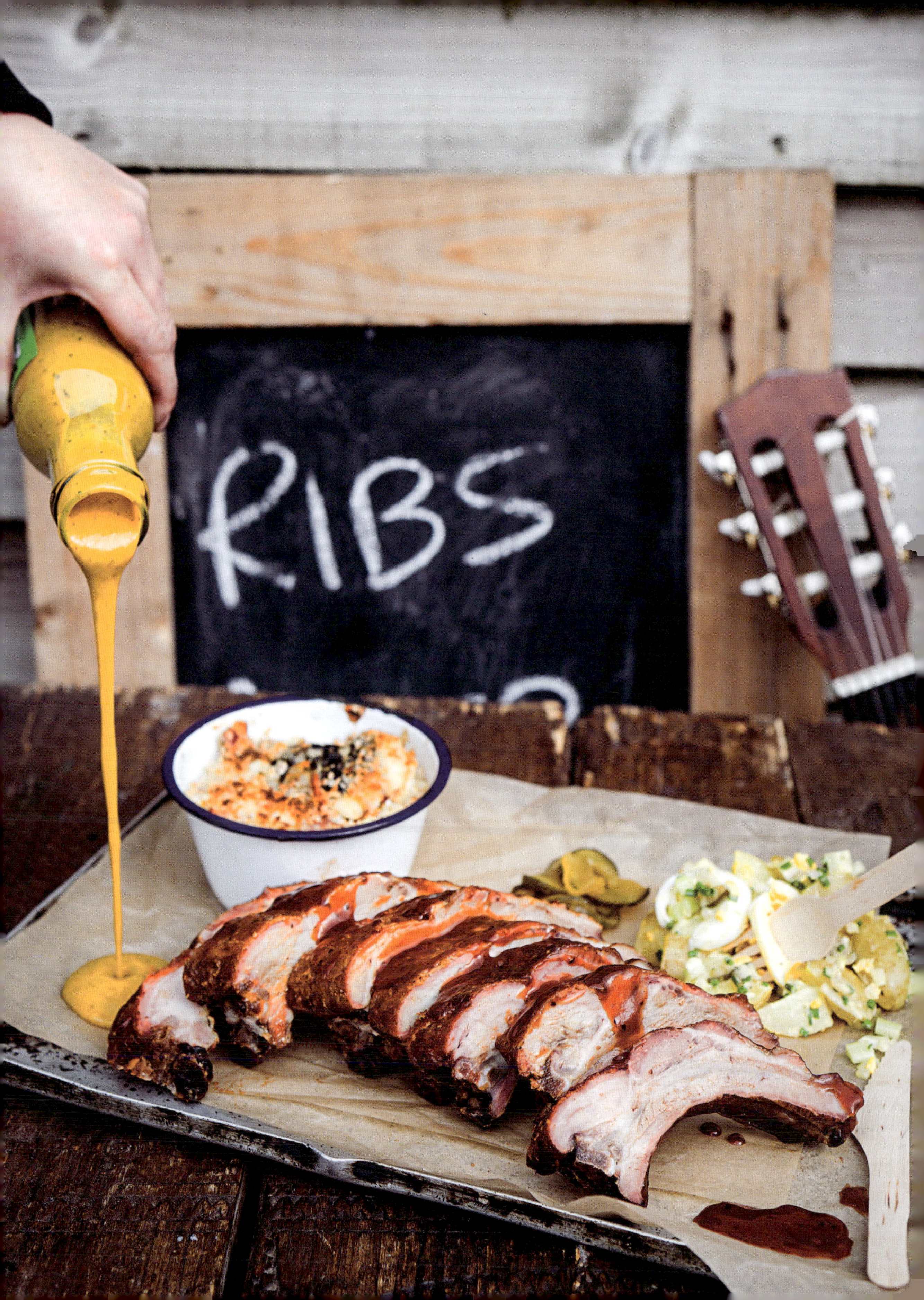
RIBS

SERVES 4

BABY BACK RIBS

Taken from the very top loin section of the pig's ribcage, baby backs have shorter, curvier bones with plenty of meat on them. Usually, you'll get a whole rack of babies per serving, leaving behind a rather impressive little boneyard, along with sticky faces and hands. We like these on the sweeter, stickier side, glazed with a rich Maple Bourbon Barbecue Sauce or our Blackberry Chipotle Barbecue Sauce.

COOKING METHODS Indirect Grilling/Smoking   **WOOD** Hickory, Oak

4 whole racks baby back pork ribs

3 tbsp olive oil or American mustard

8 tbsp Hang Fire Almost All-purpose Rub (page 26)

300g Maple Bourbon Barbecue Sauce (page 40) or Blackberry Chipotle Barbecue Sauce (page 39)

For the Basting Mixture

150ml fresh apple juice

150ml cider vinegar

4 tbsp softened unsalted butter

4 tbsp soft light brown sugar

First remove the rib membrane from the back of each rib (see page 56). Drizzle 1 tablespoon of oil or a squirt of American mustard on each side of the ribs and rub in. Dust the rub onto the surface and underneath on the bone side of the ribs, coating the edges. Be careful not to rub too vigorously otherwise you'll clog the pores that need to be open to absorb smoke. Pop in the fridge for 1 hour.

When you're ready to cook the ribs, set up your grill for indirect heat, and maintain a consistent temperature around 108°C/225°F. Place your ribs in the smoker, curve of the bone facing down. If you're using a rack to smoke your ribs in, see note on page 60. Depending on the meatiness of the ribs, you're looking at a 6-hour smoke.

After 3 hours, a decent bark should have formed and you can wrap the ribs up in foil boats. Place a rack of ribs in the centre of two sheets of foil large enough to wrap over the top (the double layer prevents the bones from poking through). Make a little lip all round, turning the foil up at the edges. Mix together the apple juice and vinegar and divide between the foil boats. Distribute the butter on top of the ribs and sprinkle with brown sugar. Wrap up tightly and crimp the edges. Return to the smoker for 2 hours.

After 2 hours, remove the ribs from the foil and discard the foil and the liquid. The steaming stage will have tenderised the meat and the end bones should be showing through nicely. Return the ribs to the smoker for another hour. Warm the barbecue sauce with a knob of butter, over low heat until, the butter has melted. Don't let it boil or bubble. Glaze the ribs twice all over during their final hour of cooking.

Your ribs should be done by the 6-hour mark. When they come out of the smoker, brush them liberally with the sauce then let them rest for 5–10 minutes. Carve evenly between the bones to serve.

MEAT

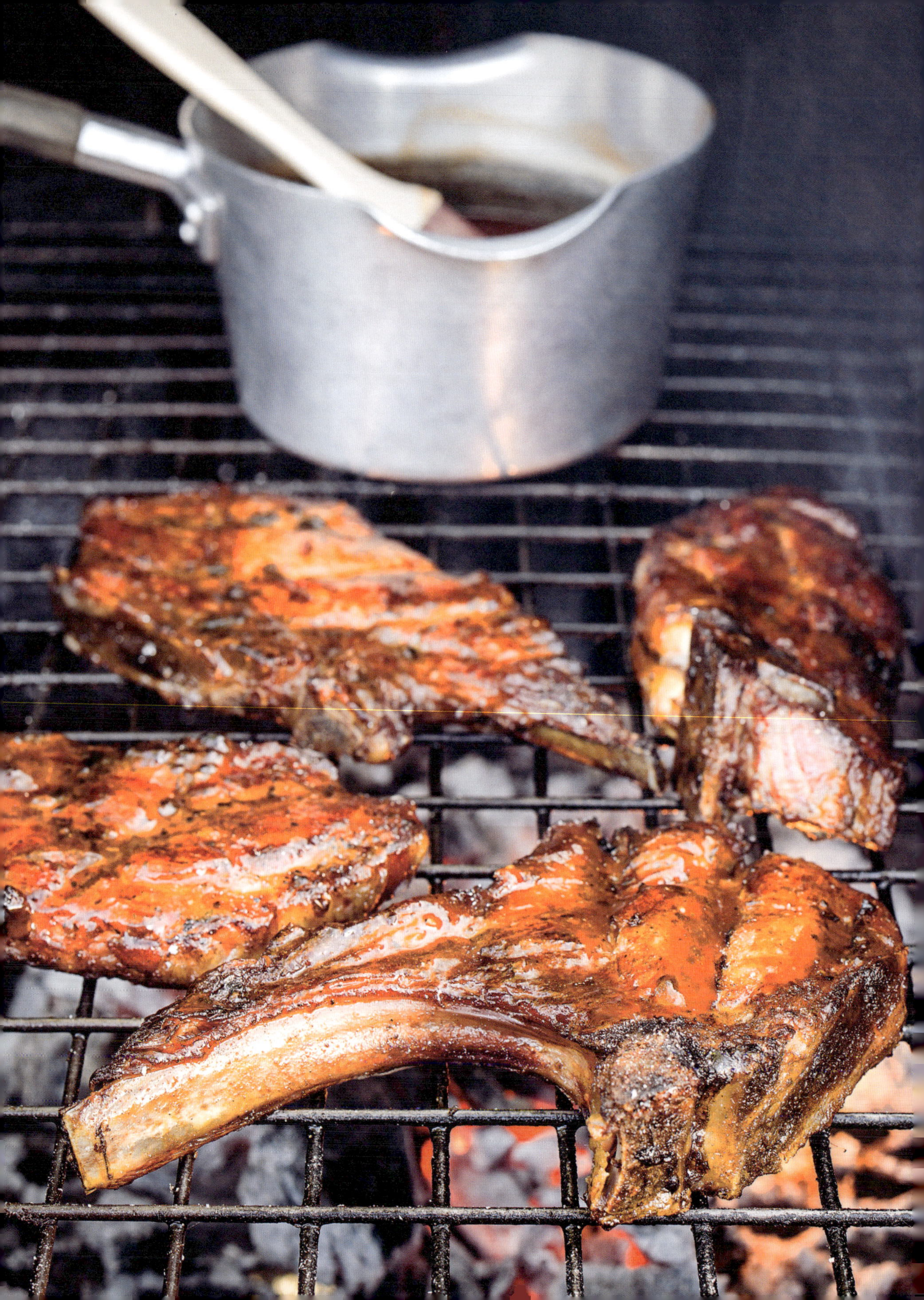

SERVES 5-6

COUNTRY-STYLE PORK RIBS
WITH WEST COUNTRY CIDER LIQUOR

Country-style ribs are meatier than other rib cuts and are from the blade end of the pork loin, close to the shoulder. It's like a small baby back rib and pork tenderloin all in one. We especially like this cut for its flavour, tenderness and value. Plus you can switch up the flavour profile to pretty much anything you like. Here, we make the ribs West-country style, with a little still sweetened cider and English mustard for balance.

COOKING METHODS Indirect Smoking/Grilling & Grilling

WOOD Oak, Beech or Cherry

- 300g South Carolina Mustard Sauce (page 38)
- 1.5kg bone-in, country-style pork ribs, cut into 6 pieces
- 40g Hang Fire Almost All-purpose Rub (page 26)
- 1 large onion, thinly sliced
- 3 garlic cloves, roughly chopped
- 300ml medium West Country style cider
- 100g soft light brown sugar
- 1 tbsp English mustard powder
- 1 tsp onion powder
- 2 fresh bay leaves
- 3 fresh thyme sprigs
- ½ tsp crushed red pepper flakes
- sea salt flakes and freshly ground back pepper
- groundnut oil, for greasing

Rub a teaspoon of mustard sauce on each side of the pork ribs. Cover and pop in the fridge for at least 1 hour while you prepare your braising liquor and set up your grill.

In a heavy-based pan, combine all the remaining ingredients, except the oil and keeping aside 150g of the South Carolina Mustard Sauce. Bring to a simmer over low heat – do not let it boil – for 10 minutes. Pour into an ovenproof dish with a lid, or disposable foil tin (with a foil lid), large enough to accommodate your ribs.

Set your smoker up for indirect heat at 120°C/250°F. Grease the grill with a little oil and arrange the ribs on top. Cook for about 1½ hours, or until the internal temperature of the loin end reads 65°C/150°F on an instant-read thermometer. Transfer the ribs to your dish with the braising liquor. Evenly coat the ribs with the liquor, making sure the onions stay on the bottom of the dish. Cover tightly and return to the smoker for 2 hours, or until the internal temperature of the ribs is between 108°C/195°F and 110°C/200°F. The cider helps tenderise the ribs and they will take on a wonderful fragrance.

Carefully remove the dish from the smoker and drain the braising liquor back into your heavy-based pan. Set over medium heat and simmer for about 15 minutes, until reduced by about half.

Meanwhile, return your ribs to your grill and sear on direct heat, brushing the ribs all over with the reserved South Carolina Mustard Sauce. Grill for 2–3 minutes each side to set the sweet mustard glaze. To serve, line up the ribs and pour over your reduced cider mustard liquor. Serve with pickles (pages 182–86), German-style Potato Salad (page 155) and Lexington-style Red 'Slaw (page 150).

MEAT

NORTH CAROLINA-STYLE PULLED PORK

SERVES 8

Pork is the cornerstone of traditional, Carolina-style barbecue. We sell a ton of this, and just when we think people are 'over' pulled pork, we sell a ton more. There is an insatiable appetite for pulled pork right now, but nothing beats real pulled pork – and for us, it's solely a smoked meat.

Pulled pork is fairly straightforward to make when you understand the process and principles. And for the novice pit boss, it is by far one of the most satisfying things to cook out on your smoker. Combine your pulled pork with some delicious side dishes like coleslaw and potato salad.

COOKING METHODS Indirect Grilling/Smoking

WOOD 50/50 Hickory/Cherry mix

- 1 x 3–4kg bone-in rindless pork shoulder (Boston butt)
- 4 tbsp groundnut oil or 4 tsp American mustard

For the Mop Sauce

- 400ml cider vinegar
- 100ml Worcestershire sauce
- 3 tbsp ketchup (page 35)
- 2 tbsp dark brown sugar
- 1 tbsp red pepper flakes
- 1 tbsp Louisiana-style Hot Sauce (page 44)
- 1 tbsp fine sea salt
- 1 tsp ground black pepper

For the Rub

- 100g soft light brown sugar
- 100g fine sea salt
- 2 tbsp paprika
- 1 tbsp ground cinnamon
- 1 tbsp garlic granules
- 1 tbsp onion granules
- 1 tbsp coarsely ground black pepper
- 1 tbsp chilli powder
- 1 tbsp fennel seeds

First, make the sauce. Combine the ingredients in a saucepan over medium heat for 5–10 minutes. Remove from the heat and reserve about half of the sauce to mix with your pulled pork meat at the end of the cook.

Next, combine the ingredients for the rub in a bowl and put your pork shoulder in a baking tray. Rub the pork all over with oil or American mustard, then sprinkle liberally with the rub, making sure it is evenly coated. Give it a pat all over but don't rub vigorously as you'll end up clogging the fine pores in the pork, which we need open to absorb smoke. Let the pork sit for 2 hours in the fridge while you get your smoker ready.

Set your smoker up for indirect smoking – you want to hold a temperature of 108°C/225°F before putting in your pork, fat side up. Add your wood. You're in for a long smoke, about 18–23 hours, so think about your coal-adding strategy to make sure your smoker floats around 108°C/225°F. Add in a couple more wood chunks/chips every hour or so for the first 5 hours, or as and when they burn out, to get a good smoky flavour; this is a dense piece of meat, so can take a good hit of smoke.

After the 14-hour mark, start basting the pork with your mop sauce, every hour until it is done. You'll want to get pretty quick at doing this as your smoker will drop in temperature every time you open it. See also our note about 'The Meat Stall' (opposite).

There are two ways to tell when your pork is done. Firstly, using heat-proof gloves, grab the bone and give it a tug. If it starts to come away easily, you're there. Alternatively, if you have an instant-read thermometer, you're looking for an internal temperature of about 95°C/203°F.

When the pork is done, carefully remove from the smoker, transfer to a clean roasting tin, cover tightly in foil and leave to sit for 30–40 minutes. After this time, use some claws or heat-proof gloves to pull the pork meat, discarding the bone and anything that looks like fat or connective tissue. We like to keep as much of the bark in the mix as possible. Gently heat up some of the reserved mop sauce and mop it over the shredded meat to keep it nice and moist before serving.

THE STALL – DON'T PANIC!

Your pork shoulder will undoubtedly hit the 'meat stall' (that is, it appears to stop cooking) when the internal temperature reaches 65°C/150°F–75°C/170°F and it'll stay there for hours. This is normal and there are plenty of theories why this happens. If you want to understand the science, we recommend visiting amazingribs.com and checking out their in-depth section on 'meat stall'. For us, the stall is akin to suddenly being stuck on the crest of a rollercoaster ride. All the connective tissues, fats and collagens and moisture are physically and chemically changing all at one time-consuming apex. As the moisture evaporates from your hunk of meat, the muscle will start to heat up again, setting the rollercoaster cart back in motion. This can take anything from 3–6 hours. Don't whip the pork out and stick it in the oven (unless you're really pushed for time) and don't crank up the smoker heat – you can't rush good things. If you are desperate to jostle it along, make a 'Texas Crutch' (see Brisket and Burnt Ends, pages 92–93). We prefer to open another beer, not worry about it and let it take its own sweet, smoky time.

NO IFS, NO BUTTS

We've found one of the more consistent ways to communicate this pork cut to your British butcher is by calling it a 'bone-in pork shoulder, neck end'. Resist the temptation to ask an old-school butcher for a 'Boston butt' (as it's called in the States) because you'll invariably be met with a blank expression. You can, of course, use a boneless shoulder, but sometimes the finesse required to tunnel the bone out can be hit and miss and you may not end up with a solid barrel or butt shape. Plus cooking for a long time on the bone is sure to impart a little more flavour.

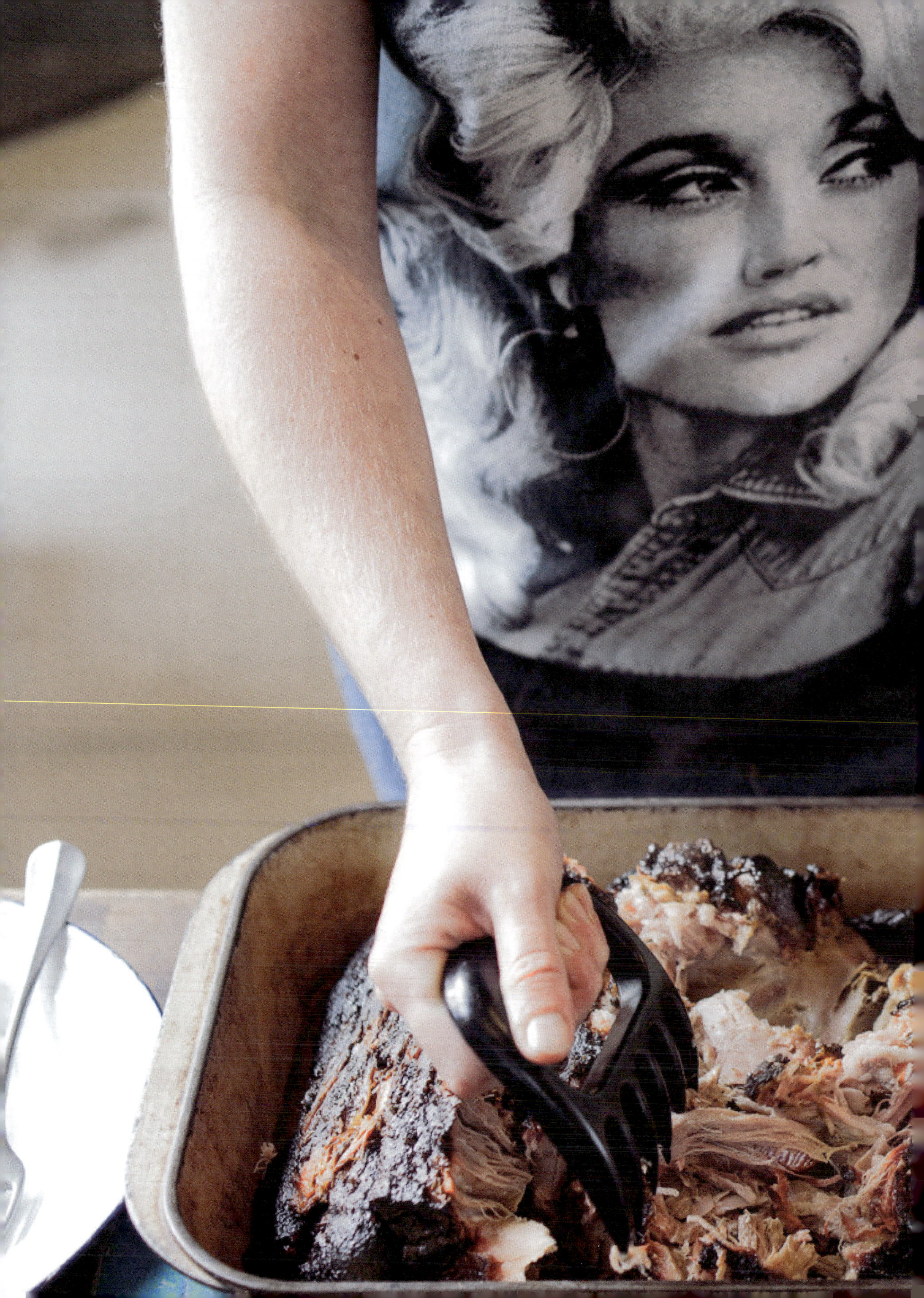

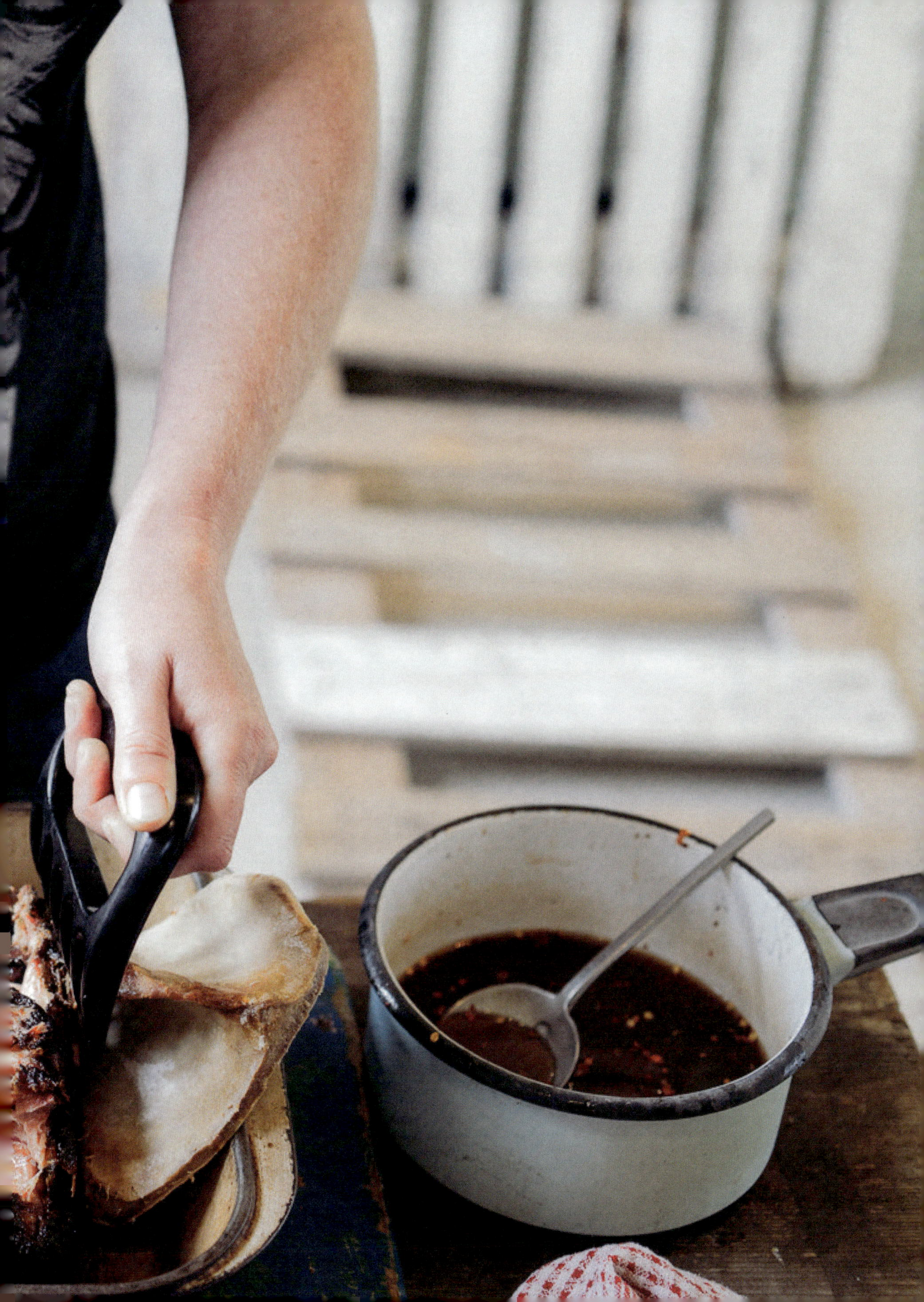

SERVES 8–10

COMPETITION PULLED PORK

We went along to several regional barbecue competitions while we were in the States; it's a fascinating world, full of tips, tricks and determination to gain the edge over the competition and make the judges giddy with one bite of meat (as that's often all they take). We observed this pork recipe in action at the '40th Annual World's Oldest BBQ Cooking Contest' in Covington, TN. The pit boss of one particularly successful team kindly talked us through his recipe, and we even got to take it to their 'turn in' entry to the judges' table with a crew member (way more nerve-wracking than it sounds). They humbly requested to remain nameless as a team because they use a very similar recipe for most competitions. All we can say is, thanks to the pit master we called 'Soda Pop Bob', we hope we've done your recipe justice.

Anyone that makes, or is interested in, competition barbecue won't be put off by this process, but it can feel intimidating to attempt for the first time, plus if you look at the timings, you'll be working on this piece of meat every few hours, so you won't get much sleep. Take your time and go through the recipe stage by stage, we're sure you'll enjoy the final product.

COOKING METHODS Indirect Smoking/Grilling

WOOD 50/50 Hickory/Cherry mix

1 x 4.5kg bone-in, rindless pork shoulder (aka Boston butt)
100ml groundnut oil
fine sea salt, to taste

For the Flavour Injection

150ml apple juice
5 tbsp soft light brown sugar
2 tbsp Worcestershire sauce
1 tbsp light soy sauce
1 tbsp fine sea salt

continued over there...

STAGE ONE

In a pan, combine the flavour injection ingredients with 100ml water over low heat. Cook, stirring, for 4–5 minutes until the salt and sugar dissolve. Remove from heat and allow to cool.

Trim off any excess fat from the pork – you only want to leave about 3mm on the top. Place in a baking tray while you inject the flavour injection. Fill a basting syringe with the flavour injection mixture and, working in straight lines about 5cm apart, push the needle in and slowly pull the needle from the pork as you squeeze the plunger. Repeat, until you have used all of the mixture. If you plan on handing in what's known as 'The Money Muscle', see the notes on page 70 before you make a start on preparing the shoulder. Wrap in cling film and refrigerate for 2 hours. Bring the pork out of the fridge to allow it to rest at room temperature while you prepare your smoker.

STAGE TWO

In a bowl, combine the ingredients for the competition rub. Pat the pork dry with kitchen towels and rub the oil in, liberally sprinkle on about half the competition

For the Competition Rub

50g dark brown sugar

30g paprika

30g garlic salt

30g onion powder

20g fine sea salt

20g ancho chilli powder

20g toasted fennel seeds, ground

10g cayenne pepper

10g ground black pepper

For the Spritz Juice

100ml apple juice

100ml cider vinegar

For the Wrap Juice

50g South Carolina Mustard Sauce (page 38)

50g soft light brown sugar

50ml cider vinegar

2 tbsp unsalted butter

For the Finishing Sauce and Glaze

100g Hang Fire Smokehouse Barbecue Sauce (page 45)

100g Crab Apple Butter (page 33)

50ml cider vinegar

100g unsalted butter

1 tsp fine sea salt

Hey cowboy, the recipe continues on the next page...

rub, reserving the other half for later. Make sure it's well coated, lightly patting the rub into the oil as you go. Bob kindly reminded us that 'it ain't no massage parlour' – so don't rub in too vigorously! Put the pork back in the fridge for 2 hours. After this time, take the pork out of the fridge for 30 minutes before you put it in the smoker.

Set your grill up for indirect heat at 108°C/225°F. As it starts to come up to temperature, it's time to add your wood. Arrange your pork shoulder on the grates, fatside down. Cook for 3 hours. Meanwhile, combine the spritz juice ingredients in a clean spray bottle. After the 3-hour mark, flip your pork so the fat is facing upwards and spritz all over with your apple and cider vinegar mix. Continue to cook for another 5 hours, spritzing and adding wood every hour or so, or as and when needed for up to 5–6 hours. Spritz the pork again, then continue to cook for another 3 hours. At this stage, use an instant-read thermometer to check that the internal temperature of the pork is about 77°C/170°F (careful you don't hit the bone when you are checking the temperature of the pork). This is the temperature you want to hit before thinking about removing the 'Money Muscle' (page 70).

NEXT, PREPARE YOUR WRAP JUICE

In a small pan, warm the ingredients and stir well until fully combined. Remove your pork shoulder from the smoker and put in a disposable foil tin. Pour the wrap juice all over the pork, make a foil tent with a double layer of foil over the tin, and ensuring there are no holes. The foil should be crimped tightly around the tin but should not touch the pork. Transfer to the smoker, crank the heat up to 121°C/250°F and cook for 6 hours. Carefully remove the pork and set it back in the smoker. Cook for a further 2–3 hours, or until the internal temperature of the pork reaches 93°C/200°F.

THE FINAL STAGE

While your shoulder is just coming to temperature, prepare your finishing sauce and glaze.

In a small saucepan, combine the ingredients and warm through over medium-low heat. Strain through a metal sieve into a bowl, using a spoon to push through to get a smooth spreadable glaze and sauce.

Remove the shoulder from the smoker and carefully remove the foil tent – it will be piping hot – and reserve this if you can. Brush on some of the finishing glaze and sprinkle over some of the reserved championship rub, then return to the smoker for 30 minutes. Remove your pork from the smoker, cover tightly with a fresh sheet of foil and put it in a cool box for 1 hour.

With either bear claws or heatproof gloves, start to pull the shoulder blade bone out. Shred the meat into small and medium pieces, being careful to remove and discard any connective tissue and excess fat. Don't over-shred the meat – you want to get plenty of bark in there and some pieces that show off your smoke ring. Mix through some of the finishing sauce so each piece is beautifully glazed. If you are serving the 'money muscle', brush some sauce onto each slice of that, too. Finish with a light sprinkling of fine sea salt.

Place a loose ball of pulled pork, about fist size, in the top of your perfect 'putting green' parsley box and lay your glazed slices of money muscle below. Most importantly, get to the turn-in well on time. You really don't want to have to sprint and squeeze through crowds with your precious cargo, so plan your route and have a dedicated person do this. We'll pass on the final piece of advice that 'Soda Pop Bob' gave us... 'Don't drop it, girls!'

SHOW ME THE MONEY (MUSCLE)

It seems to be the modus operandi for today's competition teams to hand in the 'money muscle' with their pulled pork boxes. However, we did notice that not all teams did, and we also noticed their names weren't called. We're assuming that it shows the judges an extra level of skill and expertise. The money muscle is pretty easy to identify – it's the long muscle on the side of the pork shoulder that has evenly spaced stripes of fat running horizontally down it. Most Kansas City Barbecue Society sanctioned barbecue competitions prohibit any separation of a 'whole' piece while it's uncooked. You'll want to work with a flexible boning knife to try and separate this muscle as much as possible from the main shoulder, leaving a little at the base so it remains connected. Sneaky huh? Trim any excess fat from around the muscle.

Just before the wrapping stage, cut the muscle off and make a separate foil parcel for it. Add a large knob of butter, Hang Fire Smokehouse Barbecue Sauce and a sprinkling of brown sugar to the foil parcel and put the muscle on top. Wrap tightly and return to the smoker along with your shoulder.

After 30 minutes of cooking, open the money muscle foil parcel so the bark reforms (you may want to brush the contents of the parcel all over the muscle). Return to the pit for 15 minutes. Take it out again, discard any excess liquid from the foil parcel, and wrap back up again in foil and return it to the pit. Keep an eye on the temperature and remove it when it hits 82–85°C /180–185°F. Set the parcel in your thermal box until you're ready to carve into slices and serve with your competition pulled pork.

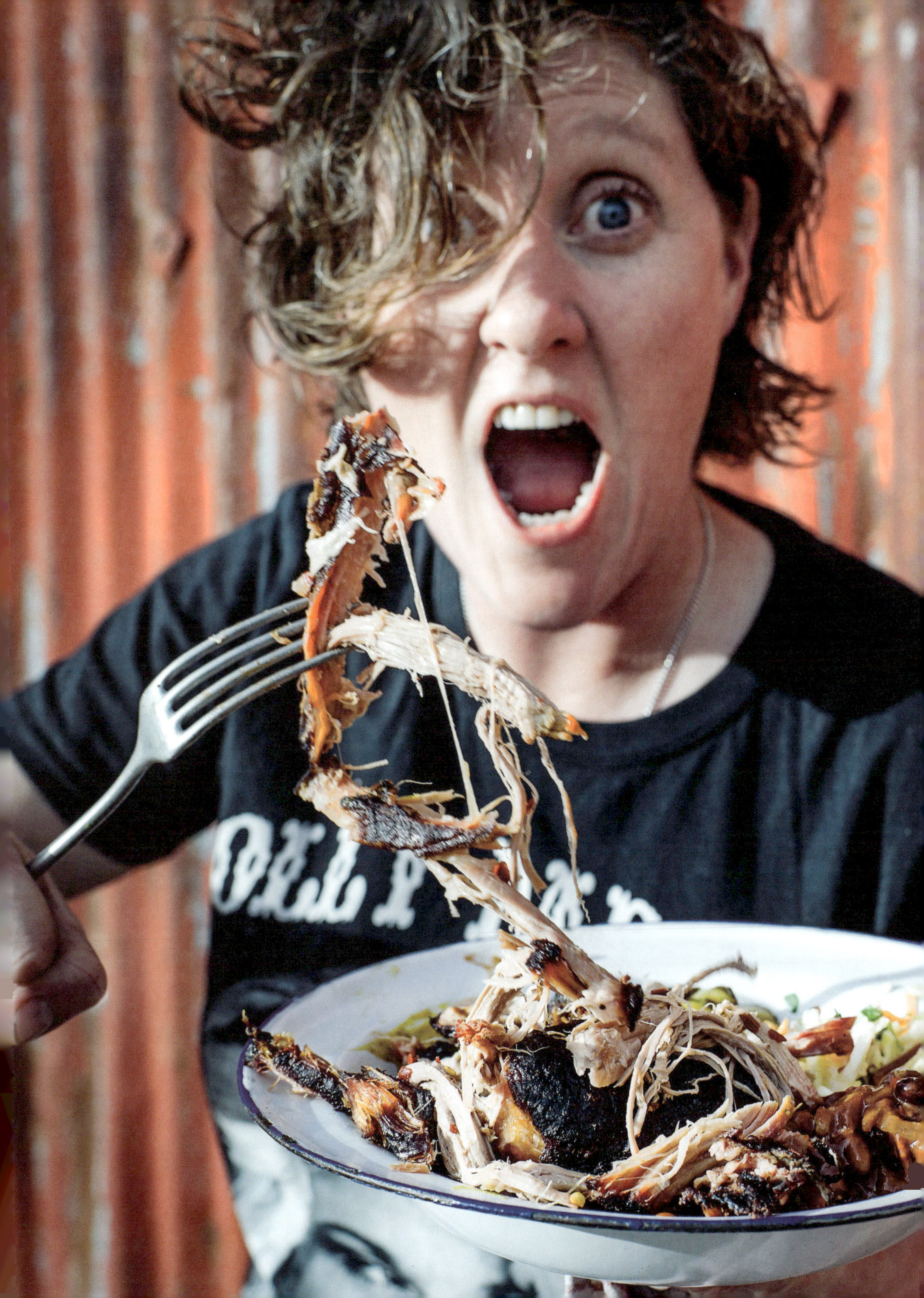

SMOKED PORK CHOPS
WITH WEST INDIAN-STYLE SALSA VERDE

This makes for a great dinner and is fairly quick to make – by slow and low standards that is. We love this take on salsa verde, with its fiery heat and delicious earthy thyme flavour. Brine your pork chops for a minimum of three to five hours, and you'll lock in the juicy pork flavour. Goes great with Hoppin' John (page 170), Hasselback Potatoes (page 156) and a dollop of sour cream.

COOKING METHODS Brining, Indirect Grilling/Smoking

WOOD Cherry

4 boneless pork loin chops, about 5cm thick
1 tbsp coarse salt
1 tbsp freshly cracked black pepper

For the Brine

25g sea salt flakes
25g soft light brown sugar
1 tsp ground cinnamon
½ tsp allspice
2 sprigs of fresh thyme
1 fresh bay leaf

For the West Indian-style Salsa Verde

1 tsp soft light brown sugar
150ml olive oil
juice of 4 limes
small bunch flat-leaf parsley, chopped
1 tbsp finely chopped fresh thyme leaves
small bunch coriander, chopped
1 large garlic clove, finely chopped
4 spring onions, finely chopped
1 tsp finely grated lime zest
1 scotch bonnet chilli, deseeded and finely chopped
½ tsp fine sea salt
½ tsp chopped fresh ginger

First, brine the pork chops. Add all the ingredients for the brine to a pan along with 500ml water. Heat gently over low heat for about 5 minutes, until the salt has dissolved. Take off the heat and allow the brine to cool to room temperature. Put the pork chops in a plastic tub or ziplock bag and pour over the cooled brine. Refrigerate for at least 3 hours, or ideally 5–6 hours.

To make the salsa verde, pulse the sugar, oil and lime juice in a food processor. Add the remaining ingredients and blitz for a few seconds until loosely blended. Pour into a bowl, cover with cling film and set aside.

Remove the pork chops from the brine and pat dry with kitchen paper. Season with a little salt and pepper and let them come to room temperature.

Meanwhile, fire up your grill for indirect heat using cherry wood for the smoke flavour and stabilise the temperature at 113°C/235°F. Add the pork chops and smoke for about 1 hour or so, until the pork chops reach an internal temperature of 74°C/165°F on an instant-read thermometer. Remove and let them rest on a warm plate for 10 minutes.

Thinly slice the pork chops and pour over the salsa verde to serve, approximately 3 tablespoons per chop. You can keep any salsa verde you don't use for up to a week in the fridge.

SERVES 6-8

CUBAN MOJO HAM HOCK

Much like a lamb shank, a ham hock has the leg bone running through it, and it takes a slow and low cook beautifully. It's an often forgotten cut of the pig, but give this recipe go – you'll love the Latino flavours and it makes a fantastic alternative to regular ham hock recipe. Not to mention that ham hocks are pretty good value, too. You can get fairly small hocks that make up one large portion, and these look great on the plate when served. Ask your butcher to give you 'uncured' hocks, and to remove the skins for you; the skins can be used to make pork crackling. Plan ahead with this dish if you get pre-cured hocks, as you'll need to remove the saline in the hocks overnight before using them (see below).

COOKING METHODS Indirect Grilling/Smoking or Oven   **WOOD** Apple, Oak

4 rindless ham hocks (about 400g each), preferably uncured

For the Mojo Marinade

250ml fresh orange juice

120ml freshly squeezed lime juice

1 garlic head, cloves separated, peeled and finely sliced

1 tbsp toasted cumin seeds, ground

1 tbsp dried oregano

1 tbsp sea salt flakes

1 tbsp paprika

1 tsp freshly cracked black pepper

For the Glaze

100g soft light brown sugar

50g honey

100ml cider vinegar

Start by mixing the marinade ingredients in a bowl. Place the ham hocks in a ziplock bag large enough to accommodate the hocks and marinade. Pour over the marinade and refrigerate for at least 24 hours, ideally 48 hours.

To smoke the hocks, set up your grill for indirect heat at 108°C/225°F. The hocks will take around 4 hours to reach 72°C/160°F. Rest the hocks in a foil tent for 10–15 minutes before serving.

If you want to roast the ham hocks in the oven, preheat the oven to 180°C/350°F/gas mark 4. Place the hocks in a medium-sized roasting tin (about 25 x 30cm), cover with foil and cook for 3½ hours, or until the meat is deliciously tender and falling off the bone. Turn the hocks two or three times during cooking to baste with the juices and get all those beautiful flavours into the meat.

These ham hocks go wonderfully with some Pineapple Chow-Chow (page 181), Maque Choux (page 173) and a bowl of Hush Puppies (page 160).

SALTY HOCKS

For this recipe, it is best to use uncured hocks, however, they are often sold pre-cured. If using cured ham hocks, simply put them in a bowl with plenty of water. Add half a potato (to speed up the osmosis a little) and leave to soak overnight before using.

It's also worth cooking an extra ham hock to use in other dishes. Take the meat off and freeze in a ziplock bag. You can then make a delicious mid-week pot of Hoppin' John (page 170).

HOT PIG WINGS

SERVES 10–12 AS AN APPETISER, OR 4–5 AS A MAIN

Pig wings are technically from the fore shank of the pig and they're basically mini ham hocks using the closest and smallest, cluster of muscles to the bone. Your butcher should be able to get you some of these but make sure you give them advance notice and you'll probably have to talk them through it – prepare for 'pigs don't fly' jokes.

They not only taste great, they look impressive – like Jurassic chicken wings! We like to make a big plate of them and serve them as appetisers before a barbecue dinner. In this recipe, we give the pig wings a little heat with both the rub and the glaze, and go the 'whole hog' by making a tasty blue cheese dip on the side. We also like to serve these with our Louisiana-style Remoulade (page 45) – the creamy, vinegary sauce works really well.

COOKING METHODS Indirect Smoking/Grilling   **WOOD** Oak, Beech or Cherry

10–12 pork shanks (about 350g each)
1–2 tbsp groundnut oil
150g Sweet Chipotle Barbecue Sauce (page 36)

For the 4-3-2-1 Hot Rub
4 tbsp fine sea salt
3 tbsp soft light brown sugar
2 tbsp cayenne pepper
1 tbsp paprika

For the Blue Cheese Dip
100ml soured cream
100g mayonnaise
50ml buttermilk
85g blue cheese, crumbled
1 garlic clove, finely chopped
2 tbsp finely chopped flat-leaf parsley
¼ tsp fresh cracked black pepper
fine sea salt, to taste
pinch of paprika

Mix all the ingredients for the blue cheese dip in a large bowl, cover and refrigerate until ready to serve.

Next, combine the ingredients for the rub in a bowl. Make sure your pig wings have about 6cm of exposed bone at the top. Rub your pig wings in groundnut oil and coat evenly with the rub. Cover the bowl with cling film and refrigerate overnight.

The next day, take the pig wings out of the fridge and allow them to come up to room temperature for 30 minutes before smoking.

Wrap the exposed hock bones in squares of foil. Set your grill up for indirect heat and regulate to 108°C/225°F, add in your wood and place the pig wings on the grates. They'll take around 5 hours to smoke and you're looking to hit a fairly high internal temperature of 90°C/195°F. When the pig wings have reached this temperature, remove the foil and glaze all over with warmed Sweet Chipotle Barbecue Sauce, return to the smoker for a further 15 minutes then repeat once more. Allow the pig wings to rest for 15 minutes before serving with the blue cheese dip.

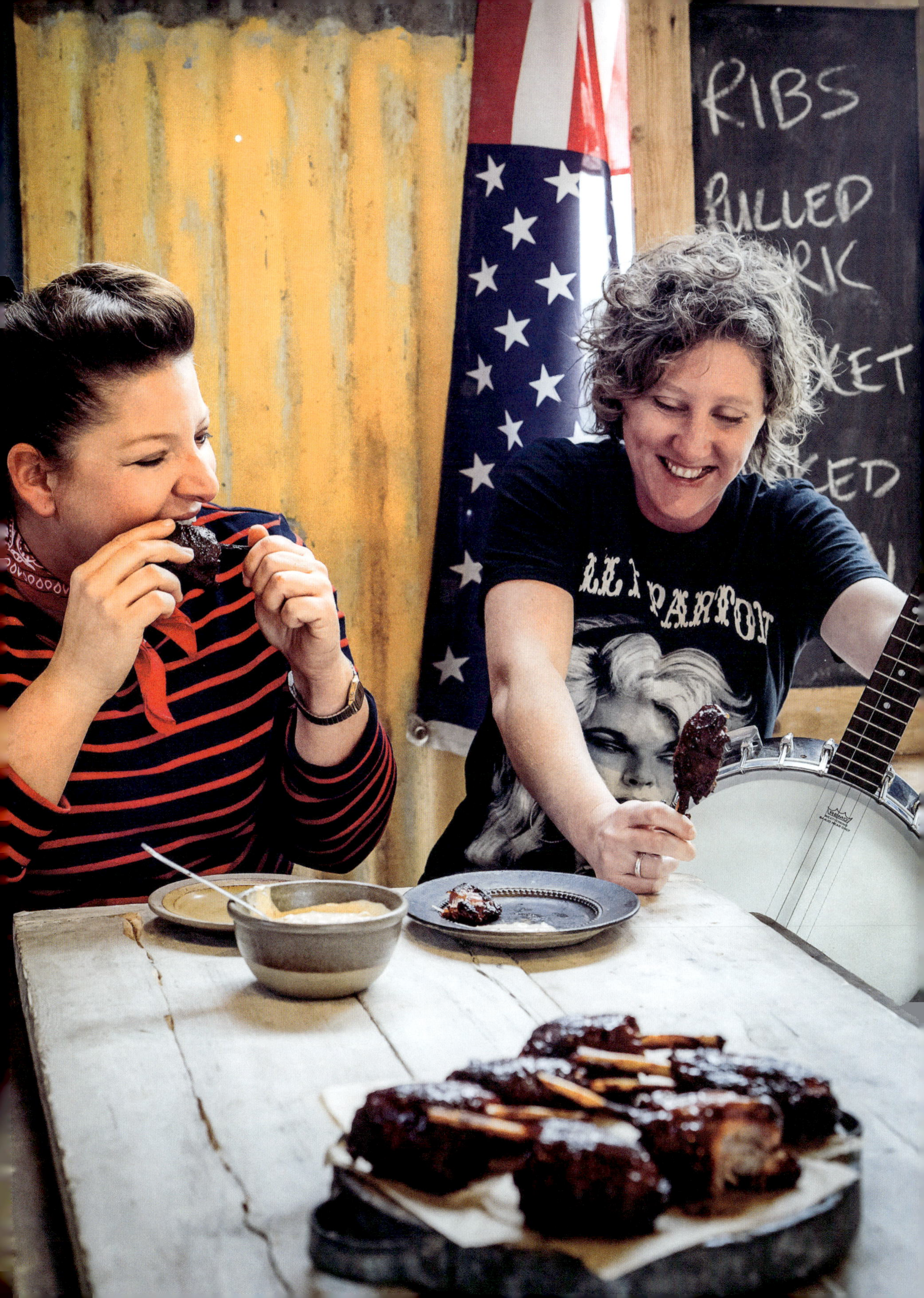
RIBS
PULLED

MAKES ABOUT 12

ANDOUILLE SAUSAGE

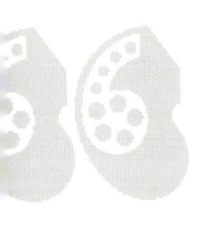

Pronounced 'and-oo-ee' this spicy Cajun-smoked pork sausage will set your taste buds alight. This truly is one of our favourite sausages to make and smoke, and to use in any of our Louisiana side dishes. Much like chaurice, this sausage is ubiquitous throughout Louisiana. However, unlike its French origin, we won't be making this with tripe and intestines, but with prime pork shoulder and pork back fat. Read our helpful notes (opposite) before you start making the sausages.

COOKING METHODS Indirect Grilling/Smoking

WOOD Oak, Hickory or Cherry

- 1 tsp Prague Powder #1
- 1.25kg boneless pork shoulder, cut into 5cm cubes
- 225g pork back fat, cut into small cubes
- 60g Cajun seasoning (page 29)
- 2 tbsp paprika
- 2 tbsp fat-free milk powder
- 3 garlic cloves, finely chopped
- 2 tsp freshly cracked black pepper
- 1 tbsp fine sea salt
- 2 tsp filé powder (Filé powder is made from the ground leaves of the North American Sassafras tree. It adds a distinctive, earthy flavour and is also used as a thickening agent in Louisiana cooking.)
- 1 tsp chilli powder
- 1 tsp crushed red chillies
- 1 tsp ground cumin
- natural hog casing, 5m x 36/40 (soaked overnight in water and drained)

First, put the coarse blade of your meat grinder in the freezer. In a large bowl, combine the Prague Powder #1 with 1 tablespoon of water to dissolve. Add the pork shoulder, pork fat, Cajun seasoning, paprika, milk powder, garlic, black pepper, salt, filé, chilli powder, red chillies and cumin and mix well. Refrigerate for at least 1 hour.

Pass the meat through a meat grinder fitted with your coarse blade. Return the mix back into the bowl, cover tightly with cling film, and refrigerate overnight.

The next day, test the seasoning of your sausage mix. Heat a dash of oil in a frying pan and add a small piece of the sausage mix. Fry over medium heat for a few minutes, until thoroughly cooked. Have a taste and add more seasoning if necessary.

When you're ready to make your sausage, turn your kitchen tap on to a slow, steady flow. Hook the hog casing over the end of the tap and flush with water for a few minutes. Squeeze all of the water out of the casing. This is a good time to check the casing for any holes in the casing, if any water comes spouting out, cut that bit out and check another piece.

Using the sausage attachment on a stand mixer, push about 1 metre of casing on the hose attachment and tie the end. Start slowly feeding your mix into the casing, holding the sausage as you go. (You might find it useful to have a large bowl handy for the sausage to drop into.) When you have the individual sausage length you're after, stop feeding the meat through, pinch the sausage casing with your thumb and forefinger and twist to whatever length you like – 15cm is about right.

The next stage is to smoke the sausages. We use sausage sticks to smoke our sausage, which are basically stainless steel pieces of dowelling, and we wrap the sausages around them. When you've made your links, you need to allow them some drying time. You can either hang them in your fridge for 2 hours or hang your sausages in front of a fan for 1 hour before smoking. The skins should be dry to the touch and the sausages should look a little darker in colouring.

This stage will test your smoking skills a little. You want to creep the temperature of your smoker up from 60°C/140°F to 71°C/160°F throughout the cook time, which could be around the 3–4 hour mark, to get maximum smoke flavour without overcooking and rendering the fats too quickly. Add your wood (oak, hickory or cherry) at the start and again as and when it burns out. Check the temperature of the sausages after 2 hours. You're aiming for the internal temperature of your sausage to reach 74°C/165°F. Remove them from the smoker at this point and immediately spray liberally with cold water. Hang at room temperature in front of a fan for 1 hour, then refrigerate overnight, uncovered, before eating.

The sausages will keep for 3–4 days in the fridge and freeze very well for up to 3 months.

SAUSAGE-MAKING TIPS

When making sausage, it's helpful to keep the blades and the chopping bowl in the freezer. We go as far as to stand the chopping bowl in an ice bath to keep the minced meat as cold as possible. Be methodical and keep your equipment clean and sanitised, washing it immediately after use, and keep work surfaces free of debris. Making sausage can be a messy business.

FAT TASTES GOOD: There are a couple of options with adding pork fat: either add chopped up pieces to your sausage mixture (think black pudding fatty bits), or grind the pork fat as in the recipe above depending on the texture you want. We like to freeze the fat before it's cut, making it easier to chop up or go through the grinder.

GIMME SOME SKIN: We always recommended using natural casings. Collagen skins, although much easier to work with, won't really give you that sausage 'snap' bite, or that authentic sausage texture. Hog casings are a little easier to work with than sheep casings. However if you want a thinner sausage, try switching to the smaller, sheep casings. You'll likely need to soak the natural casings overnight.

A NOTE ON PRAGUE POWDER #1:

We recommend using this so you can keep your sausage making adventures safe for you and anyone else eating them. It has a combination of table salt and sodium nitrite, which not only helps prevent the build up of nasty bacteria but also preserves the colour of the meat, preventing it from looking grey when cooked. Read the instructions on your packet of Prague Powder #1 carefully, it's potentially harmful if not used in the correct way.

CHAURICE SAUSAGE

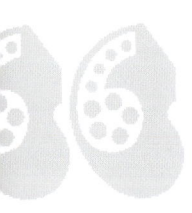

MAKES ABOUT 12

We're big fans of Louisiana sausages. Pronounced 'sha-rees', the intense spice is the key characteristic of this traditional, fresh Creole sausage. Chaurice is similar to Spanish chorizo but without the curing process, and is a main ingredient of jambalaya and gumbo. This sausage is a spicy one, bear that in mind when you're adding it to your dishes. Have a read of our helpful sausage-making tips on page 77 before making these.

COOKING METHODS Indirect Grilling/Smoking   **WOOD** Oak, Beech or Cherry

- 1 tsp Prague Powder #1 (page 77)
- 1.25kg boneless pork shoulder, cut into 5cm cubes
- 225g pork back fat, cut into small cubes
- 1 medium onion, finely chopped
- 4 tsp paprika
- 3 tsp chilli powder
- 3 tsp finely chopped garlic
- 1 tbsp fine sea salt
- 1 tsp chopped fresh thyme leaves
- 1 tsp chilli flakes
- ½ tsp cayenne pepper
- 1 tsp ground cumin
- 1 tsp fresh cracked black pepper
- ¼ tsp ground allspice
- natural hog casing, 5m x 36/40 (soaked overnight in water and drained)

First, put the coarse blade of your meat grinder in the freezer. In a large bowl, combine the Prague Powder #1 with 1 tablespoon of water to dissolve. Add the remaining ingredients apart from the hog casing and mix well. Refrigerate for at least 1 hour.

Pass the meat through a meat grinder fitted with your coarse blade. Return the mix back into the bowl, cover tightly with cling film, and refrigerate overnight.

The next day, test the seasoning of your sausage mix. Heat a dash of oil in a pan and fry a small piece of the sausage mix over medium heat for a few minutes, until thoroughly cooked. Taste and add more seasoning if necessary.

When you're ready to make your sausage, turn your kitchen tap on to a slow, steady flow. Hook the hog casing over the end of the tap and flush with water for a few minutes. Squeeze all of the water out of the casing. This is a good time to check the casing for any holes in the casing, if any water comes spouting out, cut that bit out and check another piece.

Using the sausage attachment on a stand mixer, push about 1 metre of casing on the hose attachment and tie the end. Start slowly feeding your mix into the casing, holding the sausage as you go. (You might find it useful to have a large bowl handy for the sausage to drop into.) When you have the individual sausage length you're after, stop feeding the meat through, pinch the sausage casing with your thumb and forefinger and twist to whatever length you like, about 15–20cm is about right.

You can smoke your sausages according to the instructions on page 77 or grill or pan-fry them with a little water added and use them in any dish you want. The sausages will keep for 3–4 days in the fridge and freeze very well for up to 3 months.

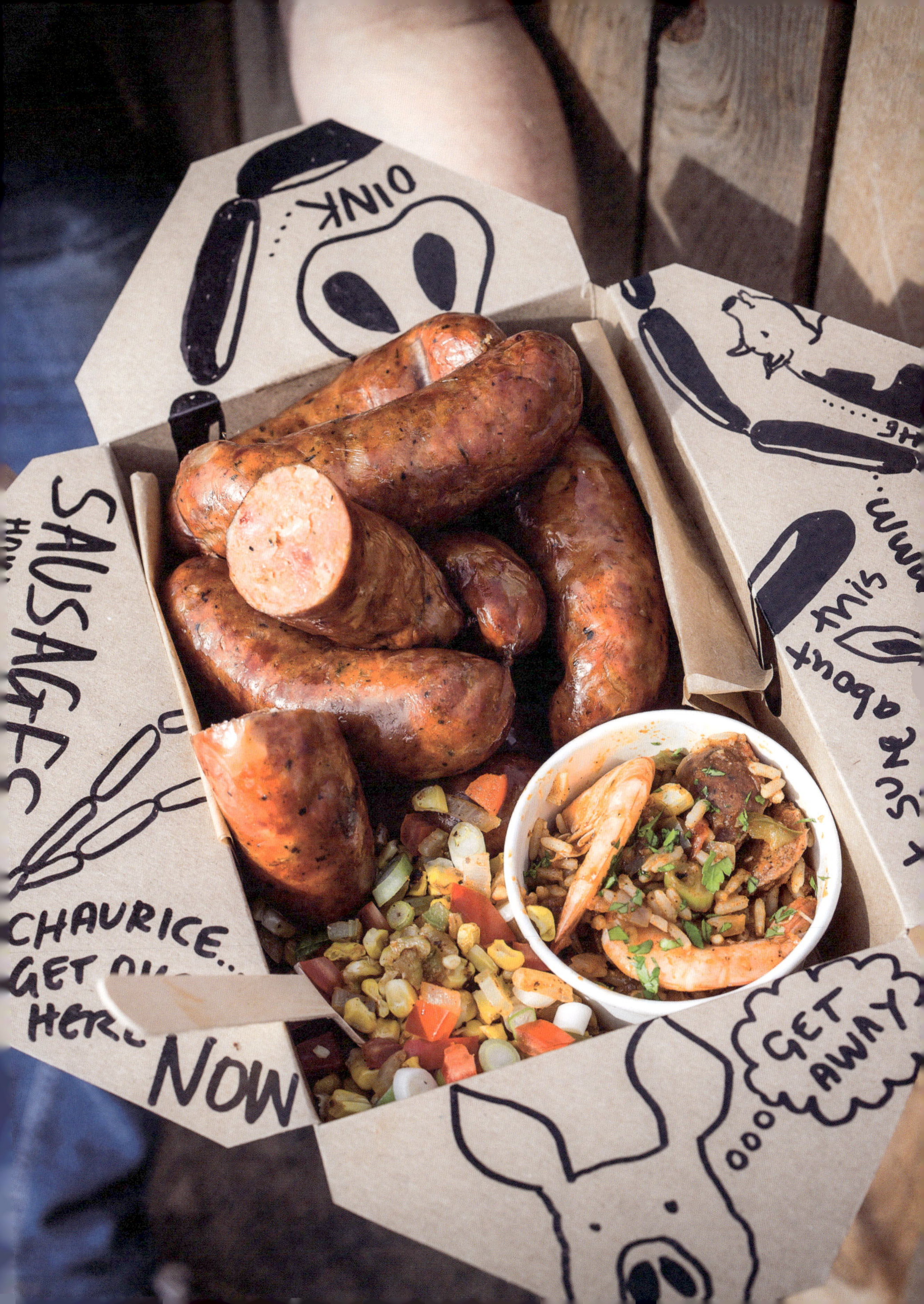
OINK
CHAURICE...
NOW
GET AWAY

SERVES 10–12

DOWN-HOME SMOKED BACON

Everything's better with bacon, right? This is a fairly straightforward recipe for how to cure and smoke your own bacon. When you get the hang of the curing process and have a firm grasp of how to safely use curing salts, you can pretty much make any style of bacon you want. Like all good things, this one is going to take some time. Start the recipe 7–12 days before.

COOKING METHODS Curing, Cold Smoking

WOOD Beech, Apple, Cherry, Maple

1 x 2.5kg boneless rind-on pork belly

For the basic dry cure

3 bay leaves

240g fine sea salt

200g soft light brown sugar

1 tbsp coarsely ground pepper

2 tsp Prague Powder #1 (page 77)

Using a sharp knife, trim your pork belly to make an even shape, close to a rectangle or square. Put in a baking tray large enough to give you a little room around the sides.

Put the bay leaves in a spice grinder and blitz to a powder. Add the remaining ingredients to a bowl, making sure they are well combined (it's important that the Prague Powder #1 is evenly distributed). Press the cure firmly and evenly all over the pork and rub well into the belly. Place the pork in a large ziplock bag, expel as much air as possible (or use a vacuum sealer if you have one). Pop it in the fridge and leave it there for 7 days. (If your piece of pork is thicker than 4cm, leave in the fridge for about 10 days.) Turn it over every day. You should see some osmosis at work as the salt breaks down the cells causing liquid from the meat to accumulate in the bag – the pork will feel firmer as the days progress.

Once the pork is cured, remove from the fridge and gently rinse under the tap. Pat dry with kitchen towels and keep out of the fridge for about 30 minutes to bring it back to room temperature before you put it in your smoker.

TO HOT SMOKE

Prepare your smoker for indirect heat, setting it pretty low at 94°C/200°F. Put the pork belly in, followed by a handful of wood chips or a couple of chunks of wood. Smoke until the internal temperature of the pork belly reaches about 74°C/165°F on an instant-read thermometer, about 12–14 hours.

TO COLD SMOKE

Using a cold smoke generator, fill with sawdust and light the corner with a tea light as per the manufacturer's instructions. Bullet-style smokers are great for this job as they often have a bar in the lid you can hang meat from. Use two meat hooks to hang the belly from the lid. Cold smoke for a minimum of 12 hours. Keep an eye on your cold smoke generator as you may need to refill it depending on its size.

AFTER YOU'VE HOT- OR COLD-SMOKED YOUR BACON

Wrap the pork belly in cling film, or preferably cut it in half and vacuum seal, then put in the fridge for 5 days. This allows the smoke flavour to mature. After 5 days, we usually portion the belly into around 200g of thick (3mm) slices, keep what we want to eat for the next day or two and vacuum pack and freeze the rest. It will keep for another week in the fridge and freeze for 3 months.

MAKING YOUR OWN FLAVOUR PROFILES

You can add pretty much anything in the curing stage. We like fresh, oily herbs such as thyme, sage or rosemary. You can add chilli flakes, cracked black pepper, maple syrup, honey, black strap molasses or juniper berries, celery seeds, fennel seeds, cumin seeds and caraway seeds. Find flavours that you really like and try some of them out. Just try not to go overboard – test out just two or three extra ingredients with the basic cure above and see which additions give your ultimate side of bacon.

SERVES 4-5

MAPLE BACON WEAVED PORK TENDERLOIN
WITH CHORIZO AND APPLE STUFFING

This is a decadent little dish that uses a fillet of pork or pork tenderloin, and is almost a more refined version of the barbecue classic, bacon explosion. The bacon weave still makes an appearance, mainly because the more reasons you have to make a mat out of bacon in your life, frankly, the better. You really can just wrap the tenderloin in bacon, but where's the fun in that? The apple and chorizo make a rich, flavourful stuffing.

COOKING METHODS Indirect Grilling/Smoking   **WOOD** Apple, Maple, Cherry

500g Down-home Smoked Bacon (pages 80–81) or good-quality streaky bacon

350g pork tenderloin or fillet

50g maple syrup

1 tbsp freshly cracked black pepper

2 tbsp Hang Fire Almost All-purpose Rub (page 26)

1 tbsp groundnut oil

For the Chorizo and Apple Stuffing

1 tbsp unsalted butter

1 eating apple, peeled, cored and diced

1 tsp soft light brown sugar

100g fresh chorizo sausages

1 small onion, finely chopped

1 garlic clove, crushed to a paste with 1 tsp fine sea salt

1 tsp fresh thyme leaves

sea salt and freshly ground black pepper

Weave the bacon (see opposite) on a large sheet of cling film. Transfer to a flat baking tray and put in the fridge until ready to use. Next, let's get the stuffing ready.

Melt the butter in a large frying pan over medium heat and add the apple. Cook for 4–5 minutes, then add the sugar. Continue to cook, tossing for 4–5 minutes, until the apple starts to caramelise. Remove from the pan and set aside.

Slice open the skins of the chorizo sausages and put the chorizo meat into the same pan you fried the apples in. Fry for 3–4 minutes over medium-high heat, breaking up the chorizo a little and letting it brown. Add the onion, garlic and thyme and gently fry with the chorizo for 10 minutes, until the onion is soft, and the chorizo is cooked and has released its oils. Season with salt and pepper. Remove the pan from the heat and drain the chorizo fat away, and discard from the pan. Add the caramelised apple back into the pan with the onion and chorizo, and set aside to cool for 30 minutes.

Now prepare the tenderloin and the stuffing pocket. Using a sharp knife, make an incision in the side of the tenderloin, and down the length, being careful not to go all the way through to the other side. Start the incision 1cm from the thick end and stop before the loin tapers too thinly. Pack the tenderloin with the stuffing. Remove the bacon weave from the fridge, and place the stuffed tenderloin in the centre, then fold the tapered end on to itself. Start by folding the ends of the bacon weave onto the ends of the tenderloin – it'll be a bit tricky and won't look totally perfect, but it'll turn out looking great. Use a little pressure to fold the bacon weave around the loin, take one side of the cling film and fold over, same with the other side so the bacon overlaps itself. Wrap the cling film around and flip it over so that the seam of the bacon weave is underneath.

Rub the oil on the weave and sprinkle with the rub.

Set up your smoker and regulate the temperature to 108°C/225°F. Put the loin in the smoker, add in the wood (apple, maple or cherry wood are all good), and smoke for 3–4 hours, or until the internal temperature of the loin meat (not the stuffing) reaches 72°C/160°F on your instant-read thermometer. Just before the tenderloin is ready, in a bowl, mix the maple syrup and cracked black pepper and brush it all over the top of the bacon weave. Allow this to set for 20 minutes in the grill.

Carefully remove the loin, wrap loosely in foil and let rest for at least 15 minutes before cutting and serving.

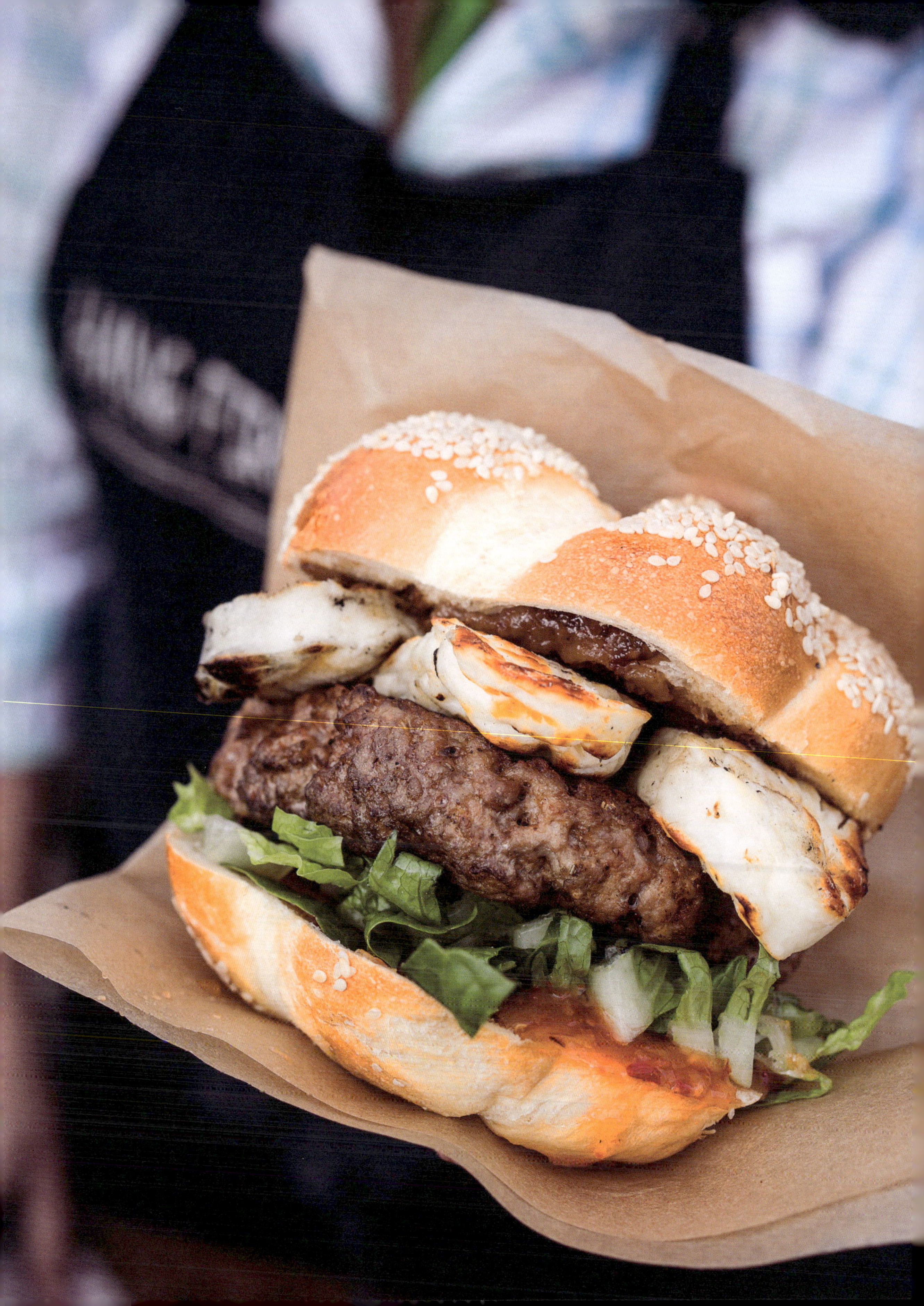

SERVES 6

PERFECT PORK & HALLOUMI BURGERS

Wherever we went in the States, burgers were always a sure-fire hit. Every town or city seemed to have numerous impressive burger joints filled with hungry diners of every demographic, from grandparents to hipsters. This particular burger recipe was standout for us. We ate something similar in an Aspen skier's diner, nestled in the Rocky Mountains of Colorado.

COOKING METHOD Grilling

- 3 banana shallots, finely diced
- 2 garlic cloves, finely chopped
- 1 tsp groundnut oil, plus extra for frying and brushing
- 2 tbsp Creole seasoning (page 29)
- 1½ tsp ground cumin
- 1½ tsp ground coriander
- 1kg minced pork shoulder
- 3 rashers cooked bacon (pages 80–81) or any good streaky bacon, finely chopped
- small handful fresh thyme leaves
- small handful chopped flat-leaf parsley leaves
- 1 tsp fine sea salt
- 1 tsp freshly cracked black pepper
- ½ tsp chilli powder

For the Burger

- 6 Kaiser Rolls (page 192), or good brioche or burger buns, halved
- 6 tbsp Bacon Jam (page 30)
- 6 tbsp Chilli Jam (page 31)
- 6 slices halloumi (about 250g packet)
- 1 tbsp smoked paprika
- Little Gem lettuce or fresh rocket
- freshly cracked black pepper, to taste

Gently fry the shallots and garlic in the oil for 5–7 minutes over medium heat, until softened. Turn the heat to low and stir through the Creole seasoning, cumin and coriander for 1–2 minutes. Cool to room temperature.

In a large bowl, using wet hands, combine the minced pork, bacon, fresh herbs, salt and pepper, chilli powder, and the cooled shallot mixture. Refrigerate for 1 hour.

Heat a dash of oil in a frying pan and add a small piece of burger mix. Fry over medium heat for a few minutes, until cooked, then taste and add more seasoning if necessary.

Form the meat mixture into six even-sized patties and press your thumb into the middle of each one to create a dimple. Place the patties on a plate, cover with cling film and refrigerate for 1 hour for the flavours to mature.

Set your grill up for direct heat but leave a 'cool zone' i.e. an area without coals (see indirect grilling, pages 18–19). Toast the cut sides of the rolls so they are golden, around 15 seconds. Spread a tablespoon of bacon jam on one half, and a tablespoon of chilli jam on the other, and top with a handful of rocket or chopped lettuce.

Season both sides of the patties and cook for 3–5 minutes on the grates over the direct heat, then flip. Make sure you get a good Maillard reaction (chemical reaction between amino acids and sugars that gives a beautiful, chargrilled colour and flavour) before turning. They will take around 8–10 minutes to cook, but use your instant-read thermometer to ensure the middles reach 74°C/165°F.

As you flip your burgers, start grilling the halloumi. Brush each slice with a little oil and sprinkle on the smoked paprika. Grill for 1–2 minutes, until they have a golden, slightly charred texture. Rest the cooked burgers on the indirect side of your grill for about 5 minutes. Place each patty on top of the rocket, followed by grilled halloumi. Enjoy!

MEAT

SERVES 4–6

SMOKED PORK BELLY

This awesome piece of fatty pig takes to smoking like a duck to water. With all its fat keeping it moist, the pork belly makes for a forgiving piece of meat to cook. It's pretty simple to do and will yield great results. Depending on the size of your smoker, you may want to cut the loin in half if you are using a whole piece and use the remaining to make some of our down-home smoked bacon (pages 80–81).

COOKING METHODS Indirect heat

WOOD Hickory, Cherry, Oak, Beech

- 1 x 2kg bone in, rindless pork belly (see below)
- 3 tbsp groundnut oil
- 75g Hang Fire Almost All-purpose Rub (page 26)
- 100ml Hang Fire Smokehouse Barbecue Sauce (page 45)

Slice off some of the thick fat from the top of the pork belly, you'll want a maximum of 5mm fat. Rub the oil on both sides of the belly and liberally sprinkle with the rub.

Set up your grill for indirect heat and regulate at 108°C/225°F. Put your wood chunks in, and, as soon as they start smoking, place your pork belly fat side up on the indirect side. Smoke for about 5–6 hours, check the pork belly has reached an internal temperature of approximately 88°C/190°F on your instant-read thermometer, then brush the top of the belly with some warmed barbecue sauce. Keep smoking until the internal temperature reaches 90°C/195°F.

You can of course cook the pork belly until it pulls, but we like to slice it into thick slabs and finish them off on the direct side of the grill.

KING OF THE RIB

To make King Ribs, slice between the bones as you would regular pork ribs. These massive meaty ribs look impressive and taste great – no wonder they have been a hit on the streetfood scene. We like to finish them on the grill, as they are, and slather them in warm barbecue sauce and a good dousing of Memphis dry shake (page 29).

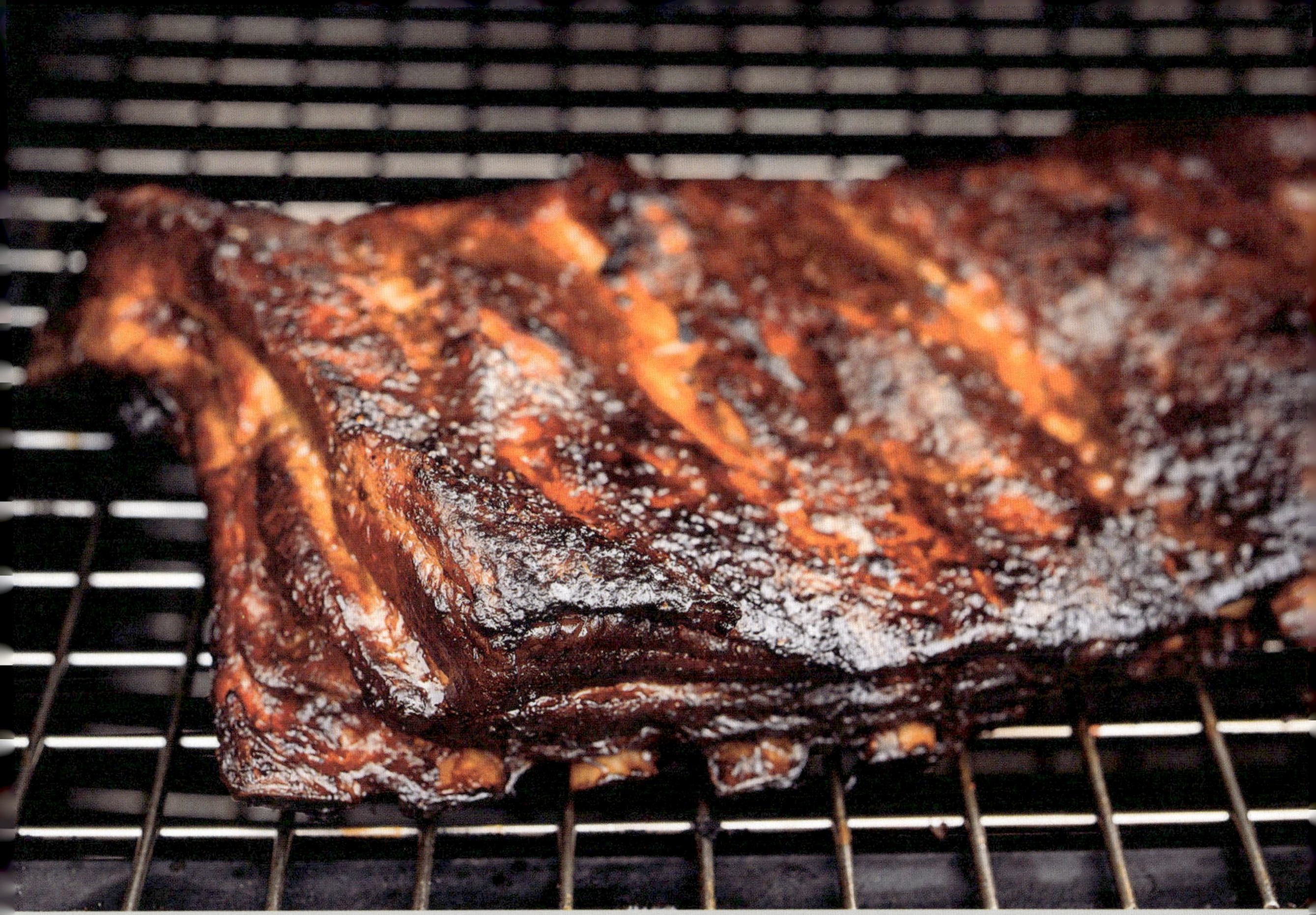
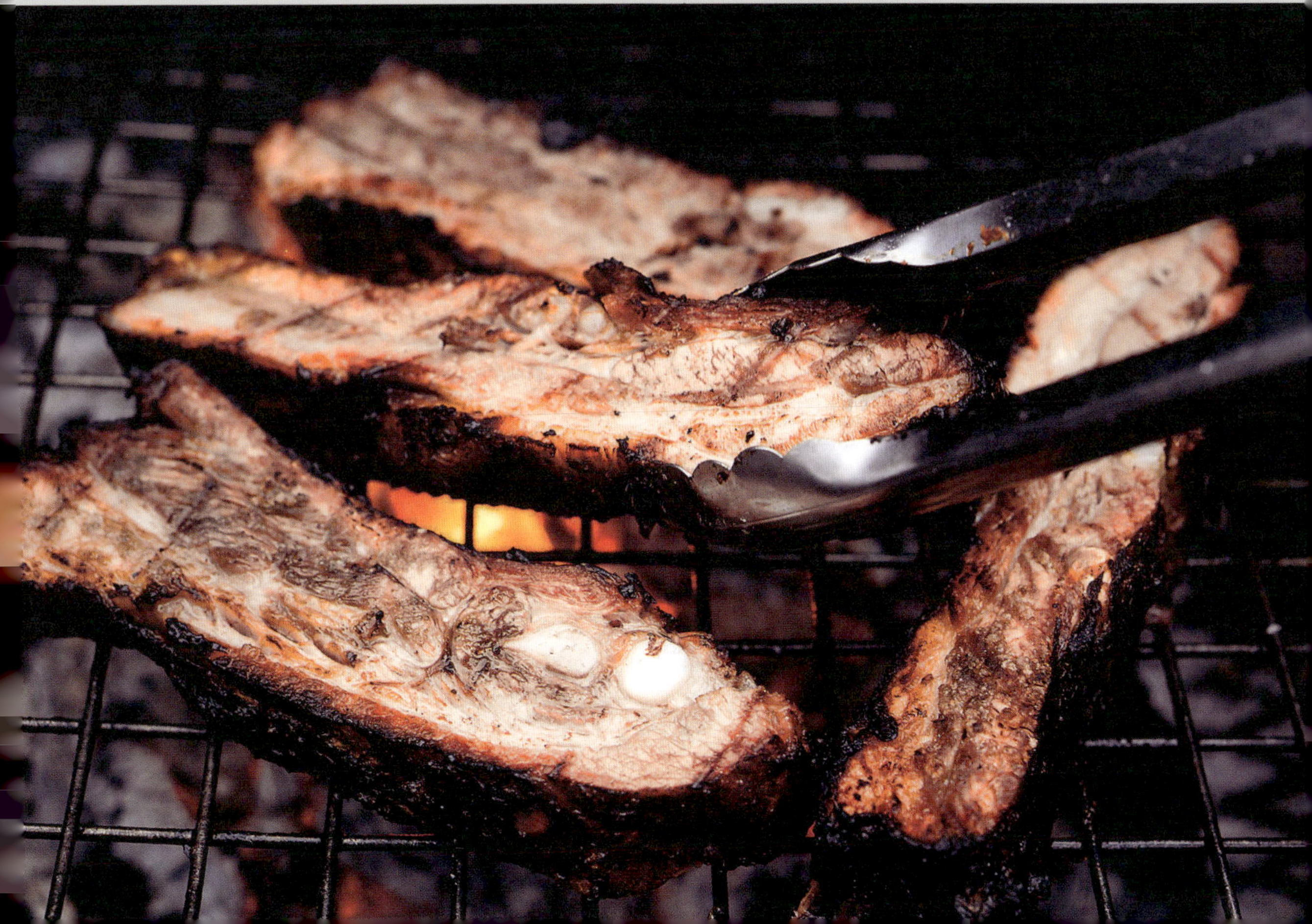

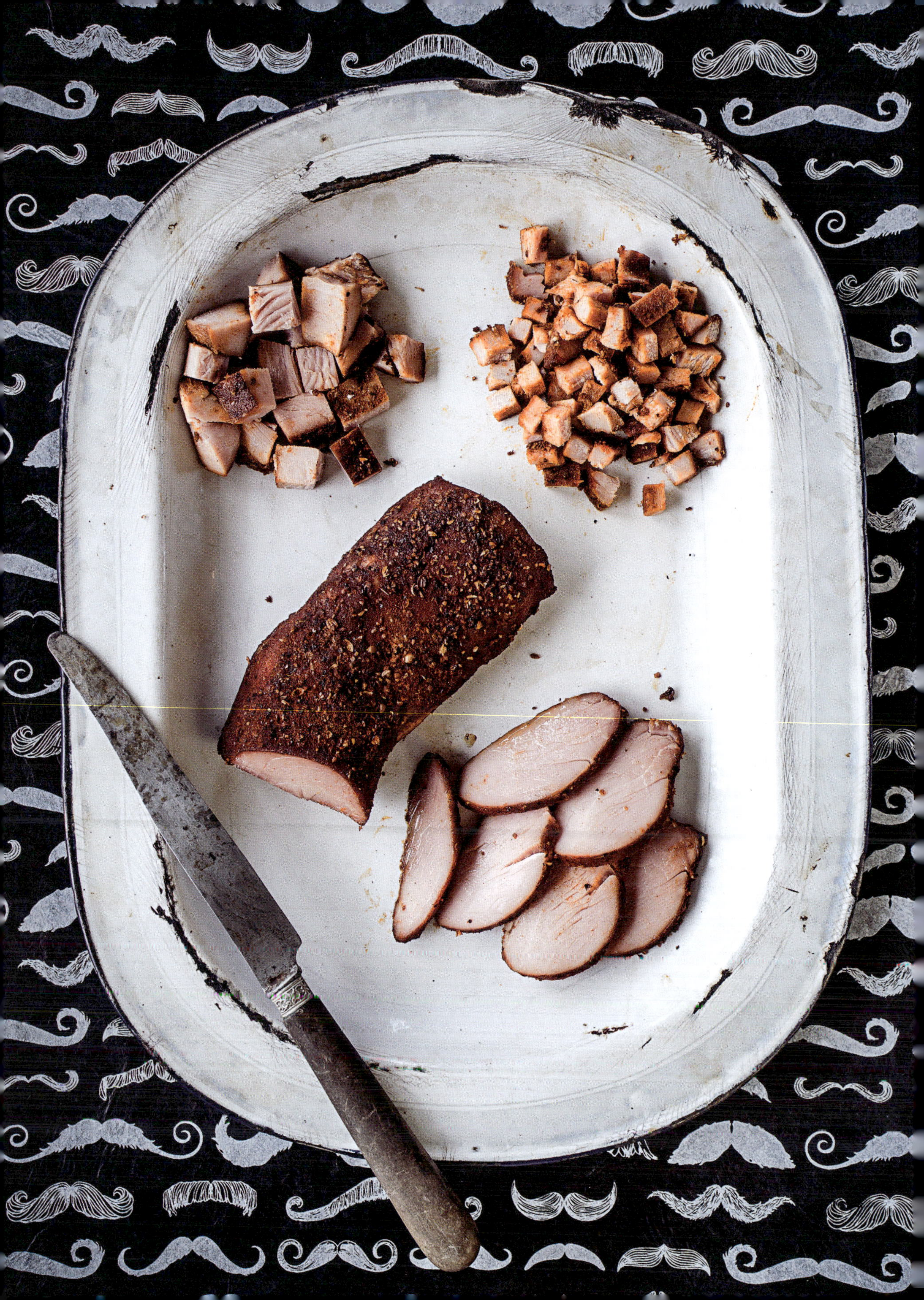

MAKES ABOUT 600G

TASSO HAM

As in much of Louisiana cooking, getting that exact ingredient is integral to the authentic flavour of the dish. Tasso is essentially a cured, spicy ham that you can use in Gumbo (page 169), Red Beans & Rice (page 162), soups, salads, sandwiches and to serve as charcuterie. It's such a versatile meat to have around that you'll always want to have a little stock of tasso in your fridge, and because it's fairly straightforward to make, there's no excuse not to have this amazing ham to hand.

COOKING METHODS Curing, Indirect Grilling/Smoking

WOOD 50/50 Hickory/Oak mix

- 80g fine sea salt
- 2 tbsp paprika
- 3 tbsp garlic powder
- 2 tbsp onion powder
- 1 tbsp cayenne pepper
- 2 tsp coarsely ground black pepper
- 1 tsp ground cinnamon
- 1 tsp ground cloves
- 1 tsp freshly cracked black pepper
- 2 x 350g pork fillets or tenderloins

In a large bowl, add all the dry ingredients and mix until fully combined. Put in the pork and coat liberally and evenly in the spice mixture. Place in a ziplock bag, expel as much air as possible, or vacuum-pack the strips, and refrigerate for 3 full days.

Remove the cured pork from the fridge and arrange the pork on a wire rack over a baking tray. Get a fan on them and leave to dry for an hour or so, turning them over now and again.

Next, you're going to smoke the cured pork on a low temperature, forcing further dehydration while absorbing maximum smoke. Regulate your smoker to about 93°C/200°F. Place the cured pork in the smoker and add your first lot of hickory and oak wood. Cook for about 3–4 hours, adding more wood as it burns out every hour, until the tasso reaches an internal temperature of 74°C/165°F on your instant-read thermometer.

Remove the tasso from the grill and allow to rest for 10 minutes. Put into ziplock bags (or vacuum pack them) and refrigerate for at least 24 hours before using (this will lock in the smoke flavour). The tasso will keep, well wrapped, in the fridge for 5 days and also freezes brilliantly for up to 3 months.

FRESH IS BEST

Make sure you pick up the freshest pork for this as we're not using any curing salts. You can also use pig cheeks or thick strips of pork shoulder instead. Bear in mind if using more meat, you would need to increase the ratios of salt and spices.

MEAT

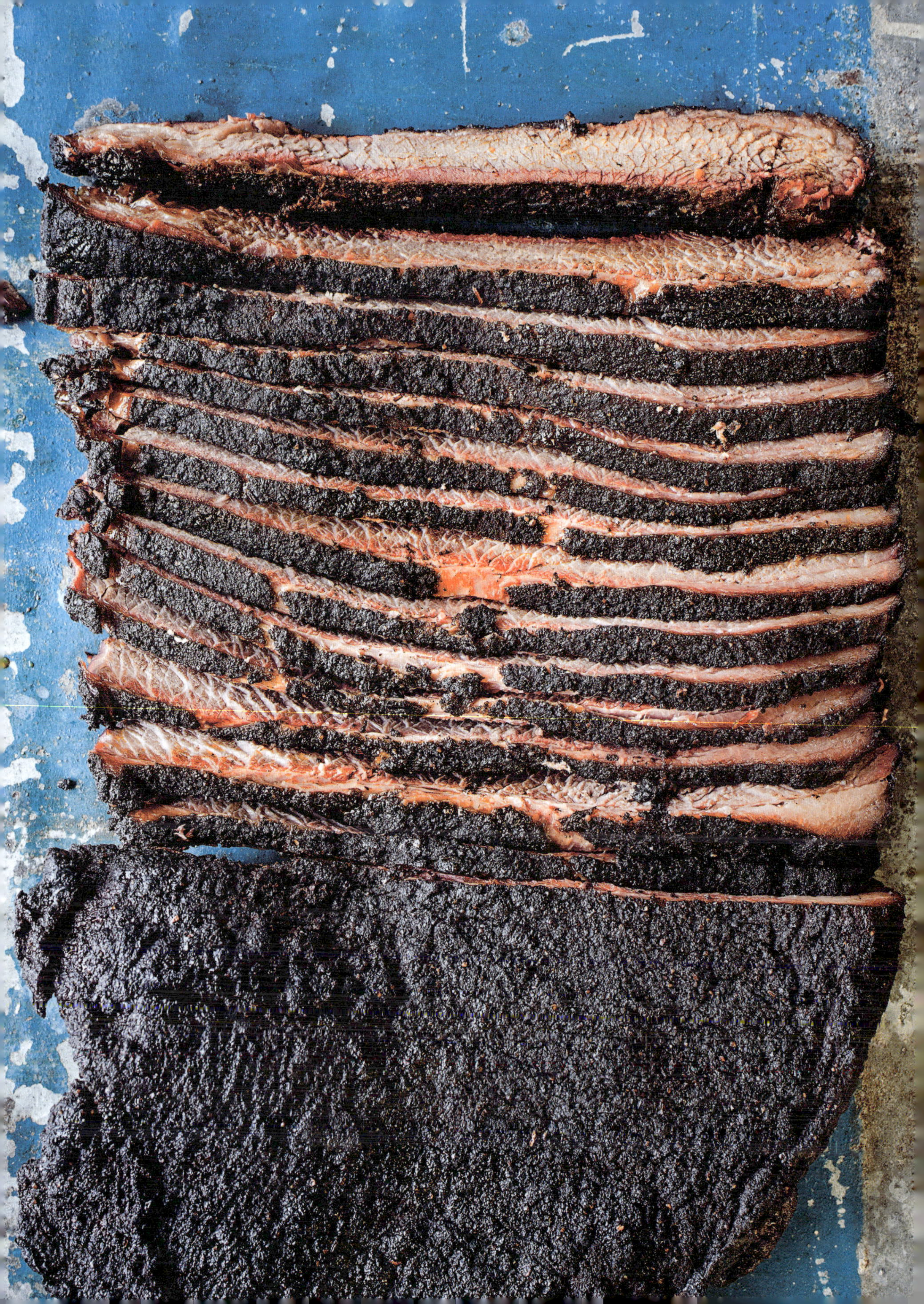

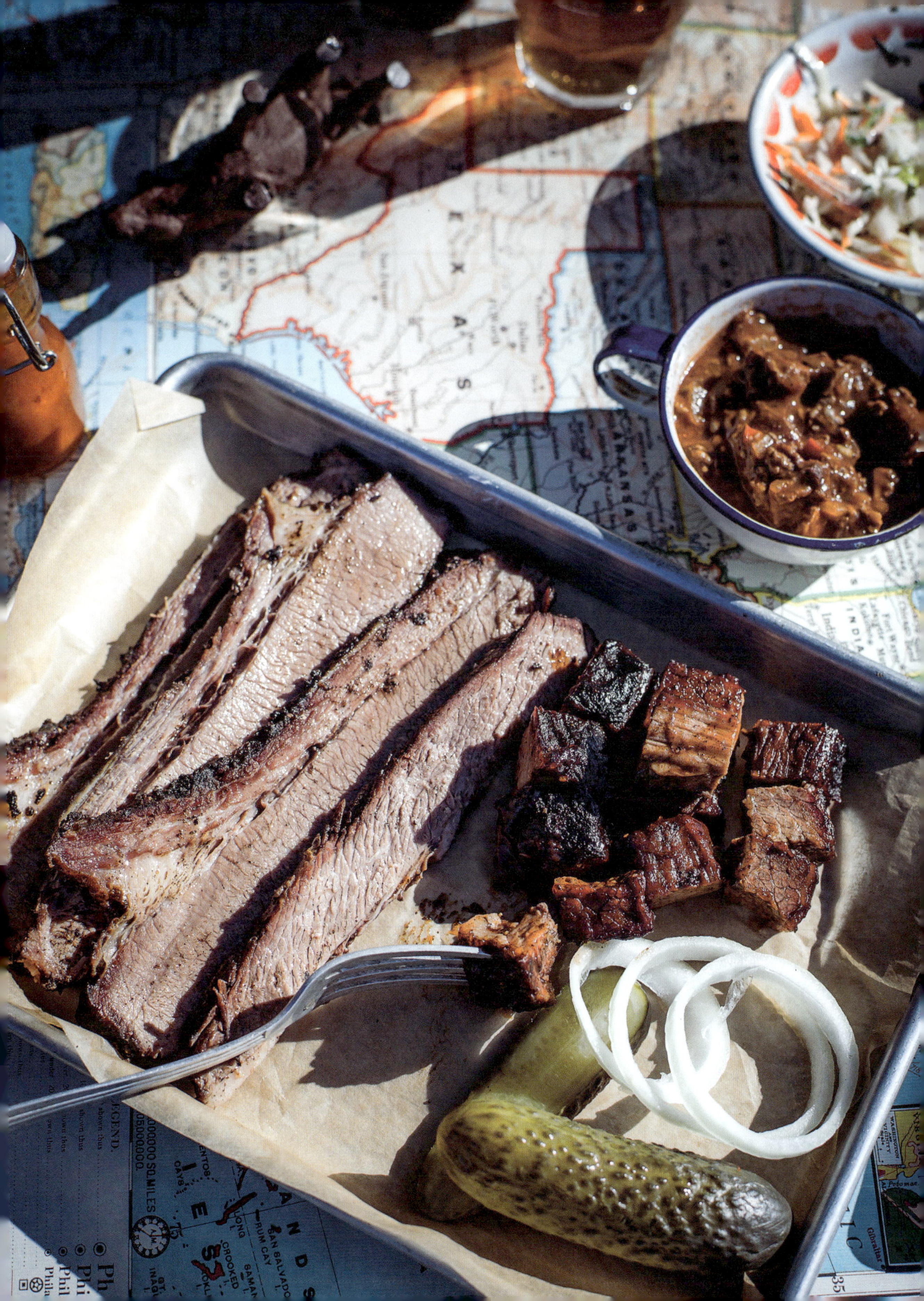

BRISKET & BURNT ENDS

SERVES 8-10

Cooking brisket has been by far one of the most difficult cuts for us to get right. Our first taste of real brisket was in Texas. We ate a lot of it there and it was truly life changing. In particular, king of 'cue, Aaron Franklin's barbecue is, to date, one of the finest plates of barbecue we've had the pleasure of eating. The brisket was wobbly, buttery and beefy. It was held together perfectly by a firm peppery bark and was dripping with juices. Eating that brisket almost caused a table-thumping When Sally Met Harry moment right in the middle of his restaurant!

Trying to replicate this standard of cooked brisket in the UK is not without its challenges. We'd love to offer a fool-proof formula here, but that's not going to happen as this unmarbled, tough cut is an equally tough cookie to crack. You need to persevere with this one, cook many, make notes and learn from each cook. Trust us, you'll be on cloud nine when you crack it.

COOKING METHODS Indirect Grilling/Smoking   **WOOD** Oak

1 x 4 kg beef brisket, point end attached and fat cap intact
2–3 tbsp groundnut oil
200ml brown ale, at room temperature
100ml beef stock, warmed
100g Barbecue Sauce (page 45)

For the Rub

50g coarse ground black pepper
50g sea salt flakes
10g garlic granules
1 tbsp chilli powder

First, mix the rub ingredients together well in a tub or shaker and set aside.

Next, trim off any hard, or particularly thick, areas of fat from the brisket. Don't be overzealous though, as you need to leave a decent fat cap on the top of the brisket, about 3mm, so that it renders into delicious beef 'caramel'. Turn the brisket over and remove any silver skin or sinew. Put the brisket in a foil tray or roasting tray and rub it all over with the groundnut oil. Dust both sides, catching the edges, with the rub.

Set your smoker up for indirect heat and regulate the temperature between 108°C/225°F and 120°C/250°F. If you're using an offset smoker, point the thickest part (the point end) towards the heat source. Throw in a handful of oak chips or a couple of oak wood chunks at this point and put in your brisket. You're looking at about 12 hours to smoke, think of it as roughly 3 hours per kilogram of meat. Add another handful of oak chips or a couple of oak chunks as and when it burns out for the first 6–8 hours.

At the 7-hour mark, you want to think about the Texas crutch (where the beef is wrapped in foil with stock or beer). It is a little controversial, however with lean, grass-fed beef, we've found this a necessary step in producing a tender, juicy brisket. To make a Texas crutch, take 3 metres of foil, fold it twice into thirds, with the remaining third as a flap. Bring the edges of the foil up a little, put your brisket in the middle and pour in the stock and ale. Bring the flap over, wrap tightly, expelling as much air as possible, and crimp the edges like a giant pasty. Pop the brisket back in the smoker. Obviously, don't add any more wood after this point.

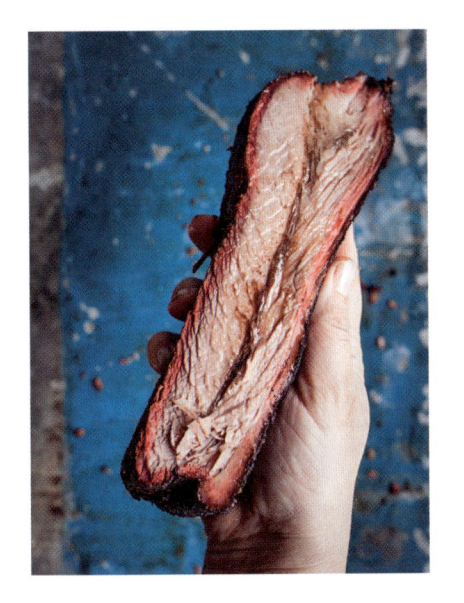

At the 12-hour mark, you want to start taking the temperature. Careful where you poke the instant-read thermometer – you don't want holes in the sides of the foil as the liquor will to start spouting out. Take the temperature using your instant-read thermometer from both the point and the middle of the flat. You're testing for tenderness here, as opposed to the temperature. Does the tip of the thermometer slide into the meat easily, or does it still feel a little tough? Most folks, including us, recommend a minimum temperature of 90°C/195°F but we've had briskets take until 98°F/208°F before they've felt tender.

When you're happy with the tenderness of the brisket, you're on the home straight! Just a few more steps before you reach brisket nirvana…

Undo the seam of the foil carefully (as that steam is going to be piping hot) and pour the braising liquid into a pan. Reduce over low heat to make a gravy. At this stage, you might want to make Burnt Ends: holding the brisket with heat-proof gloves, slice off the point end (which should be a very visible, raised muscle that sits on top of the flat) and cut the meat against the grain into 5cm cubes on a chopping board. Glaze the cubes in the barbecue sauce and place in a new foil tray in the smoker for a further 4–5 hours, or until it is fork-tender.

Reseal the foil seam and put the brisket in a cool box and wrap the foil parcel in tea towels. Let it rest for anywhere between 1 hour and 2 hours. Take it out, remove all the foil and place on a chopping board. Let it breathe for 10 minutes while the bark starts to dry out. Take a sharp carving knife and slice the brisket, against the grain, into 5mm thick slices. Serve with white onions, pickles and a little pot of the reduced gravy for dipping the slices in – and crack open another beer, heck you deserve it.

YOU GOT BEEF?

So, imagine our surprise when we discovered that not all briskets smoke the same or taste the same. We're up against it a little in the UK as our beef is generally grass fed and often grain finished. In the US, they are almost entirely grain fed, making for way more marbling and bigger bovine. However, times are a-changing and with the demand for brisket growing in the UK, many butchers are sourcing cattle with longer grain-fed finishing times. We have great ones in the UK from Wagyu, Dexter, Angus and other prime cattle varieties. If you want something special, find a good butcher that will help you. It's fun to try a USDA brisket to see the difference, however, we'd always push for supporting the hardworking British farmers.

BEEF RIBS

SERVES 4

We ate some epic beef ribs in the States, and for real beef flavour nothing touches a short rib. Short ribs, thin ribs, Jacob's ladder, English cut, we've smoked them all. They're called short ribs because they come from the short plate, and we ask our butcher to trim them to a square as a joined four-bone plate. These not only look great, but are fairly forgiving to smoke, and for our money one of the tastiest cuts on a cow.

COOKING METHODS Indirect Grilling/Smoking

WOOD Oak, Hickory

- 1 x 4-bone plate beef short ribs (about 2kg)
- 3 tbsp groundnut oil or American mustard
- 4 tbsp Mocha Rub (page 28)

For beef ribs, there's no need to remove the membrane like pork ribs as they perform a fairly essential role of keeping the rib rack together. Rub a little oil or American mustard all over the rib plate and dust the ribs liberally with the rub. Put them in your fridge for 1 hour.

Set your smoker or grill up for indirect heat and regulate the temperature at 108°C/225°F. Place the ribs on the grates and add your oak or hickory wood, adding more wood every hour for the first 4 hours or as needed. Depending on the thickness of your ribs, they could take anything from 8 to 10 hours to cook. You're looking for the meat to hit around 93°C/200°F when it's done. Wrap the ribs tightly in foil and a couple of tea towels, and put in a cool box to allow the meat to rest for at least 1 hour. To serve, slice up between the bones. We usually go for one bone per portion, depending on how big they are or how hungry you are.

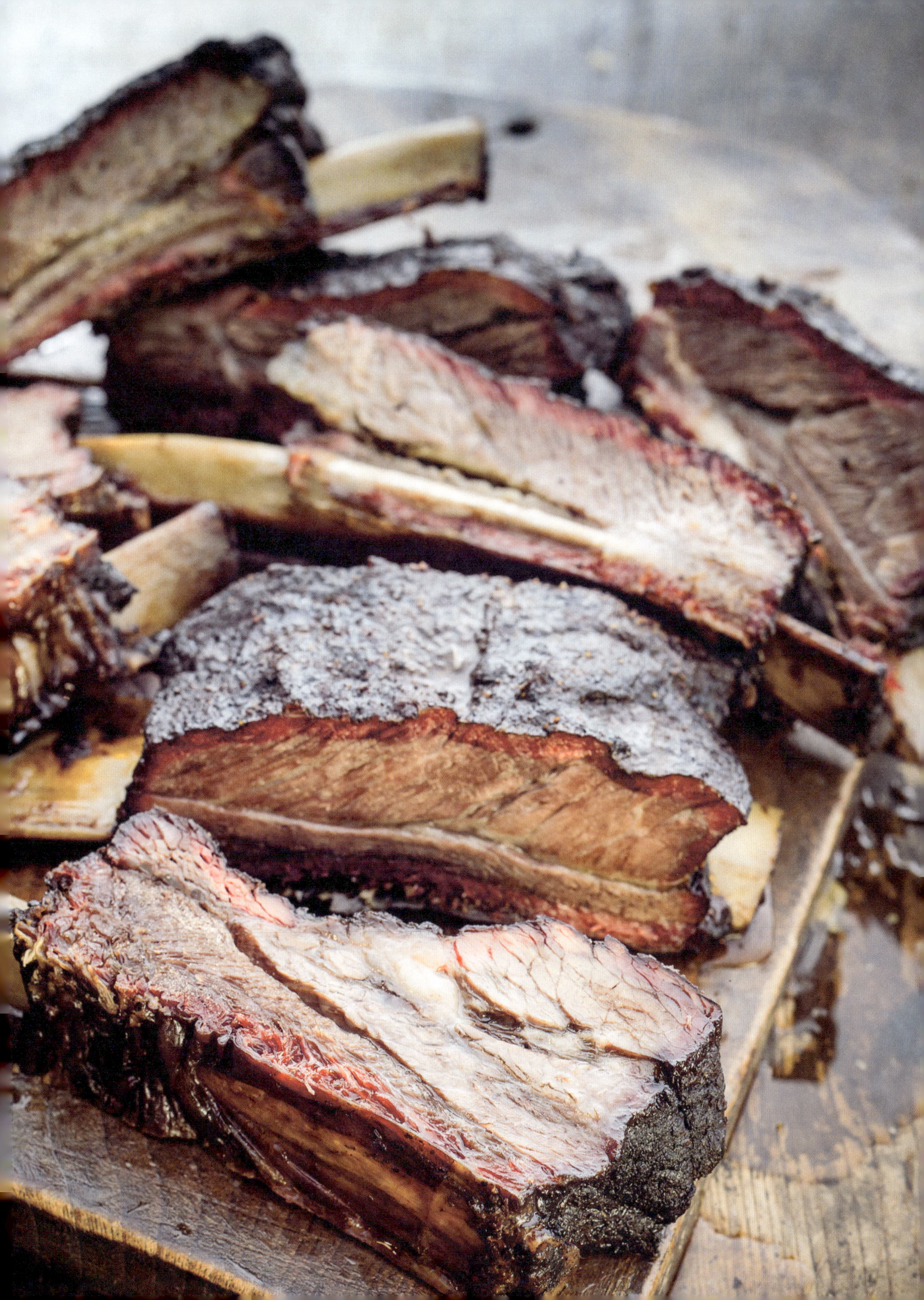

TEXAS HOT LINKS

MAKES 12–15

These sausages are ubiquitous through central market style barbecue in Texas and often called 'Hot Guts' due to the use of natural sheep or hog casings. There were a few all-beef ones that can be a bit of acquired taste. However, the spicy all-pork kind or the hot links mixed with both pork and beef were crazy good. We were the first ones to bring this sausage back to Wales and here's the recipe that we love to serve with our barbecue.

COOKING METHODS Indirect Grilling/Smoking

WOOD Oak, Hickory, Cherry

- 1½ tsp Prague Powder #1 (page 77)
- 1kg boneless pork shoulder, cut into 5cm cubes
- 400g chuck steak, cut into cubes
- 225g pork back fat, cut into small cubes
- 1 tbsp smoked paprika
- 2 tbsp garlic powder
- 2 tbsp dried sage
- 2 tbsp finely chopped flat-leaf parsley
- 1 tbsp fine sea salt
- 2 tsp toasted fennel seeds, crushed
- 1 tsp dried oregano
- 1 tsp dried thyme
- 2 tsp coarsely ground black pepper
- 1 tsp cayenne pepper
- ¼ tsp ground ginger
- natural hog casing, 5m x 36/40 (soaked overnight in water and drained)

First, put the coarse blade of your meat grinder in the freezer. In a large bowl, mix the Prague Powder #1 with 1 tablespoon of water until you have a smooth paste. Add the remaining ingredients apart from the sausage casing and mix well. Pass through a food grinder fitted with your coarse blade. Return the mixture to the bowl, cover tightly with cling film and refrigerate overnight.

The next day, test the seasoning of your sausage mix. Heat a dash of oil in a frying pan and add a small piece of the sausage mix. Fry over medium heat for a few minutes, until thoroughly cooked. Have a taste and add more seasoning if necessary.

When you're ready to make your sausage, turn your kitchen tap on to a slow, steady flow. Hook the hog casing over the end of the tap and flush with water for a few minutes. Squeeze all of the water out of the casing. This is a good time to check the casing for any holes in the casing, if any water comes spouting out, cut that bit out and check another piece.

Using the sausage attachment on a stand mixer, push about 1 metre of casing on the hose attachment and tie the end. Start slowly feeding your mix into the casing, holding the sausage as you go. (You might find it useful to have a large bowl handy for the sausage to drop into.) When you have the individual sausage length you're after, stop feeding the meat through, pinch the sausage casing with your thumb and forefinger and twist to whatever length you like – 15cm is about right.

The next stage is to smoke the sausages. We use sausage sticks to smoke our sausage, which are basically stainless steel pieces of dowelling, and we wrap the sausages around them. When you've made your links, you need to allow them some drying time. You can either hang them in your fridge for 2 hours or hang your sausages in front of a fan for 1 hour before smoking. The skins should be dry to the touch and the sausages should look a little darker in colouring.

This stage will test your smoking skills a little. You want to creep the temperature of your smoker up from 60°C/140°F to 71°C/160°F throughout the cook time, which could be around the 3–4 hour mark, to get maximum smoke flavour without overcooking and rendering the fats too quickly. Add your wood at the start and again as and when it burns out. Check the temperature of the sausages after 2 hours. You're aiming for the internal temperature of your sausage to reach 74°C/165°F. Remove them from the smoker at this point and immediately spray liberally with cold water. Hang at room temperature in front of a fan for 1 hour, then refrigerate overnight, uncovered, before eating.

The sausages will keep for 3–4 days in the fridge and freeze very well for up to 3 months.

Whisky Boys' Tri-Tip

SERVES 6–8

Tri-tip is the barbecue of choice for the Californian coast. It's a lean and delicious cut of beef that grills and smokes well, looking like a big, three-pointed steak. Our most memorable encounter was when Fresno's finest Country Rock band were recording at our friend's recording studio in Tennessee and wanted to show us 'Cali 'Cue', namely marinated and grilled tri-tip. Eating something that was more akin to medium-rare sirloin was a welcome pit stop on our slow and low road trip. This is a take on their recipe and is dedicated to the Whisky Row boys who are still rockin' in the free world.

COOKING METHOD Grilling

2 x 1–1.25kg tri-tip steaks
groundnut oil, for greasing

For the Marinade
100ml balsamic vinegar
100ml Worcestershire sauce
100ml olive oil
100ml soy sauce
2 tbsp Dijon mustard
3 tbsp ground black pepper
1 tbsp garlic powder
3 garlic cloves, chopped
3 shots of your favourite whisky or bourbon

For the Mop Sauce
100ml red wine vinegar
100ml garlic-infused olive oil
1 tbsp chilli flakes

Whisk the marinade ingredients except the whisky or bourbon in a pan over a medium heat for 5 minutes. Remove from the heat and allow the marinade to cool to room temperature. Stir in two of the whisky shots, and sneak a shot for yourself. Put the tri-tips into two large ziplock bags, pour over the marinade in equal quantities, squeeze the air out and seal the bags. Refrigerate for at least 4 hours, or ideally overnight. Oscillate the bags every now and then to help the marinade do its job.

Take the tri-tips out of the bag, discarding the liquid, and set them on a roasting tray. Pat them dry with kitchen towels and set aside to come up to room temperature while you set up your grill. Grab a handful of oak chips and soak them in water for 30 minutes.

Set up your grill for direct heat. Get the coals white hot and a good bed of them, too. You'll need the coals to last about 30–45 minutes. We're aiming for medium-rare meat without scorching, so watch those flare-ups. Rub a little groundnut oil on the tri-tips. Now scatter your soaked wood chips over the red-hot coals to add a little smoke to the beef, wait a moment for them to start smoking before you start cooking. Place your tri-tips directly on the grates, fat-side down and close the lid for 5 minutes. After this time, flip the steaks over and close the lid again for another 5 minutes.

In a small bowl, vigorously whisk the mop sauce ingredients and get your basting brush ready. Continue to turn the tri-tips every 4–5 minutes for 30 minutes, basting each side regularly with your mop sauce.

WHAT IS TRI-TIP?

The tri-tip is a cut of beef from the bottom sirloin sub-primal cut. It is a small triangular muscle, usually 600g–1.5kg. There are two tri-tips per cow. You will undoubtedly have to pre-order these. Ask your butcher to source the largest ones he can get. As it's considered sirloin, expect to pay sirloin prices – yes, this falls into the 'treat meat' category. However, each tri-tip will serve three or four people easily. Plus you'll look super awesome searing these hunks of meat on your grill and telling all your friends that 'this is how they 'cue in Californ-I-A'.

Have your instant-read thermometer to hand, and when the tri-tips internal temperature registers at 55°C /130°F you're good to go. Remove from the grill, cover with a foil tent and allow to rest for 15–20 minutes.

Slicing the tri-tip isn't completely straightforward. You have two opposing grains here, see the picture below.

We usually cut along the yellow line so as to cut it almost in half. With cut A, we'll cut it this way against the grain. With cut B, we'll cut it this way against the grain.

Transfer the slices to a warmed serving dish and let the guests help themselves. Serve with some jambalaya (page 165) for a surf and turf experience.

STEAKS: FORGETTING THE FILLET

Both of us come from 80s working-class backgrounds, so the closest we got to steaks was one of our dads ordering very macho T-bone steaks, or a mixed grill, on rare family trips to a local restaurant. As we reached our late teens, the holy grail of steaks was seemingly the hunk of lean beef called 'fillet steak', which, apparently, we were supposed to order so rare a good vet could resuscitate it. Nowadays, the idea of lean steak is reserved for the health-conscious; the flavour-conscious seek out sub-primal cuts from loins and diaphragms of the harder working muscles. Have you ever heard a butcher declare his love of rump steak over fillet? If so, they were on to something: flavour through marbling. Here are some of our favourite cuts that pack the beefy flavour punch we crave when we want a steak, and how best to cook them.

> Before cooking any steak, allow it to come to room temperature.

MEAT

1. SKIRT / HANGAR / ONGLET STEAK

COOKING METHODS Grill, Dirty, Pan-fry

Found 'hanging' from the last rib bone, near the diaphragm of a cow, this is such a beautifully rich steak. About all you need to understand about this cut is that it was known as the 'butcher's steak' because they used to save the cut for themselves. Sneaky butchers, we're onto you! This is an amazing cut if you want to make your own Philly cheese steak – it stands up to the garlicky filling while delivering a full beefy punch. And because of its robust flavour, it can also take a good marinating. It's also incredible when cooked 'dirty' (see page 105).

2. PICANHA RUMP STEAK / TOP SIRLOIN CAP

COOKING METHODS Grill, Roast, Smoke, Pan-fry, Reverse Sear

The picanha rump steak has become quite popular on the UK barbecue circuit. It is a succulent and tender cut from the rump that is extremely popular in Brazilian churrascaria, and takes smoke particularly well. You can buy a whole hunk of this and reverse sear it on the smoker, cut it into steaks and finish them on the grill.

3. BAVETTE STEAK

COOKING METHODS Grill, Dirty, Pan-fry

This cut is from the flank muscle and sometimes called 'flap meat', but don't let its name put you off. It's grainy in texture and an extension of the T-bone; flap meat is officially part of the short loin section. Bavette steak will also hold up to a good strong marinade yet still pack a beefy punch.

4. RIB-EYE STEAK

COOKING METHODS Grill, Dirty, Pan-fry

The renaissance steak. This has crept back onto menus up and down the country. And for good reason. It's packed with marbling and benefits from being part of the cow's ribcage. The steaks can come anywhere between 5cm and 10cm thick, or they can be bought as a standing rib roast (see pages 108–109). Whichever way, rib-eye steak is absolutely delicious and very impressive looking. The only downside is that it is a bit more expensive due to its recent revival.

5. FEATHER BLADE STEAK

See our recipe on page 110 for cooking a feather-blade on the smoker.

6. TRI-TIP

COOKING METHODS Grill, Reverse Sear

See our recipe on pages 98–99 for cooking a tri-tip.

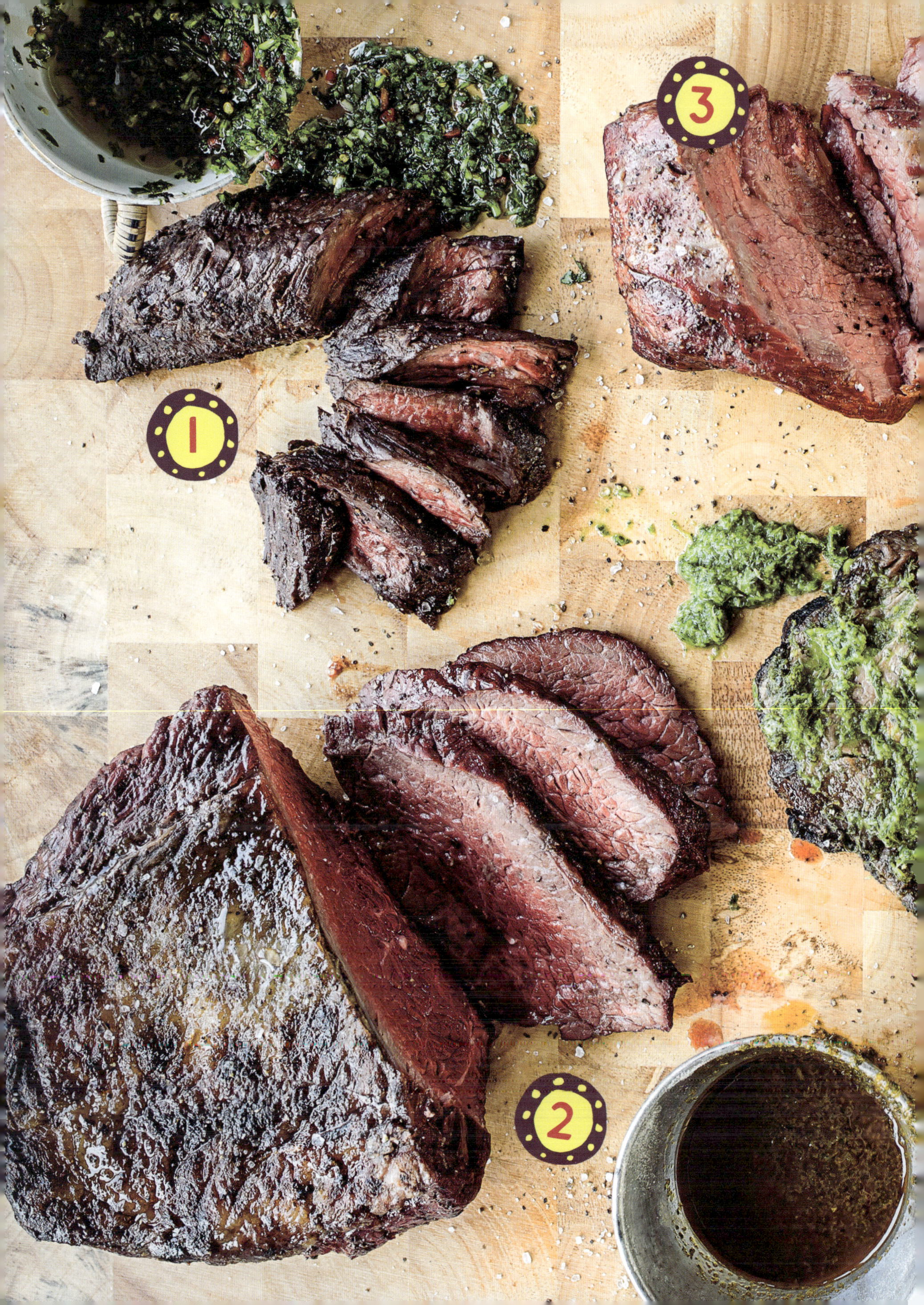
3
1
2

SEE PAGE 105 FOR OUR FAVOURITE STEAK TOPPERS TO ADD EXTRA FLAVOUR.

HOW TO COOK THE PERFECT STEAK

The timings below depend on the thickness and type of steak. We encourage using an instant-read thermometer for accuracy. All timings are approximate and aim for a medium-rare steak.

GRILL

About 20 minutes before grilling, remove the steak from the fridge and let it sit, covered, at room temperature. Heat your grill to high. Brush the steak on both sides with groundnut oil and season liberally with salt and pepper. When the grill is searingly hot, place the steak on top and cook until golden brown and slightly charred, about 3–5 minutes. Turn the steak over and grill for another 3–5 minutes for medium-rare. Transfer the steak to a chopping board or a warm plate, foil tent loosely and allow to rest for 5–10 minutes before slicing.

PAN-FRY

The trick to this method of cooking steak is butter and movement. About 20 minutes before frying, remove the steak from the fridge and let it sit, covered, at room temperature. Heat your pan to high, add 1 tablespoon groundnut oil and as soon as it is sizzling hot, add the steak. Fry for 1 minute, flip, and fry for a further 1 minute. Repeat once more, then add a knob of butter. Using a spoon, baste the steak continuously on one side for 1 minute, flip, then do the same on the other side. All in all, you're looking at 6 minutes all up. Season the steak with sea salt flakes and freshly cracked black pepper, transfer to a chopping board or a warm plate, foil tent loosely and allow to rest for 5–10 minutes before slicing.

DIRTY

A quote from NPR's Kitchen Window series, Dinner in the Fireplace:

'As with so many great culinary discoveries, this one was an accident. Johanne Killeen and George Germon, co-owners of the famed Al Forno in Providence, R.I. first put it on their menu in 1985. Killeen says that one very busy night at the restaurant, Germon unknowingly dropped a steak in the fire. When he finally found and tasted it, a dish was born.'

Although they may not have been the first people to drop meat into the fire and eat it (we're thinking cavemen), we're glad they did.

About 20 minutes before cooking, remove the steak from the fridge and let it sit, covered, at room temperature. Heat your coals until they're white hot. Place the steak directly on the coals and cook for 3 minutes or so, on each side, until golden brown and slightly charred. When you turn the steak over, make sure it sits on fresh, white coals. Generously brush one side of the steak with your chosen Steak Topper (see below), flip over onto fresh coals and cook for another 30 seconds or so. Transfer to a chopping board or a warm plate, foil tent loosely and allow to rest for 5–10 minutes before slicing.

REVERSE SEAR
(GRILL/SMOKER)

We're going to add some delicious smoke flavour to your steak. Set your grill up for indirect heat, with the coals set to one side. Heat your grill to 99°C/210°F and add some oak wood chunks/chips. Don't be shy with these as you're only going to smoke the steak for about an hour. Season the steak with sea salt flakes and freshly cracked black pepper, put on the grill and close the lid. Maintain the temperature at 99°C/210°F and cook for 1 hour, depending on the thickness of your steak. In the final 15 minutes, get a full chimney starter ready so the coals are white hot. When the internal temperature of the steak reaches 43°C/110°F, set the steak aside on a plate. Add the chimney starter coals to your grill, heating the grill until it's nice and hot. Sear your steak for 30 seconds to 1 minute per side to get some fancy line markings. Transfer to a board or warm plate, foil tent loosely and rest for 5–10 minutes.

REVERSE SEAR
(OVEN)

As with pan-frying, the trick to this is butter and movement. Remove the steak from the fridge and let it sit, covered, at room temperature for 20 minutes. Liberally season with sea salt fakes and freshly cracked black pepper. Preheat the oven to 135°C/275°F. Put the steak directly on a wire rack inside a roasting tray. Cook the steak for 30–45 minutes, depending on the thickness, until it reaches an internal temperature of 52°C/125°F. Keep an eye on the temperature at regular intervals. Allow to rest on a warm plate for 10 minutes. Now, get your griddle pan blazing hot on your hob. Brush your steak lightly with groundnut oil, and sear the steak for 30 seconds to 1 minute per side, bringing the internal temperature up to 57°C/135°F. Season the steak immediately and rest for a further 5 minutes.

STEAK TOPPERS

We're fans of steak toppings to add an extra flavour profile. Simply take your pick of one of these toppers and smear as much as you like on your steak after cooking.

Chimichurri (page 32)
Chilli & Smoked Garlic Butter (page 33)
Chermoula (page 44)
Louisiana-style Remoulade (page 45)
Rustic Harissa (page 46)
Bone Marrow Butter (page 47)

BRAISED & SMOKED CHEEKS

SERVES 4

Jowls and cheeks are probably the most well used parts of the living animal so lend themselves perfectly to slow and low due to their collagen content. We like to smoke our cheeks for a few hours before making them into a delicious stew. In this recipe you can use either pig or cow cheeks. If using beef, you'll need to braise in the liquor longer than the pig cheeks. We wouldn't recommend mixing the meats due to their varying cooking times. This is great with some Hasselback Potatoes (page 156), or mashed potatoes with Bone Marrow Butter (page 47).

COOKING METHODS Braising, Indirect Grilling/Smoking

WOOD Hickory, Oak

- 1kg pork cheeks or beef cheeks (as uniform size as possible)
- 1 litre stout or porter beer
- 50ml Worcestershire sauce
- 3 tbsp olive oil
- 50g Texas Grindhouse Rub (page 26)
- 2 medium onions, sliced
- 4 carrots, 1 left whole, 3 cut into chunks
- 1 garlic head, halved widthways
- 1 dried chipotle chilli, soaked in water overnight, seeds removed and finely sliced
- 1 fresh bay leaf
- fine sea salt and freshly ground black pepper

For the Sauce

- 500ml chicken stock (or beef stock if using beef cheeks)
- ¼ tsp cracked black pepper
- ½ tsp fine sea salt, to taste
- 3 tbsp tomato purée
- 250g tin good-quality chopped tomatoes

Remove any silver skin from the outside of the cheeks and put in a bowl. Pour over the beer and Worcestershire sauce. Cover with cling film and put in the fridge to tenderise overnight.

The next day, take the cheeks out of the marinade, reserving the liquid. Use kitchen towel to pat the cheeks dry. Rub them all over with the oil and liberally sprinkle with rub, then leave them to come to room temperature while you prepare your smoker or grill for indirect heat. Maintain the temperature at 120°C/225°F.

Add your wood and as soon as it starts to smoke, put in your cheeks. Smoke pork cheeks for about 1½ hours, and beef cheeks for about 2 hours.

Meanwhile, prepare the sauce. In a saucepan, add the reserved marinade, stock, black pepper, salt, tomato purée and tinned tomatoes. Bring to the boil over high heat, then reduce the heat to low and simmer for 15 minutes. Skim off any foam from the surface.

After your cheeks have had a hit of smoke, carefully remove them from your grill using tongs and set aside while you prepare the rest of your dish. Preheat your oven or set your grill up for indirect heat at 180°C/350°F.

Put the onions, carrots, garlic, chilli and bay leaf in a casserole dish. Place your cheeks on top, pour in your reduced sauce and add some salt and pepper. Make sure there's enough liquid to cover the cheeks, if not add a little water. Cover with a lid and braise in the oven, or your grill, for 3 hours, or until the cheeks are fork-tender. Adjust the seasoning as necessary.

Put the cheeks on a serving dish and spoon over the sauce.

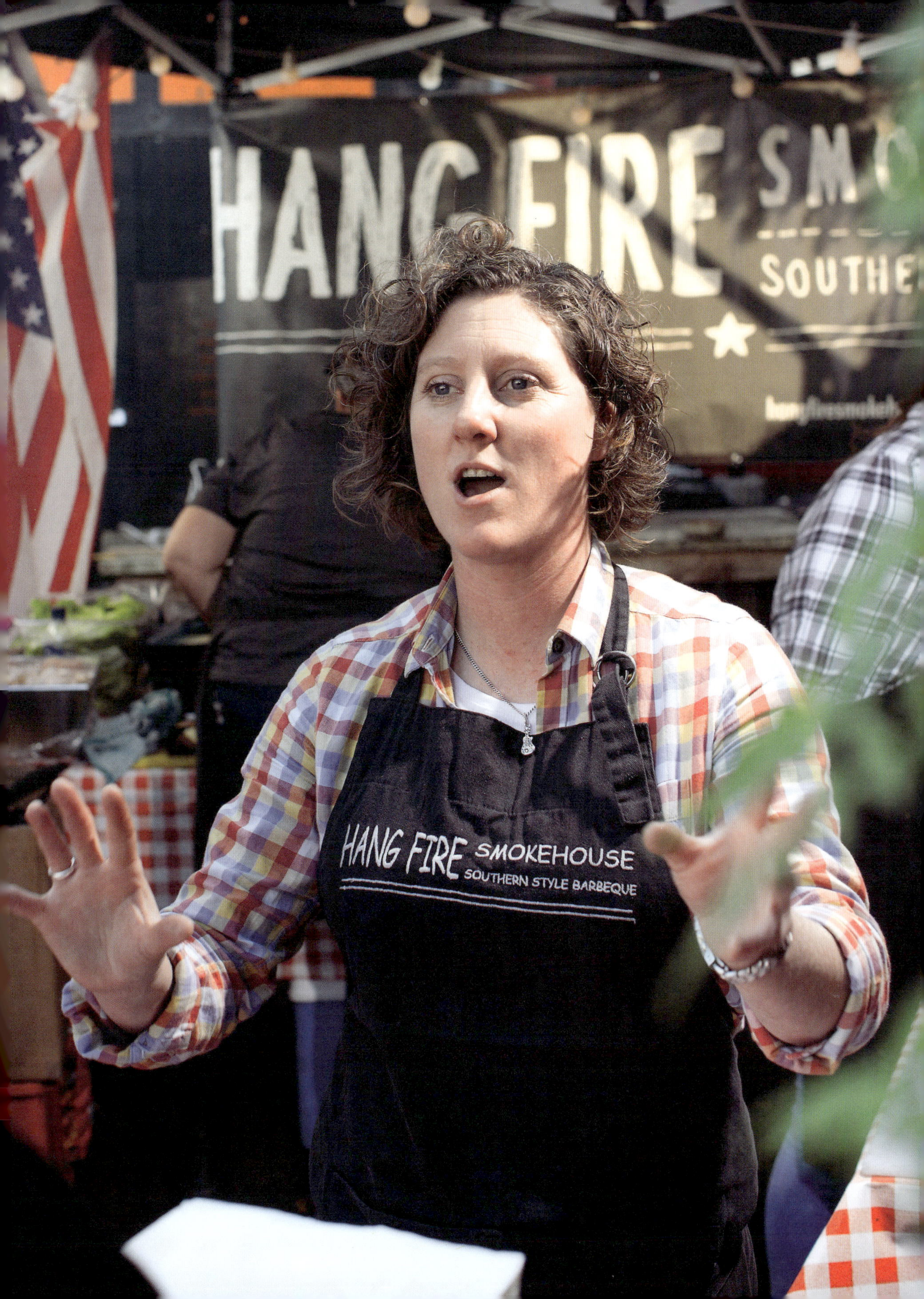
HANG FIRE
HANG FIRE SMOKEHOUSE
SOUTHERN STYLE BARBEQUE

SMOKED FORERIB

SERVES 8-10

So this is the Daddy Mac of beef roasts. The mighty forerib, or prime rib as they call it in the US. This is proper 'treat meat', not quite up there with remortgaging or selling your first born, but it can be expensive depending on how many you're feeding. However, you'll forget about all that when it forms the centrepiece to a big cook-out and looks magnificent, in all its primal, meaty glory. This recipe is inspired by two of our barbecue heroes, Kelly and Roni Wertz, who for our money pioneered barbecue prime rib at their now-closed Kansas restaurant. What we wouldn't give today for a table at that restaurant (and two extra stomachs!). You'll need to order this cut of beef at your local butchers (see opposite).

COOKING METHODS Indirect Grilling/Smoking   **WOOD** Oak

6–8kg bone-in beef forerib (about 3–4 bones)
4 tbsp sea salt flakes
3 tbsp olive oil

For the Rub

1 tbsp ground cumin
2 tbsp coarsely ground black pepper
1 tbsp chilli powder
1 tbsp fine sea salt
2 tbsp soft light brown sugar
2 tsp garlic granules
2 tsp onion powder
2 tsp paprika
1 tsp dried rosemary
1 tsp dried oregano

Start by mixing all the rub ingredients together in a bowl. Set aside. Scrape the bones clean, if they aren't already, with a paring knife. Leave about 3–5mm of thick fat along the back of the roast and diagonally score through the fat, then repeat in the opposite direction, being careful not to cut through the binding string, creating a diamond-shaped pattern.

Generously coat the meat with your rub mixture, rubbing the seasoning into the joint and pressing it firmly into the scored fat section on the back. Cover with cling film and rest in the fridge overnight.

The next day, bring your forerib out and let it come to room temperature for about 15 minutes. Sprinkle with the salt flakes.

Prepare your smoker for indirect heat. You want the temperature to settle at 108°C/225°F before you put your joint in. Put in a handful of woodchips, or a couple of blocks of oak (you can repeat this hourly or as and when the wood has burned out). You're looking at a 5–6-hour smoke time, and an internal temperature for the meat to be no greater than 60°C/140°F on an instant-read thermometer.

When your forerib is medium rare, add some extra coals to your grill. With heatproof gloves and some tongs, move the joint over to the direct-heat side of your grill and sear all over for 5 minutes on each side. Loosely tent the joint in foil and let it rest over a wire rack in a pan for 20 minutes. The juices in the pan can then be used to make a tasty gravy.

MEAT

FLINTSTONE FORERIB

When ordering the forerib, you'll probably be asked how many bones you want or if you want it boneless. Sometimes the butcher will 'French trim' the bones, remove the meat from the shin and tie it all back together so the cut stays in shape through its cooking process. You can, of course, use a boneless rib roast, just make sure it's tied up so it doesn't start to unravel and dry out during the smoking process. You may find that a boneless joint will go further as you can cut the slices thinner, however, you won't get that 'Flintstones' effect with all those magnificent bones!

Transfer the forerib to a chopping board, slice thinly and wait for the 'ooohs' and 'aaaahs' from your hungry guests. Serve with mashed potatoes with Bone Marrow Butter (page 47) or some Hassleback Potatoes (page 156), Southern-style Barbecue Greens with Pork (page 179) and Maque Choux (page 173) for a beautifully vibrant dinner table.

MEAT

SERVES 4

SMOKED FEATHER BLADE STEAK

We made this dish a few times at one of our kitchen takeovers and it went down a storm. We really wanted to do steak but didn't want to serve a ton of T-bones, so we reverse-seared feather blade by smoking it a little then finishing it off in a pan with plenty of rub-seasoned butter. The light smokiness really adds to the sweetness of this super-flavoursome cut, and the bonus is that it is fairly inexpensive by steak standards.

COOKING METHODS Indirect Grilling/Smoking and Grilling

WOOD Hickory, Oak

- 1 x 1.5kg whole feather blade beef steak
- 2 tsp groundnut oil

For the Rub
- 2 tbsp paprika
- 1 tbsp sea salt flakes
- 1 tbsp coarsely ground black pepper
- 1 tbsp soft light brown sugar
- 1 tbsp garlic granules
- 1 tbsp onion granules
- 1 tsp cayenne pepper

First, combine the ingredients for the rub in a bowl.

To prepare the steak, using a sharp knife, remove any silver skin from the outside of the steak. Rub a little oil all over the steak, then liberally sprinkle both sides with the rub, reserving half the rub for later.

Set your smoker up for indirect heat at 108°C/225°F. Add a small handful of oak or hickory chunks/chips, get them smoking, then add your steak and cook for up to 1½–2 hours, until the internal temperature hits 55°C/130°F on your instant-read thermometer.

Carefully remove the steak from the smoker and allow to rest for 45 minutes. Using a sharp knife, cut through the steak lengthways, slightly above the centre and straight through the middle. The sinew should be visible so slide your knife under it and slowly work the knife through to remove the entire sinew. Discard.

Brush a little oil on both sides of the steak pieces and sprinkle with the reserved rub.

Set your smoker or grill up for direct heat on medium-high. Put the steaks on the grill and sear for 3–4 minutes, on each side, until beautifully chargrilled. They should be medium rare. Serve with some Bone Marrow Butter (page 47) Southern-style Potato Salad (page 154) and Southern-style Barbecue Greens with Pork (page 179).

FEATHER STEAK, AKA THE FLAT IRON

This tender, juicy steak is cut from the oyster blade – old-school butchers know them as 'butlers' steak' or 'feather steak'. They are called 'feather' steaks because of the intricate marbling running throughout. The whole feather steak is really two identical muscles with a tough sinew running down the centre. The light smoking adds to the natural sweetness of this super flavoursome cut, and the bonus is that it is fairly inexpensive by steak standards.

MAKES 2.5KG

SALT BEEF

We love a bit of salt beef at Hang Fire HQ and it's relatively straightforward to make. You just need the following ingredients and a bit of time. The brining takes seven days, so a little effort now will pay maximum reward later.

COOKING METHODS   Curing and Poaching

For the Brine

270g soft light brown sugar
350g coarse sea salt
2 tsp whole black peppercorns
8–10 juniper berries
6 cloves
2 fresh bay leaves
53g salt petre (optional)

For the Beef

1 x 2.5kg boneless beef brisket (flat only)
1 large carrot, roughly chopped
1 onion, chopped
1 celery stick, roughly chopped
1 bouquet garni
½ garlic head, unpeeled

Put all the brine ingredients into a very large pan, pour in 2.5 litres water and slowly bring to the boil over medium-high heat, stirring to help the sugar and salt dissolve. When it comes to the boil, allow to bubble away for 2 minutes. Take off the heat and leave to cool completely.

Put the meat in a large, clean glass dish or a non-reactive container and cover the meat with the brine; it must be totally immersed. You might need to weight it down with a plate. Leave covered, in your fridge, for seven days.

Take the beef out of the brine and rinse it under cold running water. Roll and tie the beef with kitchen string and put it in a pan with the vegetables, bouquet garni and garlic, adding enough cold water to cover. Bring the water to the boil over medium heat, reduce the heat to low, and leave to poach gently – and we mean gently – for 2½–3 hours. Cook until the beef is completely tender (check this with a skewer). Serve in thick, steaming slices with mashed potatoes and Southern-style Barbecue Greens with Pork (page 179) or make a killer sandwich with pickles and South Carolina Mustard Sauce (page 38). You can serve it hot (reheat it in the broth in which it has cooked) or cold. To store, wrap well in cling film and keep in the fridge for up to 1 week.

TINNED CORNED BEEF

Original salt beef bears little resemblance to the tinned corned beef we know (and guiltily love, with a lashing of pickle on white bread). The tinned variety is apparently a derivative from an Argentinian beef trimming dish, set in its own fat and jelly. You can make a fancy version, more like a terrine, by shredding your salt beef with finely chopped dill pickles and melted, unsalted butter and leave in the fridge to set.

MEAT

PASTRAMI

MAKES 1.5 KG

Recently, we've made a lot of pastrami as we've been serving it in our wonderfully chewy, artisan pretzel buns (pages 190–91) at our streetfood events. There are not many pleasures in life that compare to a perfect Reuben sandwich, or making your own pastrami. Do bear in mind that good things take time. This recipe takes about six days but it will be well worth the wait, trust us.

COOKING METHODS Curing, Indirect grilling/smoking **WOOD** Oak, Hickory

1 x 2kg boneless beef brisket, trimmed of any hard fat
2 tbsp groundnut oil

For the Cure

225g fine sea salt
75g soft light brown sugar
2 tsp Prague Powder #1 (page 77)
2 bay leaves, ground
2 tbsp garlic powder
2 tbsp ground allspice
1 tbsp ground black pepper

For the Rub

2 tbsp paprika
1 tbsp soft light brown sugar
2 tbsp garlic granules
4 tbsp coarsely ground black pepper
3 tbsp coriander seeds, roughly ground
1 tbsp ground allspice

Combine all the cure ingredients in a large pan, pour in 1.5 litres water and warm through over low heat, stirring, until all the salt and sugar has dissolved. Remove from the heat and allow to cool to room temperature. Put your brisket in a ziplock bag and pour over the curing liquid. Expel any air from the bag, seal, and place in a dish. Refrigerate for 5 days, turning the brisket over daily to ensure the cure penetrates the meat fully.

After 5 days, remove the brisket from the brine, and rinse well in cold water. Soak the brisket in clean water for 1½ hours, changing the water every 30 minutes. Drain. Use kitchen towels to pat the brisket dry. In a bowl, combine the ingredients for the rub. Using your hands, rub a little groundnut oil on the brisket and sprinkle the rub mixture evenly and liberally on both sides, patting it into the meat. Put the brisket back in the fridge for at least 24 hours or 48 hours if you can; this will help the rub adhere.

Set your smoker up for indirect heat and regulate at 121°C/250°F. Pop in your brisket, along with some chunks/chips of oak or hickory wood. Add more wood as it burns out for the first 3 hours. Smoke the brisket for 6–8 hours, until it reaches an internal temperature of 74°C/165°F on your instant-read thermometer.

The final stage is to steam your pastrami and give it the final cook. (If you skip this step, smoke your pastrami as you would a brisket until it reaches 90°C/195°F.) Preheat your oven to 170°C/340°F. Using a large roasting tin with a wire rack, fill with warm water, so it's about 5cm deep. Place your brisket on the rack and make a foil tent, leaving some air between the top of the brisket and the foil. Crimp the edges tightly to the roasting tin. Put it in the oven for around 3 hours. The temperature of the pastrami should be around 94°C/200°F. Remove the foil and let it cook for a further 10 minutes so the bark reforms. Let it rest for 15 minutes, then slice it right into an awesome sandwich with sauerkraut, Russian dressing and lots of dill pickles.

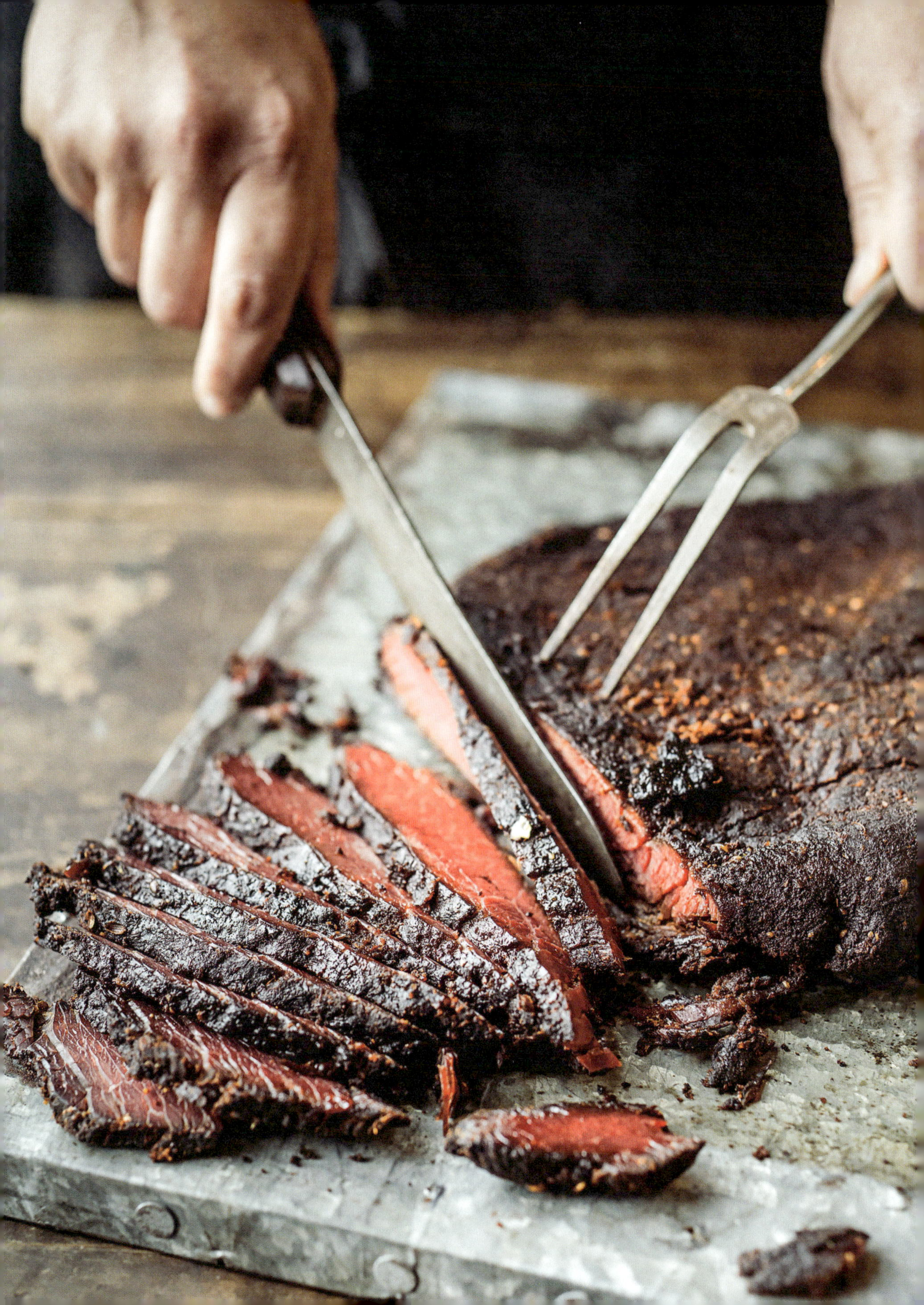

MAKES 5 LARGE BURGERS

HANG FIRE'S AA BACON CHEESEBURGER

It seems you can't move these days without burger recipes filling buns with everything from goat's cheese to peanut butter – kind of like burger white noise. In saying this, we are big fans of a simple bacon cheeseburger with a deliciously juicy, fall-apart patty. Our thoughts stray to the Californian leg of our road trip where we ate a lot of In-N-Out Burger. And up through Utah and Denver, where we ate the most simple, and exquisitely executed, burgers from many 'mom and pop' joints. It's tough to beat a classic, so here's how we make our AA (All American) bacon cheeseburger.

COOKING METHOD Grilling

75g raw bone marrow
800g coarsely minced chuck steak (80% lean/20% fat)
100g coarsely minced skirt steak
100g coarsely minced beef brisket
1½ tsp fine sea salt
2 tsp cracked black pepper

For the Burger Sauce

3 tbsp Hang Fire's Homestyle Ketchup (page 35) or good-quality shop-bought ketchup
2 tbsp mayonnaise
1 tbsp South Carolina Mustard Sauce (page 38)
1 tbsp Hang Fire Smokehouse Barbecue Sauce (page 45) or 1 tsp American mustard
1 tsp Dijon mustard
½ tsp freshly cracked black pepper
dash of your favourite hot sauce
sea salt flakes and freshly cracked pepper, to taste

Start by carefully removing the bone marrow from the bone if this hasn't been done for you. We recommend placing the removed marrow in the freezer for 30 minutes. Put your minced meat into a bowl. Then, with a coarse grater, grate the marrow into your mince, making sure it's distributed evenly, along with the salt and pepper. Trying not to overwork the mince (it will make your burgers chewy not juicy) divide it into five 200g balls. Flatten them out until each patty is about 15mm thick. Use your fingers to press a disc-like dent in the centre of each patty – the meat will contract and shrink when it hits the heat, but the disc will ensure the patty stays fairly flat during this process and won't end up like a meatball. Put the patties on an oiled plate, cover, and transfer to the fridge for 1 hour.

Meanwhile, whisk the sauce ingredients together in a bowl. Adjust the seasoning to your taste and refrigerate until you need it.

Next, set up your grill so it's nice and hot. Take the burger patties out of the fridge and season both sides well with salt and pepper. Put the patties on the hot grill (you can cook your bacon at this point too), and cook for 4–5 minutes, turning when browned and removing when cooked to your liking. Place a slice of cheese on each patty and close the lid of the grill for 1 minute to allow the cheese to melt. Move the patties to the cool side of the grill while you toast the cut sides of the buns.

MEAT

To Serve

5 Pretzel, Kaiser or Brioche rolls (pages 190–193)

10 Batavia lettuce leaves or Little Gem leaves

5 large ripe tomato slices

5 slices red onion

5 slices Monterey Jack cheese

10 slices Bread and Butter Pickles (page 182)

15 slices crispy cooked streaky bacon

We're sure you know how to construct a burger, but for the record... Smear the burger sauce all over the top and bottom of the bun, put some lettuce on the bottom half followed by the tomato, top with a burger patty, the bacon, onion and pickles, and sandwich together with the bun top.

IT AIN'T BIG, IT AIN'T CLEVER

Why eat a super-thick burger? Simply double up the patties if you want more. You get double the flavour through double the delicious 'Maillard' reaction (see page 85), which is what a tasty burger is all about.

KANSAS

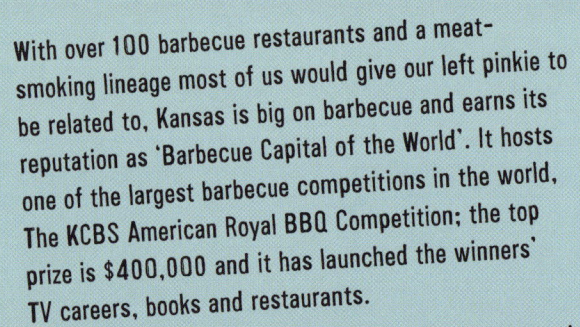

With over 100 barbecue restaurants and a meat-smoking lineage most of us would give our left pinkie to be related to, Kansas is big on barbecue and earns its reputation as 'Barbecue Capital of the World'. It hosts one of the largest barbecue competitions in the world, The KCBS American Royal BBQ Competition; the top prize is $400,000 and it has launched the winners' TV careers, books and restaurants.

Barbecue fanatics flock to Kansas City to eat slow and low morning, noon and night, 7 days a week. You're taking a risk if you rock up at the most popular places at peak time – peak time being anything between when they open and when they close. The rule is: get there early and get in the line. By the time you reach the front of the queue, you're in a barbecue feeding frenzy.

We ate at some of the best places the city has to offer: first, Fiorella's Jack Stack Barbecue, a super-smart barbecue that served the most glorious burnt ends. Variations on burnt ends cropped up on the entire menu, even in stuffed olives served with the Bloody Marys. Less swanky is Arthur Bryant's; Arthur Bryant is widely considered to be the forefather of the city's barbecue. The formica and fluro decor and menu had barely changed in decades; if it ain't broke, don't fix it. Woodyard Bar-B-Que, by contrast, is a proper little barbecue shack. Set in an old wood yard, with big red brick smokers out the back, the chimney stacks pump out good, clean smoke and wafts of smoky heaven along with it. If this place was a kid, we'd be pinching its sweet little chubby cheeks. Their brisket chilli and their baby back rib dinner absolutely blew us away. Unfussy barbecue with a perfect hit of smoke. We were fighting over the last mouthful.

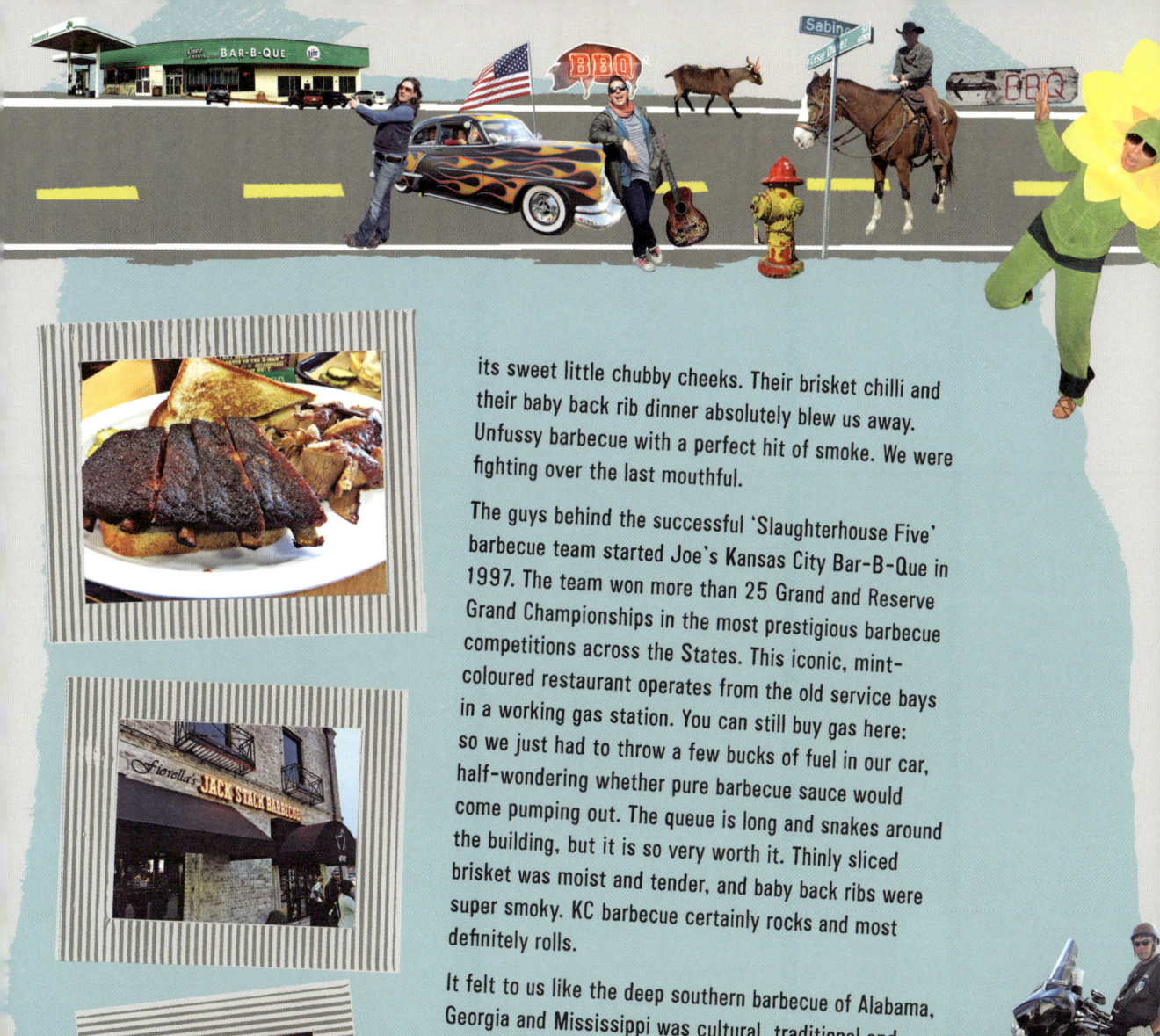

The guys behind the successful 'Slaughterhouse Five' barbecue team started Joe's Kansas City Bar-B-Que in 1997. The team won more than 25 Grand and Reserve Grand Championships in the most prestigious barbecue competitions across the States. This iconic, mint-coloured restaurant operates from the old service bays in a working gas station. You can still buy gas here: so we just had to throw a few bucks of fuel in our car, half-wondering whether pure barbecue sauce would come pumping out. The queue is long and snakes around the building, but it is so very worth it. Thinly sliced brisket was moist and tender, and baby back ribs were super smoky. KC barbecue certainly rocks and most definitely rolls.

It felt to us like the deep southern barbecue of Alabama, Georgia and Mississippi was cultural, traditional and steeped in the historic and geographical influences of music, civil rights and migration. Kansas City was a little more maverick and seemed to buck tradition: we were fascinated by the way folks like Woodyard and Joe's were approaching their craft with unique flavour profiles. At this point in our road trip, the tips and tricks we were getting from the meat carvers and pit masters about rubs, sauce wood types, smoking temperatures and cuts of meat were starting to make sense.

117

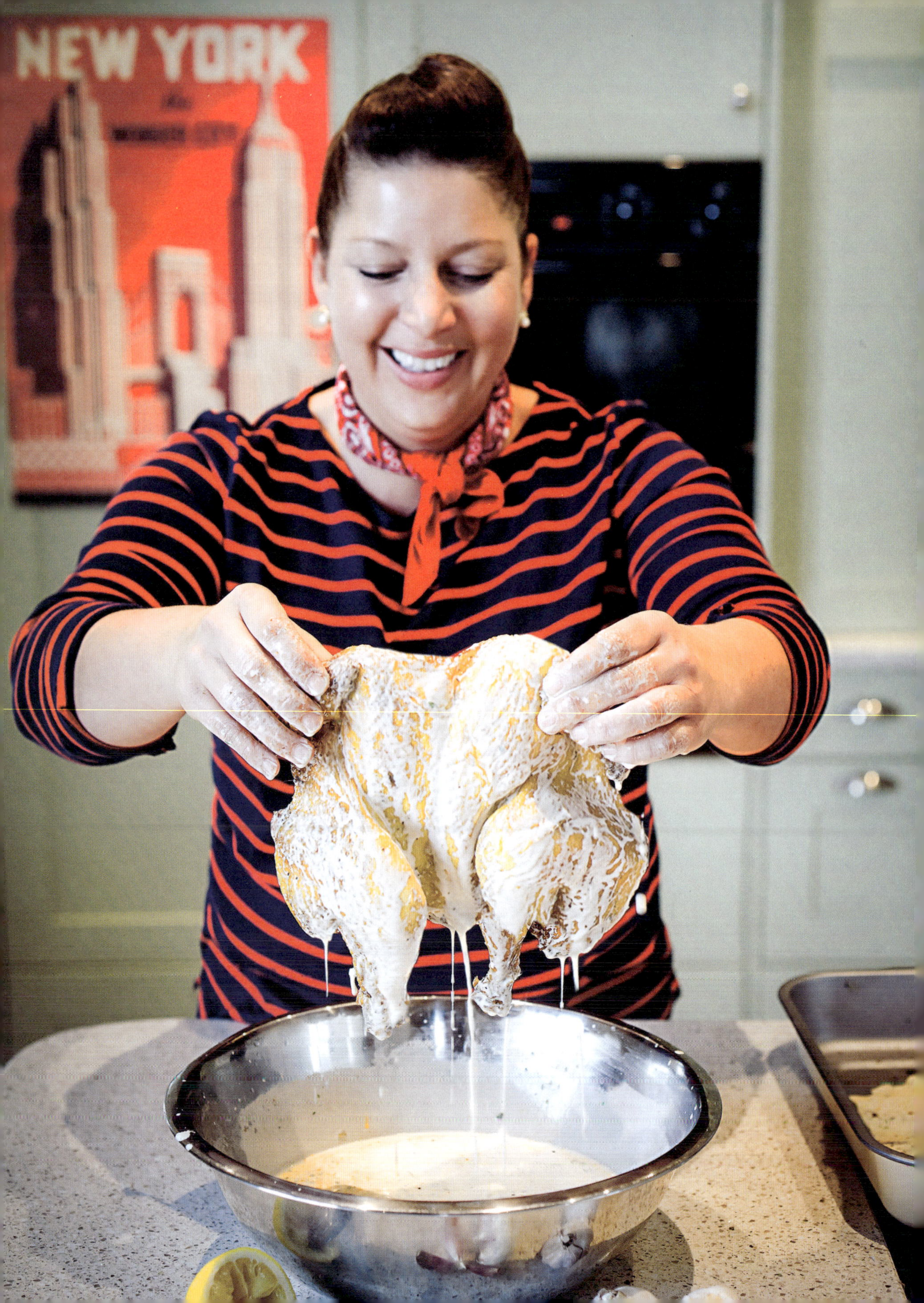
NEW YORK

HANG FIRE YARDBIRD

SERVES 4

POULTRY

This is a great recipe if you're about to begin your foray into the alchemy of slow and low barbecue. We've all heard of beer-can chicken and various other devices that will have your chicken stand to attention in your grill. But you don't really need to do this to have yourself a tasty, good-looking yardbird for dinner. We prefer to spatchcock the chicken, not only because you get more surface area for the smoke and spice to adhere to, but also because it decreases the cooking time. Make like you're in Big Bob Gibson's Barbecue joint and dip the whole smoked bird in Alabama White Barbecue Sauce (page 38) to serve.

COOKING METHODS Brining, Indirect Grilling/Smoking

WOOD Apple, Pear, Cherry, Beech, Alder

- 1 x 1.3kg whole chicken
- 1 x quantity Bird Bath Brine (page 127), cooled
- 2 tbsp groundnut oil
- 4 tbsp Yardbird Rub (page 28)
- 150g White Barbecue Sauce (page 38), to serve
- 100ml cider vinegar

To spatchcock the chicken, place it on a chopping board and use poultry shears or a sharp knife to cut along either side of the backbone. Using the palm of your hand, push the shoulder blades in opposite directions so the bird lies flat. Submerge your chicken in the prepared and cooled brine and refrigerate for at least 4–6 hours, or overnight. After the brine time, remove the chicken and pat it completely dry with kitchen towel, rub all over with the oil and sprinkle evenly on both sides with the Yardbird Rub. Put the chicken back in the fridge while you set up your grill or smoker.

Set up your grill for indirect heat; you're going start with a relatively low temperature and then after an hour, crank it up. This will ensure the bird gets a good lick of thin blue smoke and gives a nicely browned bird with crispy skin. Now, set the temperature at 108°C/225°F, and add your wood just before you put the bird in. Smoke for 1 hour, then take the temperature up to 135°C/275°F. Continue to smoke for another 2 hours, adding more wood every hour or as and when it burns out. Check the internal temperature of the thickest part of the breast with your instant-read thermometer. Once it reaches 74°C/165°F, it's done.

When the bird is cooked, remove it from the grill, cover it in the white barbecue sauce and serve with some delicious sides, such as Lexington-style Red 'Slaw (page 150), Southern-style Potato Salad (page 154) or some Hoppin' John (page 170).

MEAT

SERVES 2–3 AS AN APPETISER OR 4–5 AS MAIN

COLA HOT WINGS

These wings were the first thing we ate at our first tailgate party in Denver, CO. Right before the game started, there were fans grilling, smoking, making tacos and hotdogs and of course guzzling cold beer out the back of their trucks and cars. But these wings really stood out with their rich, sweet cola flavour and hit of heat and smoke. This recipe came from an off-duty chef and die-hard Bronco fan, and I'm sure he wouldn't mind us sharing it if we declared 'Go Broncos!'*

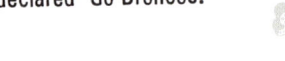

COOKING METHODS Indirect Grilling/Smoking or Oven   **WOOD** Apple, Pear, Beech, Birch

12–15 jumbo chicken wings
groundnut oil

For the Cola Brine
2 cans of your favourite cola (not a low-calorie version)
3 tbsp Louisiana Hot Sauce (page 44), or your favourite hot pepper sauce
1 tsp onion powder
4 garlic cloves, sliced
1 tbsp fine sea salt
1 tsp cracked black pepper

For the Rub
100g Yardbird Rub (page 28)
2 tsp cayenne pepper

For the Cola Barbecue Sauce
1 can of your favourite cola (not a low-calorie version)
300g ketchup
1 tbsp tomato purée
6 tbsp Worcestershire sauce
1 tbsp Louisiana Hot Sauce (page 44), or your favourite hot pepper sauce
1 tbsp smoked paprika
1½ tsp onion powder
1½ tsp garlic powder
1 tsp fine sea salt
1 tsp coarsely ground black pepper

In a large bowl, whisk the brine ingredients until totally combined. Add the the chicken wings, making sure they're well covered. Cover the bowl with cling film and put in the fridge to marinate for 3–5 hours.

After the marinating time, discard the liquid and pat the wings dry with kitchen towel. In a small bowl, thoroughly mix the Yardbird Rub and cayenne pepper and put in a shaker. Rub the wings with a little groundnut oil and sprinkle liberally, all over, with the rub mixture. Put the wings in the fridge until you're ready to grill them.

Set your grill up for indirect heat maintaining a consistent temperature of about 150°C/300°F. Add your wood and, as soon as it starts to smoke, put the wings on the grate and smoke for 30 minutes.

While you're waiting for the wings to smoke, whisk the cola barbecue sauce ingredients in a saucepan over high heat for a few minutes, until it comes to the boil and is well combined. Reduce the heat to low and simmer, stirring occasionally, for 20 minutes until thickened. Pour about a third of the sauce in a small bowl and transfer the remaining sauce to a jar and allow to cool completely before storing in the fridge for another time. It will keep for up to 1 month.

After 45 minutes, the wings should be almost done. Brush the wings with the cola barbecue sauce and close the lid to allow the glaze to set for 10–15 minutes. Check the internal temperature of the wings, making sure you don't hit the bone – it should be above 75°C/165°F.

When the wings are fully cooked, transfer to a plate, and serve with a little of the remaining cola barbecue sauce for dipping.

*At the risk of this book being burned, by NFL fans, we declare that other football teams are available to support!

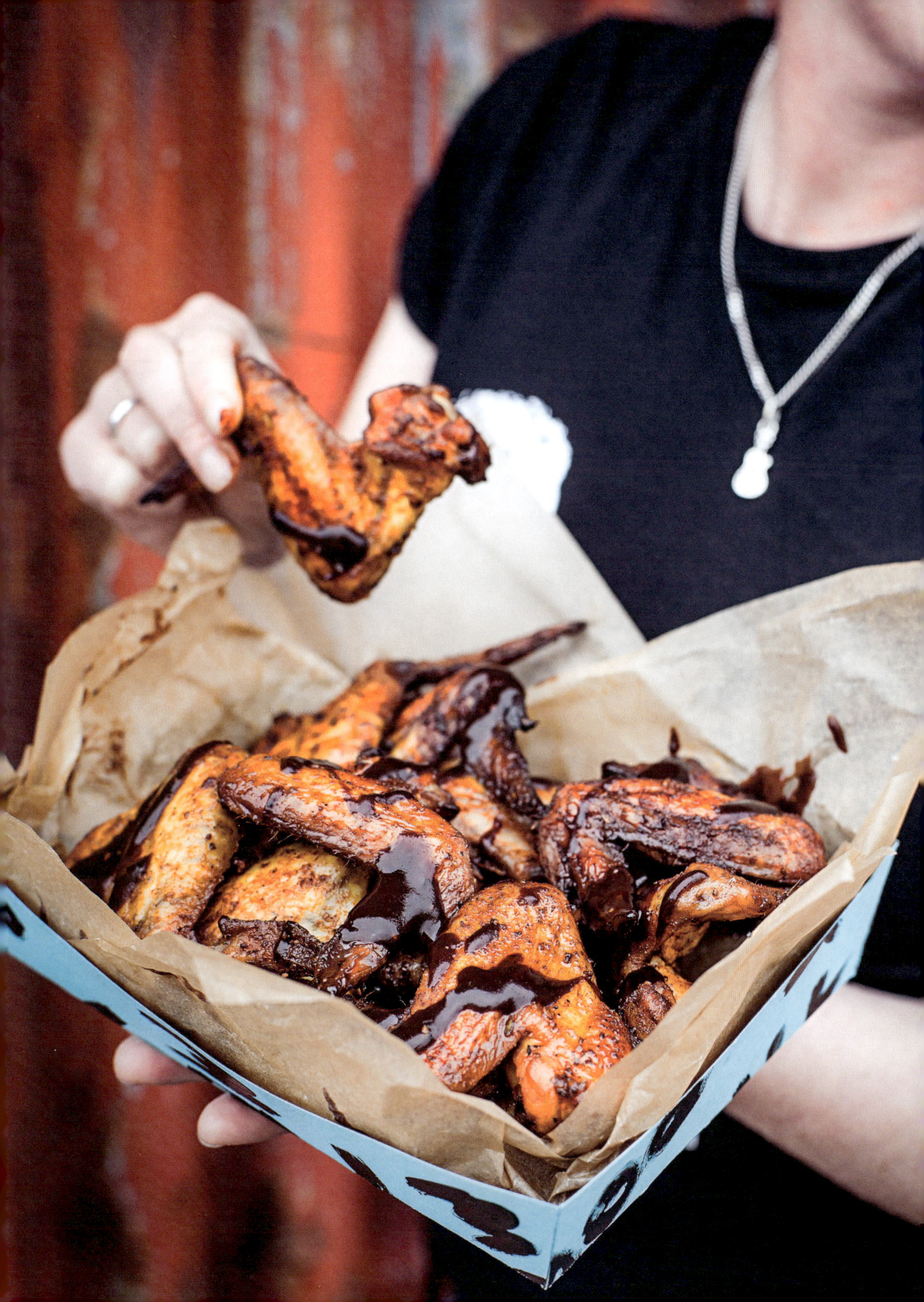

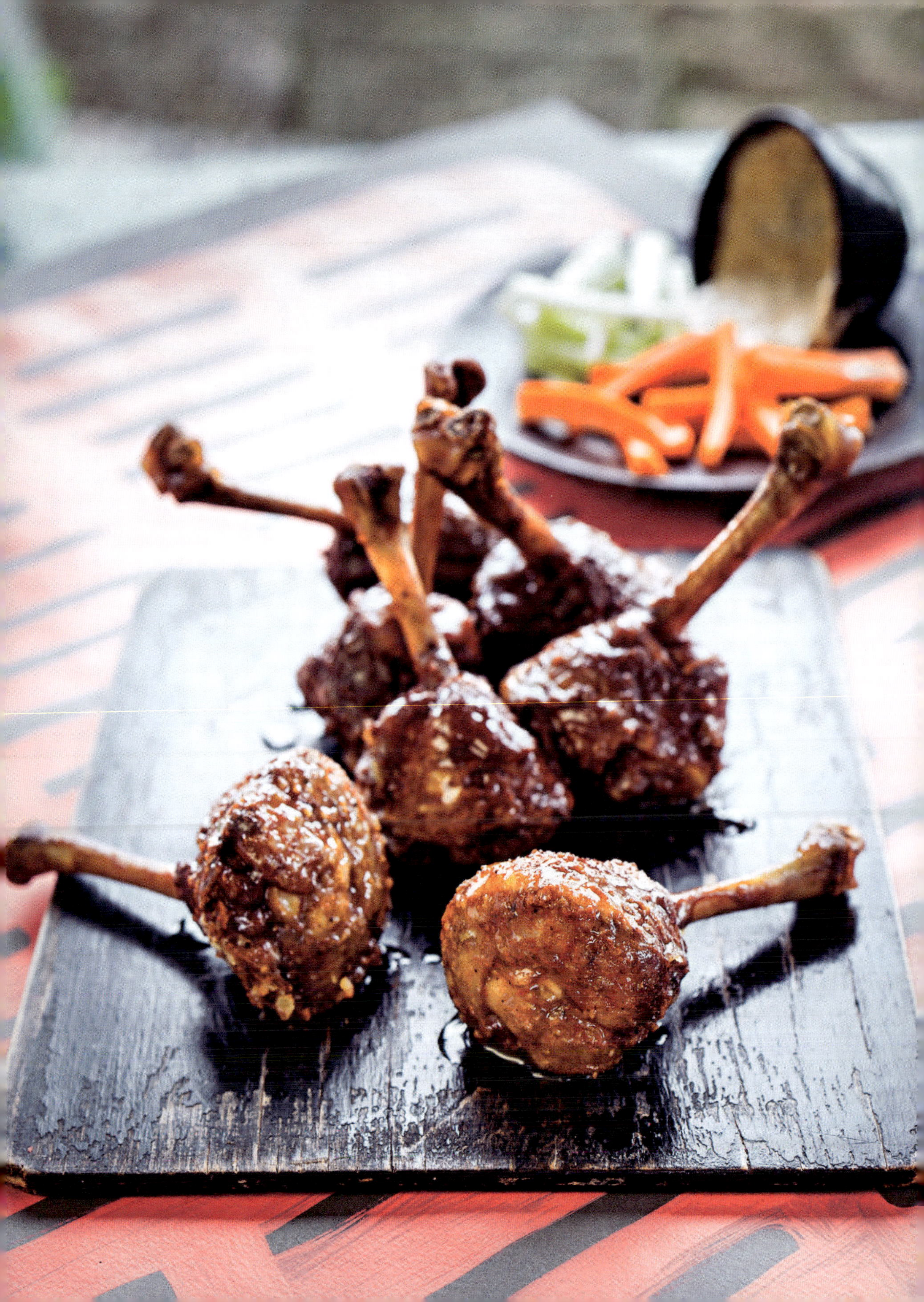

SERVES 6 AS AN APPETISER OR
4 AS A MAIN

SMOKED CHICKEN LOLLIPOPS

We've only ever seen this as an Indian dish, but it's such an awesome little appetiser that you really should have a crack at these on the barbecue. Bit fiddly, but they look impressive. The chicken lollipop is essentially a 'Frenched' chicken leg – the meat is cut loose from the small end of the bone and pushed down to create a lollipop. The leg bone is left clean and creates the lollipop stick.

COOKING METHODS Indirect Grilling/Smoking or Oven   **WOOD** Apple, Pear, Beech, Birch

12 chicken drumsticks
4 tbsp groundnut oil
50g Hang Fire's Almost All-purpose Rub (page 26)
100g Hang Fire Smokehouse Barbecue Sauce (page 45)
100g unsalted butter

To turn regular chicken legs into lollipops you'll need a sharp knife and a pair of poultry shears. Make a cut around the width of the higher part of the chicken leg just below the knuckle bone at the top, and cut through the skin and tendons. Push the meat down to the large end, making a lollipop shape. Be careful and use your fingers, or poultry shears, to remove the tiny, sharp bone nestled in the meat. Trim away the tendons as much as possible. Continue pushing the meat firmly down the bone. You're looking to make a neat little ball of meat at the end of the bone, and it should stand up on its end.

Rub a little oil on the meaty part of the lollipop and season the legs with a dusting of our Almost All-purpose Rub. Wrap the exposed bones with a little foil (this will prevent the bones from turning black during cooking and will look great for presentation). Set the chicken aside for 30 minutes at room temperature.

Meanwhile, set up your grill for indirect heat. You'll want the temperature a little higher than our usual 'slow and low' temperatures, just so the chicken skin can crisp up. Maintain a consistent temperature of 150°C/300°F.

Next, place the butter in a disposable foil roasting tin. Set the tin inside the smoker to melt the butter. When the smoker is up to temperature, place the lollipops in the tin with the butter, bones sticking up. Close the lid and cook for 2 hours. Check the internal temperature is around about 75°C/165°F. Dip each lollipop in barbecue sauce and allow the glaze to set for 30 minutes in the smoker.

Carefully remove the chicken lollipops and allow them to rest for 10 minutes before serving. Liberally brush more barbecue sauce on the lollipops and tuck in.

MEAT 123

MAI-THAI THIGHS

SERVES 10-12

This dish is an adaptation of some tasty chicken we ate at a little Thai café just off Union Street in San Francisco. It was the perfect lunch for a warm autumnal day sat in Washington Park (probably planning out our next meal). The dish borrows from classic Thai flavours and pairs with the citrus punch of a mai-tai cocktail. This marinade works well on all manner of chicken cuts, whether it be halves, whole or quarters.

COOKING METHODS Indirect Grilling/Smoking or Oven

WOOD Apple, Pear, Cherry, Beech, Alder, Birch

10–12 bone-in chicken thighs

For the Marinade
juice of 1 lime
juice of 1 medium orange
100ml pineapple juice
2 tbsp Thai fish sauce
50ml sesame oil
50g soft light brown sugar
1 tbsp sweet chilli sauce
2 tbsp chopped fresh ginger
10 garlic cloves, sliced
2 long red chillies, sliced lengthways
5 spring onions, sliced
small bunch Thai basil, chopped

For the Basting Mixture
juice of 1 lime
125ml groundnut oil
2 tbsp soft light brown sugar
1 tbsp soft dark brown sugar

Use a sharp knife to trim away any extra fatty parts from the chicken thighs and place in a large ziplock bag. Whizz the marinade ingredients in a food processor or blender and pour into the bag, massaging the marinade all over the chicken. Push out as much air as possible and seal the bag. Put in the fridge and allow to marinate overnight for maximum punch.

The next day, combine the baste ingredients in a small bowl and set aside while you prepare your smoker.

Set up your grill for indirect heat, maintain the temperature at 108°C/225°F. With the wood smoking, place the chicken on the grills, away from the coals and close the lid. Cook for a total of 2 hours, basting the chicken with your basting mixture every 20 minutes during the final 1½ hours. Crisp the skins up over the coals just before serving and check that the internal temperature of the chicken reads 75°C/165°F on an instant-read thermometer. Take off the heat and allow to rest for 5–10 minutes before serving.

NO SMOKER? NO PROBLEM

You can cook these thighs in the oven. Simply follow the recipe up until you put them in the smoker. Preheat your oven 180°C/350°F/gas mark 4. Place the thighs on a wire rack over a roasting tin and cook for 45–50 minutes, basting once during the final 15 minutes. Make sure that the internal temperature of the chicken reaches 75°C/165°F on an instant-read thermometer before serving.

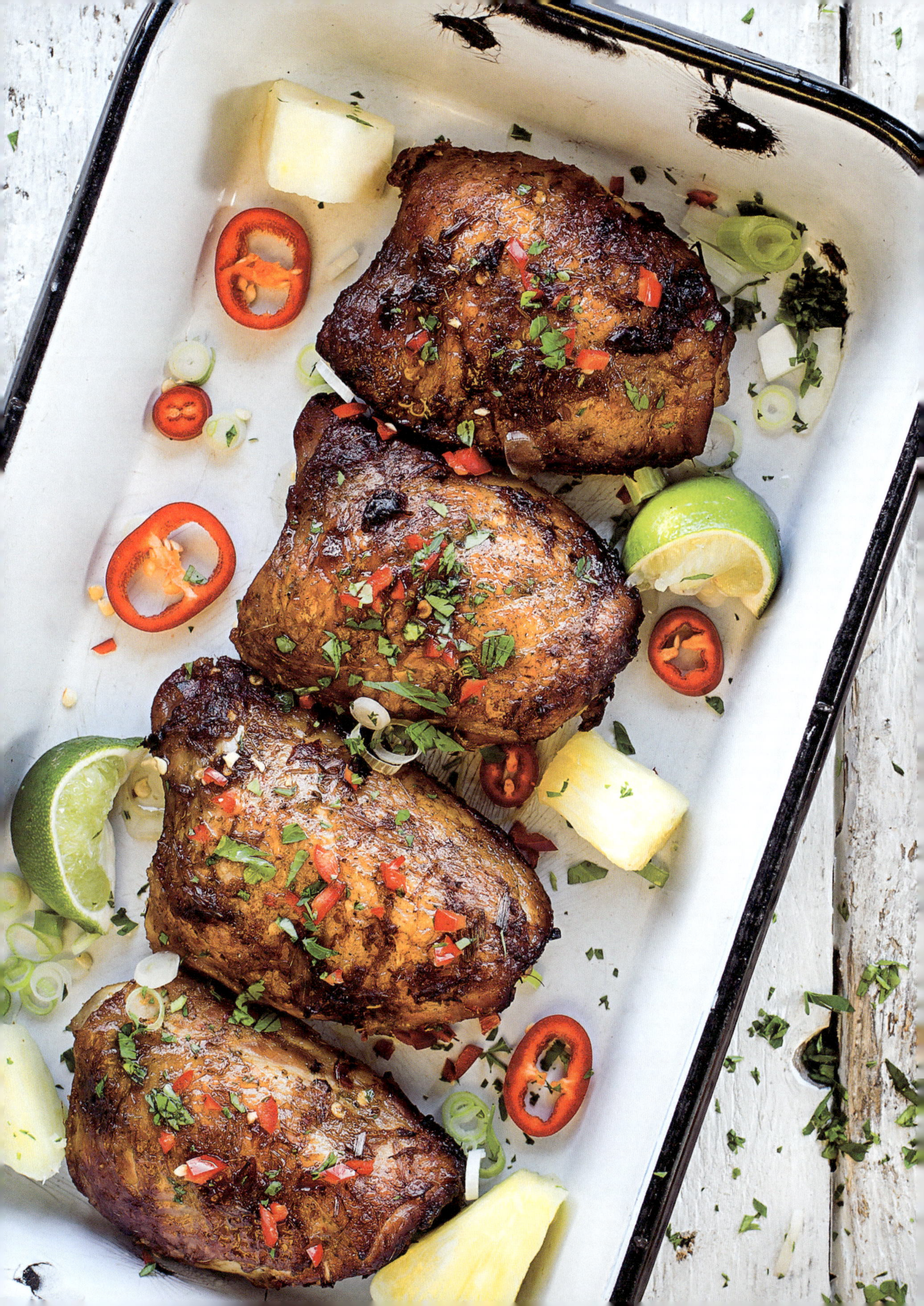

SERVES 8-10

TURKEY CROWN & WHOLE TURKEY

At Christmas time, we sell a lot of smoked turkey crowns, as well as smoking turkey throughout the year for our turkey cubanos or smokehouse club sandwiches. If you're not a fan of turkey due to memories of feather spitting, dry, festive dinners, please give this a go. It will change your mind, we promise. The subtle, smoky flavour and butter-moist breast meat will have you finding any excuse to throw a turkey in the smoker.

COOKING METHODS Brining, Indirect Grilling/Smoking

WOOD Apple, Pear, Cherry, Beech

6 litres Festive Brine (opposite)
1 x 5kg whole turkey or turkey crown
groundnut oil, to brush
1 x quantity Garden Rub (page 28)

Extra Ingredients for Whole Turkey
¼ lemon
½ garlic head (cut widthways)
½ onion, quartered
a small bunch of fresh thyme and sage leaves

Prepare your brine up to the cooling stage. Allow the brine to cool completely, then add the bird, making sure it's fully submerged. If using a whole turkey instead of a crown, put it breast side down. Refrigerate for 24 hours.

Remove the turkey from the brine and pat dry with kitchen towel. If you're using a whole turkey, stuff the cavity with the lemon, garlic, onion, thyme and sage. Brush the turkey with oil and season liberally with the Garden Rub.

Set your grill up for indirect heat, maintaining a temperature of 120°C/250°F. Add in some fruit wood (we like cherry and applewood) and when it's smoking, put in your turkey, breast side up. This will take between 4 hours and 6 hours to smoke. Take the internal temperature from the thickest part of the breast, being careful not to hit bone, and when it reaches 74°C/165°F it's ready. Remove from smoker, loosely foil tent and allow the turkey to rest for 15 minutes before carving.

MEAT

MAKES 1 LITRE, ENOUGH FOR 1 X 1.3–1.5KG CHICKEN

MAKES ENOUGH TO BRINE A 6KG BIRD

BIRD BATH BRINE

Wet brines, or rubbing with dry salt, are a great way of ensuring your poultry stays nice and moist during cooking, which is especially important when it comes to the breast meat. We all know that eating a dried-out roast chicken can have us spitting feathers!

1 litre water
50g fine sea salt
50g soft light brown sugar
2 tbsp coriander seeds
2 tbsp coarsely ground black pepper
1 tsp garlic granules
2 fresh bay leaves
1 x 1.3–1.5kg chicken

Warm the brine through by putting the ingredients (apart from the chicken) in a large saucepan set over medium heat. Bring almost to the boil to make sure the salt dissolves completely and the aromas of the herbs and spices are released. Take the pan off the heat and allow to cool completely. You don't want your uncooked chicken hanging out in the warm mixture. They call it the 'danger zone' for a reason: bacteria grows at its quickest between 5°C and 63°C. Which would make for a very dicey dining experience.

Place the bird in a large bowl or ziplock bag and pour the cooled mixture over the bird making sure it is fully submerged (especially the breast, flip it upside down if you need to). Keep in the fridge overnight before cooking any which way you like.

FESTIVE BRINE

Just like a puppy, this brine isn't just for Christmas. We call it our 'festive' brine as it has all those seasonal spices that give the poultry that sweet, subtly spiced flavour. We use this brine every time we smoke a turkey; the salt keeps the bird absolutely moist through the smoking process. You need to make sure that your bird is completely submerged in the brine, so you might need more or less water.

pared rind and juice of 1 large orange
3 fresh rosemary sprigs
250g fine sea salt
100g soft light brown sugar
1 medium onion, quartered
1 garlic head, halved widthways
1 lemon, quartered
small bunch fresh thyme
small bunch fresh sage
1 tbsp garlic powder
2 tsp finely ground black pepper
3 star anise
2 cinnamon sticks
6 litres water

Put all the ingredients in a large pan along with the 6 litres water. Stir over medium heat for 5–10 minutes, until the sugar and salt have dissolved. Take off the heat and allow to cool to room temperature. Put your poultry in a large container and pour the brine over, making sure the poultry is fully submerged. Transfer to the fridge and allow to brine for 24 hours before cooking any which way you like.

ROADRUNNER VERSION...

If you want a quick brine, 2–3 hours or so, go for 100g sea salt to every 1 litre water. Reduce the water content by half and make up the other half with ice cubes to make sure you cool your brine down sufficiently before your bird takes its bath. Pour the cooled room temperature brine over the ice cubes (don't pour boiling solution over the ice!), stir to melt, add the chicken and put immediately in the fridge to keep chilled.

DUCKSTRAMI

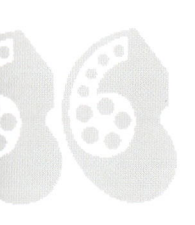

SERVES 2-4

What's not to like about duck pastrami? This is a great recipe that we've been making for the past couple of years and it really isn't as complex as you might think. You can eat it cold, shave it over salad served with a nice punchy blackberry reduction, have it as part of a charcuterie board, or make the most awesome duck Reuben's. As with all cured meats, this is gonna take patience, you're looking at starting the recipe two days in advance.

COOKING METHODS Curing, Indirect Grilling/Smoking   **WOOD** Apple, Pear, Cherry

4 good-quality duck breasts (about 250g each)

For the Cure

100g fine sea salt
2 tsp cracked black pepper
2 tsp soft dark brown sugar
1 tbsp garlic powder
8 juniper berries, ground
3 bay leaves, ground
1 tsp mixed spice
2 tsp ground coriander

For the Rub

4 tbsp coarsely ground black pepper
2 tbsp coarsely ground coriander seeds
1 tbsp garlic granules
½ tsp mixed spice

First make the cure. In a small bowl, thoroughly combine the cure ingredients. Coat the duck breasts entirely with cure and place in a large ziplock bag. Place in the coldest part of the refrigerator and cure for 48 hours, flipping the bag twice a day.

Place the duck breasts in a large container and fill with water. Allow to soak for 1 hour. Drain and pat them dry with kitchen towels.

Next, combine the ingredients for the rub in a small bowl. Coat the duck breasts entirely with the rub.

Fire up your smoker or grill to 110°C/225°F. Add chunks of cherry wood (or other fruit wood). When the wood is ignited and starts to smoke, put in the duck breasts, skin side down. Smoke for 1 hour, or until an instant-read thermometer reads 74°C/165°F when inserted into the centre of the breasts.

Remove from the smoker and allow to rest for 10 minutes. We prefer to wrap the duck breasts in cling film for at least 24 hours before we eat them, giving the flavours a chance to settle. If you want to reheat the duckstrami, we find that steaming it using a bamboo steamer is best. This warms the pastrami gently without direct heat which could cause it to dry out. Any meat you're not using can be frozen for up to 3 months, or will keep for up to 1 week in the fridge. It's a really versatile meat, and not as gamey as regular duck.

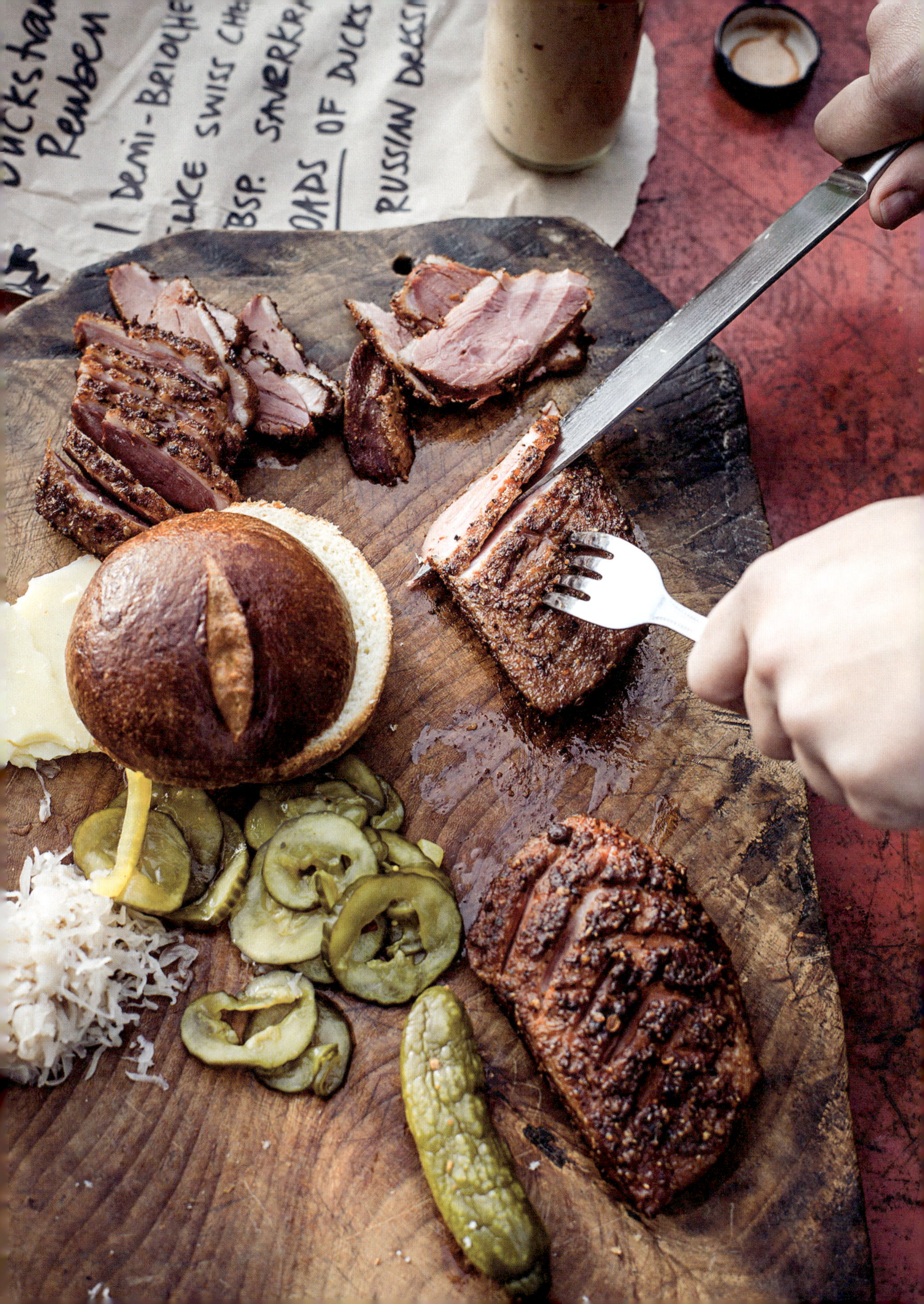

KENTUCKY

"FROM NASHVILLE TO KENTUCKY, MY HEART, IT DRAWS THE LINE"
Nashville To Kentucky, by My Morning Jacket

Our road trip to Kentucky taught us the mantra that we live by today: barbecue is a way of life.

Kentucky boasts some exports dear to our hearts: coal mining, bourbon and Bluegrass. And we couldn't help but wonder whether Welsh immigrants, working in the coal mines and farms of Louisville, could have influenced that area's favourite choice of barbecued meat: mutton.

Our first stop was Old Hickory's BBQ. A lovely little barbecue joint with worn wooden furniture and a homely vibe. Run by five generations of the same family, the aroma in this little joint was different from any other we'd visited: vaguely reminiscent of a good roast lamb dinner but with a lick of fragrant wood smoke. The locals were tucking into the mutton voraciously. We hadn't come across much lamb in our time in the States and it looked like we had struck ovine gold. After polishing off a three-meat plate of sliced and chopped mutton and mutton ribs, we were able to talk to pit boss Gary Sandefur, and he and Sam quickly bonded over their love of lamb. Gary invited us to see the Old Hickory pit, a massive 'cinder block' pit with a metal chamber on top, accessed by huge, slanted sliding doors. Large log piles of split hickory were stacked to the side and what looked like a cross between a fish slice and a snow shovel were used for moving the huge hunks of lamb, pork and beef around the smoker.

Gary's smoked mutton was a game changer. It retained its glorious, gamey flavour and tenderness, but the smoke took one of our favourite meats to another level. We had to take this one back with us. Before we left, we joined other visitors and stuck two pins in their world map, one for Wales and one for Northern Ireland.

After a visit to the International Bluegrass Museum, a mecca for us and a homage to the Grandfather of Bluegrass, Bill Monroe, we headed back to Tennessee with our bellies and minds well fed. We did find time to grab a bottle of Kentucky liquid gold from a liquor store. But Kansas, Oklahoma and Texas were calling and we refrained from spending all our meat bucks on bourbon.

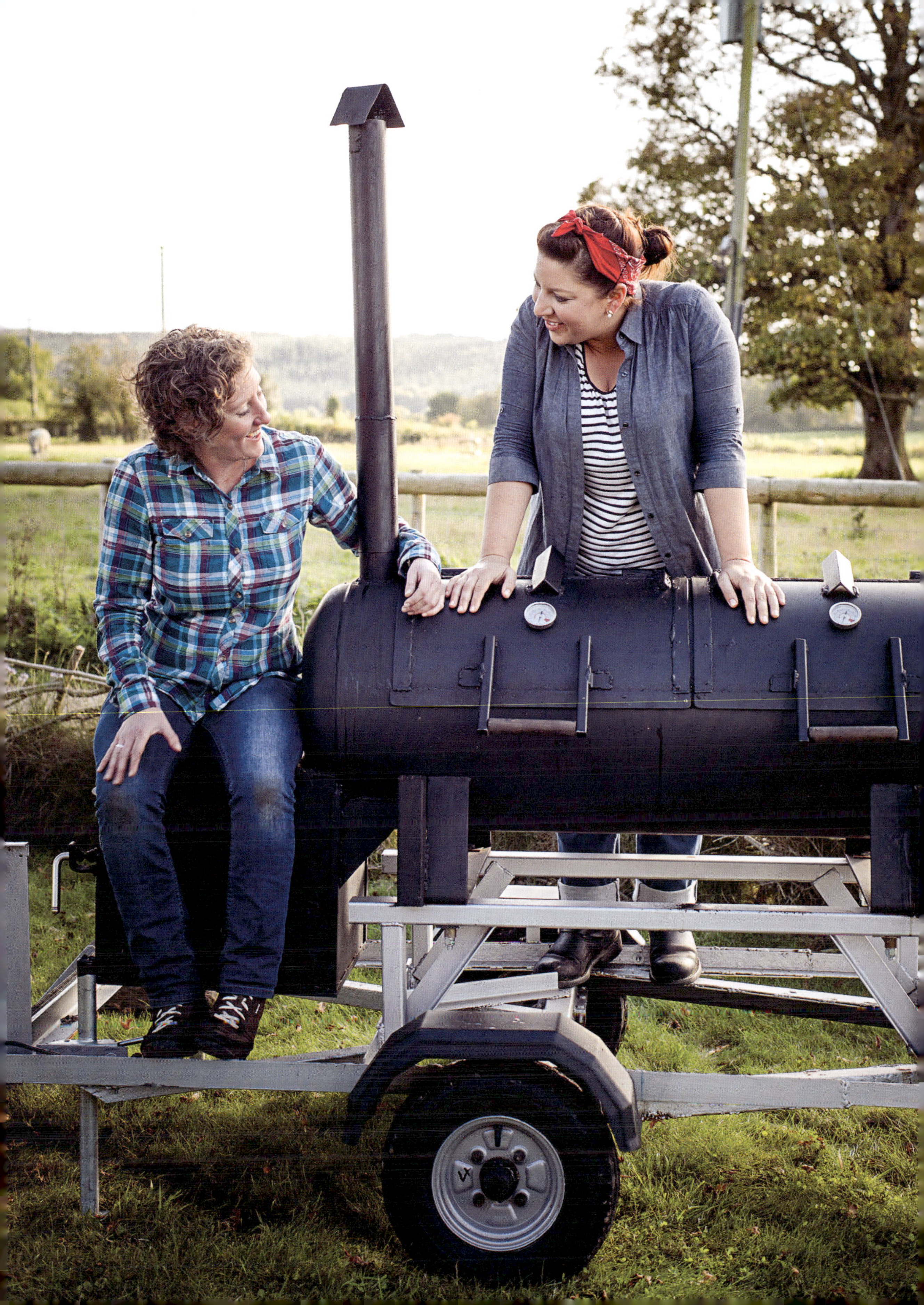

SERVES 5-8

LAMB

SMOKED LAMB SHOULDER

We get incredible lamb in the UK and there's no real reason to buy a variety from overseas. It can be expensive, depending on the time of year, so you may as well make the most of it when you can afford it and invite a few people round to dinner to share the love. This dish looks really impressive when served on a big platter or chopping board with some delicious sides. The shoulder needs to marinate in the rub overnight, so start the recipe a day before.

COOKING METHODS Indirect Grilling/Smoking or Oven   **WOOD** Apple, Pear, Cherry, Beech

1 x 3–4kg bone-in lamb shoulder
olive oil, for brushing
1 tbsp sea salt flakes
2 tsp coarsely ground pepper

For the Overnight Lamb Rub

1 tbsp English mustard powder
1 tsp garlic powder
1 tsp dried oregano
1 tsp dried rosemary
1 tsp celery salt
1 tsp ground coriander
1 tsp ground mixed spice
1 tsp fine sea salt

For the Mop Sauce

100ml distilled white vinegar
75ml Worcestershire sauce
1 tbsp soft light brown sugar
½ tbsp sea salt
½ tbsp garlic powder
½ tsp chilli powder
½ tbsp dried oregano
½ tbsp dried rosemary

In a bowl, combine the ingredients for the rub. Prepare your lamb shoulder by trimming away any excess hard fat, leaving only a thin layer (about 3mm) of fat intact. Brush the joint with olive oil then rub the the dry mix all over the lamb and place it in a non-reactive container or a ziplock bag (be sure to squeeze out the air before sealing). Put in the fridge overnight, or for at least 8 hours.

You can also make the mop sauce the night before. Put the ingredients in a saucepan with 75ml water, set over medium-low heat and whisk gently for about 5–10 minutes, until well combined and warmed through. Pour the sauce into a bowl and keep it covered until you need it.

The next day, bring the lamb out of the fridge, then sprinkle with salt and pepper. Set aside for 30 minutes to allow the lamb to come to room temperature.

Meanwhile, set up your smoker. Throughout the cooking process, you are after a temperature at the magic number of 120°C/250°F – adjust the air valves as needed. We like any fruit wood, such as apple, cherry or pear with lamb. Add the lamb to your smoker, fat side up, and smoke for 7–8 hours, brushing with the mop sauce after the 5-hour mark and every 30 minutes during the final 2 hours. Test to see if the lamb is done at the 6-hour mark by inserting your instant-read thermometer into the thickest part, being careful not to hit the bone, and checking that it reads 90°C/195°F.

When the lamb has finished smoking, carefully remove, cover with a foil tent, and put on a chopping board to rest for about 15 minutes. Use two forks to pull the meat apart, or slice into thick chunks across the grain. Serve the succulent meat topped with a few tablespoons of the mop sauce and mounds of Southern-style Barbecue Greens with Pork (page 179) and Cheddar Jalapeño Cornbread (page 189) to mop up the juices.

NO SMOKER? NO PROBLEM

Preheat your oven to 170°C/325°F/gas mark 3. Place the lamb in a roasting tin and cook for about 4½ hours, or until the meat pulls apart easily with two forks. An instant-read thermometer inserted into the thickest part of the lamb should register 91°C/195°F.

MEAT

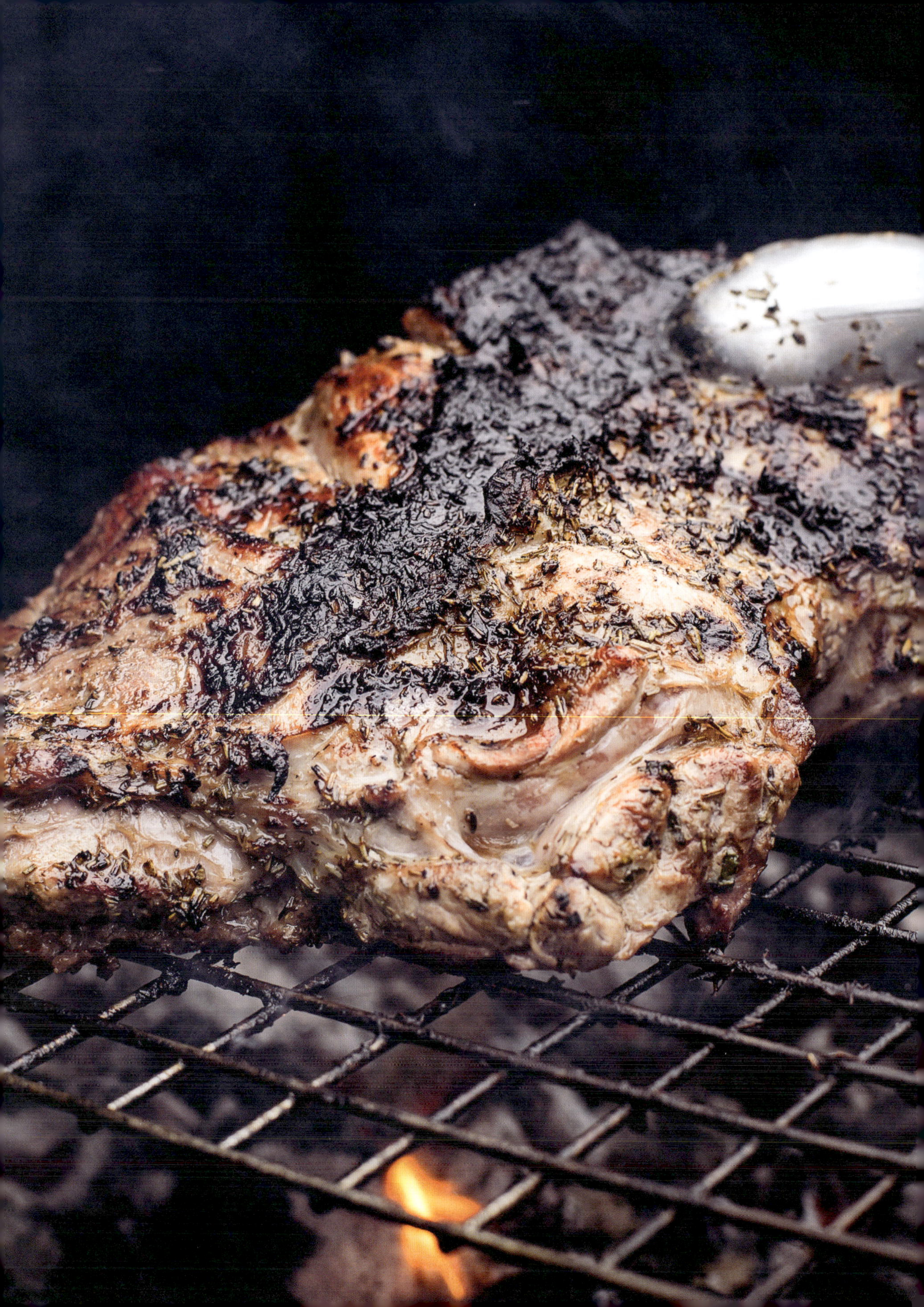

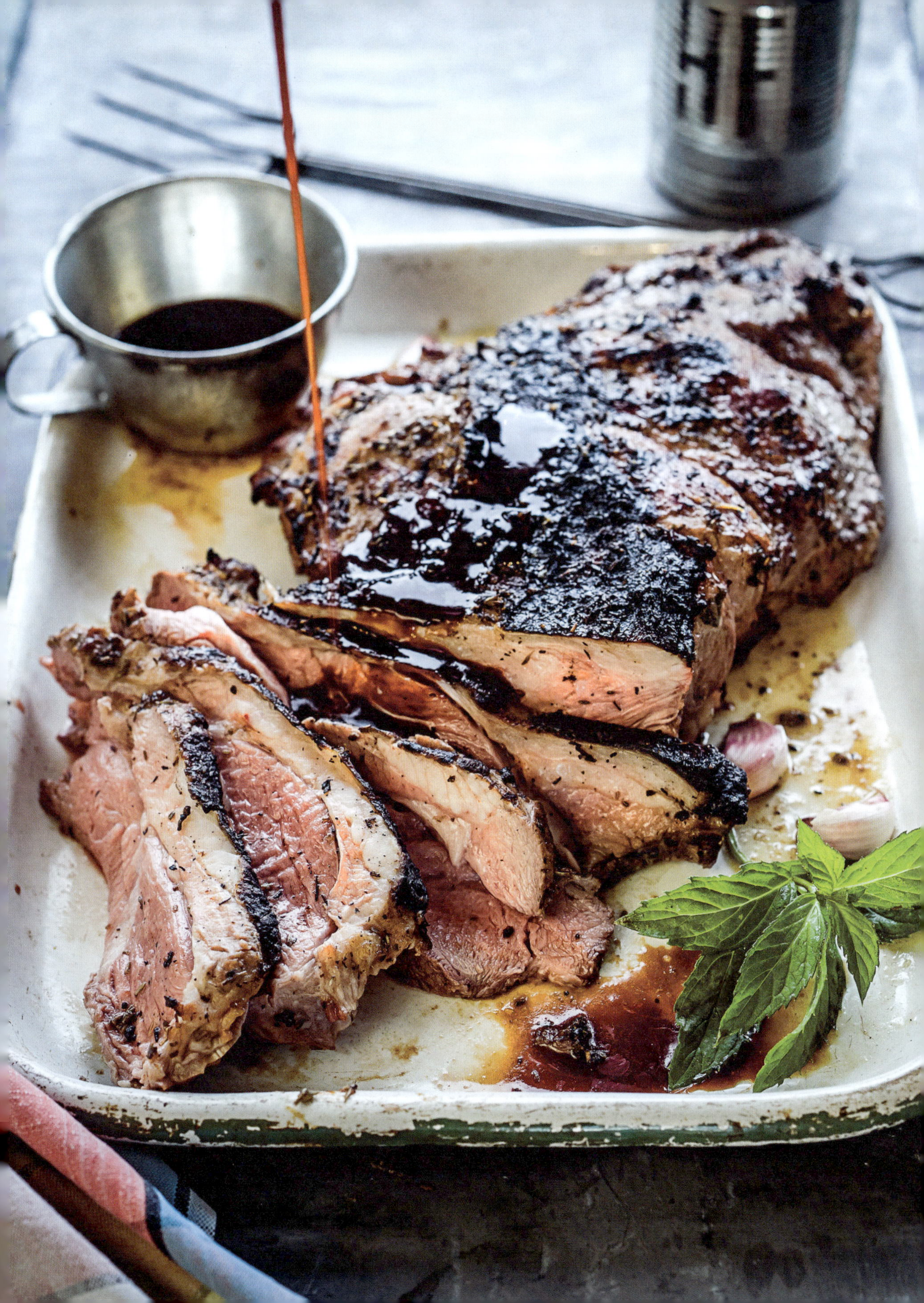

SERVES 6-8

GRILLED BUTTERFLIED LAMB LEG
WITH KENTUCKY MOP SAUCE

We really had to seek out smoked lamb while in the States. Sheep meat is so indigenous to the Welsh diet that we forget that some people find the flavour too gamey and polarising. But to us, it's the taste of green, dewy hills, early spring weather and a really delicious bowl of stew. Seems the good people of Owensboro, Kentucky, have seen the light. They'll eat 'mutton' barbecue all day long. We had some great smoked ovine from Old Hickory's of Owensboro, KY. In barbecue joints, the white sugary buns work as a vehicle for meat. But the meat, oh my, imagine, as a lifelong roast lamb eater, tasting smoked lamb for the first time. Sweet meat with a strong, homely flavour, lashings of hickory smoke and doused in a vinegar and tomatoey Worcestershire, jet-black dipping sauce. It was an out-of-body experience.

Here's our recipe for butterflied leg of lamb, Kentucky style. You can take the bone out yourself with a boning knife (see note opposite) and some patience, or you can ask your butcher to do this. Whichever way you choose, just keep the bone to use for stock. We like to marinate the lamb leg overnight.

COOKING METHOD Grilling   **WOOD** Hickory

- 1 x 4kg boneless lamb leg
- 1 tbsp sea salt flakes
- 1 tbsp coarsely ground black pepper
- 50ml groundnut oil, for greasing

For the Marinade

- 250g buttermilk or plain yoghurt
- juice of 4 lemons, plus the grated zest of 1 lemon
- 1 tbsp groundnut oil
- 6 garlic cloves, sliced
- handful fresh mint leaves, chopped
- 2 tbsp dried rosemary
- 2 tbsp dried thyme
- 2 tbsp coarse ground pepper
- 1 tbsp sea salt flakes

First, whizz the marinade ingredients in a food processor. Using a fork or sharp knife, make a few little cuts all over the outside and inside of the lamb leg and put it in a large ziplock bag. Spoon in the marinade and massage it all over the lamb, then expel any air from the bag, zip it up and refrigerate overnight.

The next day, use kitchen towels to pat as much of the marinade off your lamb as you can. Discard the marinade. Season the lamb with the salt and pepper and put it in a baking tray and leave it sit for at least 20 minutes to come to room temperature until you're ready to cook.

We're going to grill this hunk of meat indirectly, then directly, to finish. Get a hot bed of coals started on one side of your grill; you'll want it to last 1 hour at medium-high heat and maintain a temperature of about 163°C/325°F. You may want to get a chimney starter ready so you can add more white hot coals if the temperature starts to dip – just throw a couple in when you need it.

Carefully lay the lamb, fat side down first, on your grates. Sear for about 4 minutes, then flip it over, and sear again

For the Kentucky Mop Sauce

125ml Worcestershire sauce
100ml white wine vinegar
5 tbsp dark brown sugar
2 tbsp tomato purée
½ tsp garlic powder
1 tsp table salt
1 tsp ground black pepper
1 tsp onion powder
¼ tsp ground cloves
juice of ½ lemon

for a further 4 minutes. Repeat until you have diagonal charred marks.

Now, slide the meat over to the opposite side of the grates, away from the coals, and close the lid. Put in chunks of hickory wood. A piece of lamb that weighs 3–4kg will take about 1 hour to cook to medium rare. After about 35 minutes, insert an instant-read thermometer, and if it reads 60–65°C/140–145°F, your lamb is ready. Carefully remove and allow the lamb to rest, covered loosely in foil, for 15 minutes.

To make the Kentucky mop sauce, heat all the ingredients with 150ml water in a saucepan over medium-low heat. There's a lot of vinegar in this, so be careful of the fumes. Allow to simmer for around 15 minutes, until reduced by about a third.

To serve, thinly slice the lamb and arrange on a serving plate or tray. Drizzle some sauce over the slices of lamb and serve the rest of the sauce on the side for extra dipping.

DEBONING A LEG OF LAMB

To debone the leg of lamb yourself, you'll need a flexible boning knife. From the 'knee' joint, follow the bone down towards the open end of the leg. When you see the bone, open up the meat and scrape it away, leaving behind the cleaned bone. Continue to work your knife around the large bone until you have a large piece of meat and the leg bone. Even out the thickness of the lamb by making slashes in the meat, removing any extra fat or sinew as you go along.

MAKES 6

ALOHA BOYO' GRILLED LAMB KEBABS

This recipe combines the native flavours of Hawaiian barbecue – ginger and pineapple – with beautiful Welsh lamb and leeks. If you can't dig your own volcanically fuelled kalúa fire pit, then this recipe is the next best thing! Ask your butcher to debone your lamb for you.

COOKING METHOD Grilling

1 ripe pineapple
1kg boneless leg or shoulder Welsh lamb (deboned), cut into 5cm cubes
2 tbsp soft light brown sugar
50g unsalted butter
vegetable oil, for brushing

For the Lamb Marinade

3 garlic cloves, chopped
¼ small leek, roughly chopped
1 red chilli, roughly chopped (closer to a jalapeño than a finger chilli)
½ thumb-sized piece fresh ginger, peeled and chopped
250ml fresh pineapple juice
50ml dark soy sauce
3 tbsp sesame oil
juice of ½ lime
a few grinds of fresh black pepper

For the Dipping Sauce

small bunch fresh coriander, chopped
small bunch fresh flat-leaf parsley, chopped
1 red chilli, deseeded and finely chopped
zest and juice of ½ lime
100ml olive oil
2 tbsp cider vinegar
fine sea salt and cracked black pepper, to season

Place all the ingredients for the marinade in a food processor and blend until smooth. Put all the marinade and the cubed lamb into a ziplock bag or lidded plastic container. Massage the marinade into the lamb, making sure the lamb is well covered. Leave in the fridge for 3–5 hours, or overnight for a stronger flavour.

Peel and core the pineapple, and cut the flesh into 5cm cubes.

Remove the lamb from the fridge and pour the marinade into a saucepan. Bring to the boil over medium-high heat, reduce to medium-low and simmer for about 10 minutes, or until the liquid has reduced by about a half. Add the brown sugar and butter and stir through until dissolved. This is going to be a gorgeous, glossy glaze. Remove from the heat and set aside.

Now take six bamboo or metal skewers. If using bamboo, pre-soak them for a couple of hours, or even overnight in water – this will stop the skewers from burning on the grill. Thread the marinated lamb and pineapple on to the skewers, alternating the meat and pineapple.

Set your grill up, whether gas or charcoal. Brush the kebabs in a little oil and make sure your coals are white. Now let's get to grilling! Depending on how you like your lamb, you can grill the skewers for 3 minutes on each side, brushing on your reduced marinade as you turn the kebab. We like our lamb medium rare, but if you like yours a little more well done, add another minute on the grill time per side.

Lastly, combine the dipping sauce ingredients in a bowl. Arrange your skewers on a plate, drizzle the sauce on top, or serve as a dipping sauce on the side.

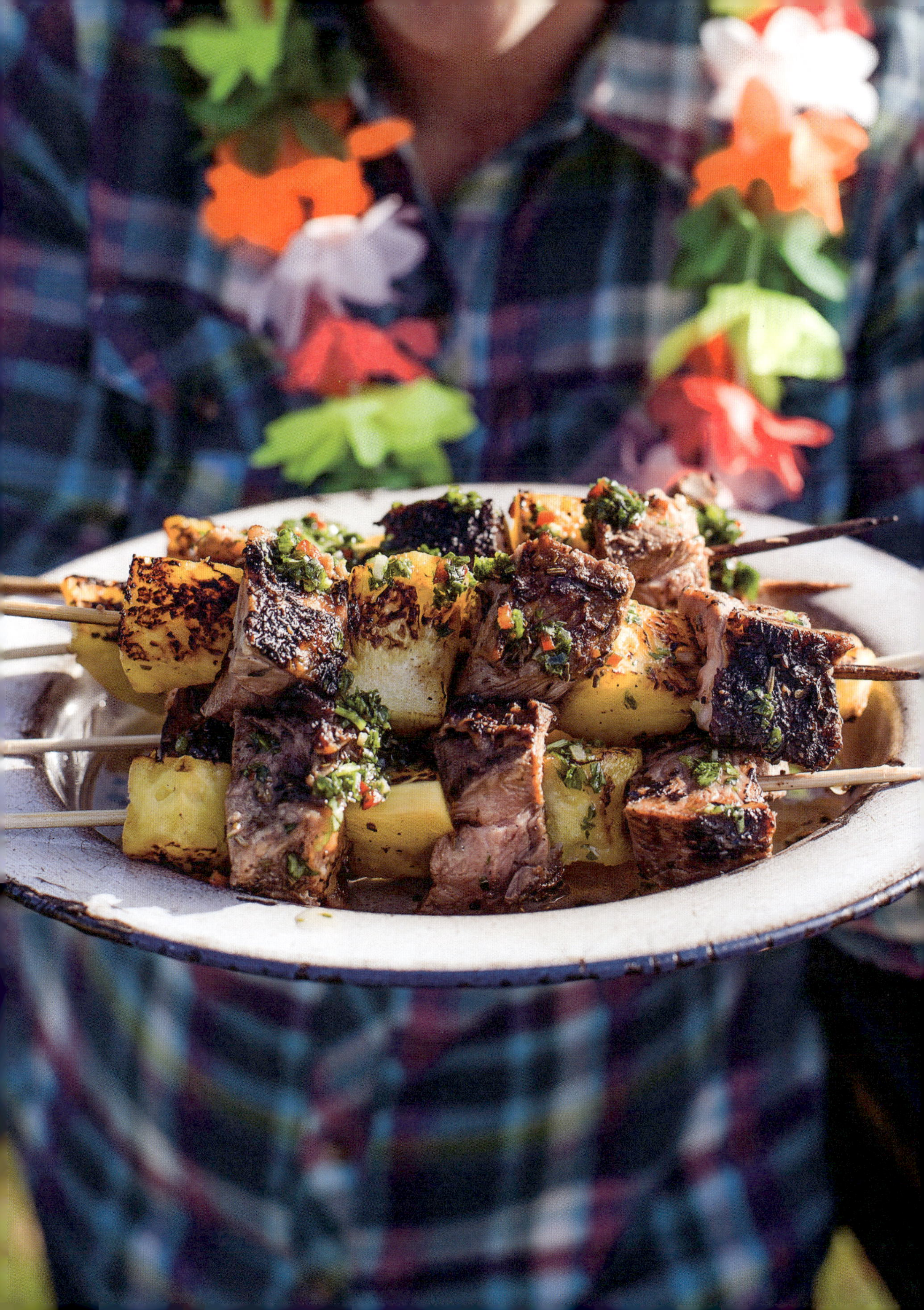

LOUISIANA

> "STATELY HOMES AND MANSIONS, OF THE SUGAR BARONS AND THE COTTON KINGS, RICH PEOPLE, OLD PEOPLE, ALL GOT DREAMS. DREAMS DO COME TRUE IN NEW ORLEANS"
>
> Down in New Orleans, Dr John

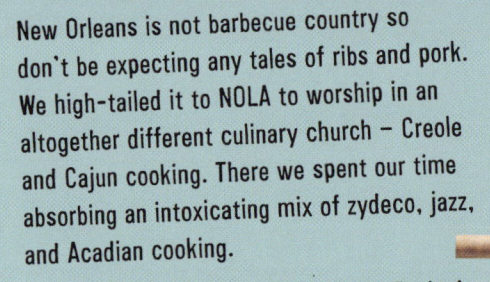

New Orleans is not barbecue country so don't be expecting any tales of ribs and pork. We high-tailed it to NOLA to worship in an altogether different culinary church – Creole and Cajun cooking. There we spent our time absorbing an intoxicating mix of zydeco, jazz, and Acadian cooking.

Driving down a highway that's level-flanked with the Bayou is an amazing experience. You drive through wetlands on what seems like a gravity-defying raised road, passing stilt house after floating house as you go.

Cornmeal-fried catfish, gumbos, Po'Boys, gulf oysters, étouffée, beignets, mufaletta sandwiches, iced teas, and cocktails were all very much on the agenda. We knew a little about the local meats like tasso, chaurice and andouille sausage and boudin, not to mention their incredible crawfish boils: newspaper laid out on big trestle tables and steamed crayfish, potatoes, corn and sausage poured into a huge pile in front of us. The 'bug boils' at New Orleans Market's Cajun Seafood were particularly good. Plus we ordered a 'medium' fried shrimp Po'Boy and it was nearly half a metre long!

The traditional dishes of Louisiana were some of the most delicious and exciting cooking we had the pleasure of eating in the States. From big soupy bowls of andouille and shrimp gumbo to homely stews at little Mom and Pop cafes, dozens of oysters (fried, grilled, fresh, deep-fried in breadcrumbs, kilpatrick, rockerfella etc). The hallmark of French colonialism still runs through the cooking with their roux base for their stews; French bread for Po'Boys and traditional herbs like thyme and rosemary; then it's all given a mighty kick with cayenne peppers. Where else can you get that heady mix of flavours and spices coupled with lashings of good old-fashioned southern hospitality?

This wonderful mix influences everything from music to architecture to the arts and the city's general 'joie de vivre'. The music scene is electrifying too: we danced off many a feast in after dark bars on Frenchmen Street, wobbling home with sore feet and sweaty t-shirts. We loved every minute and promise you you'll also fall head over heels with Louisiana's dishes: try to source the right ingredients to give that unique flavour that you just don't get anywhere else in the world.

141

SIDE KICK AND RUN

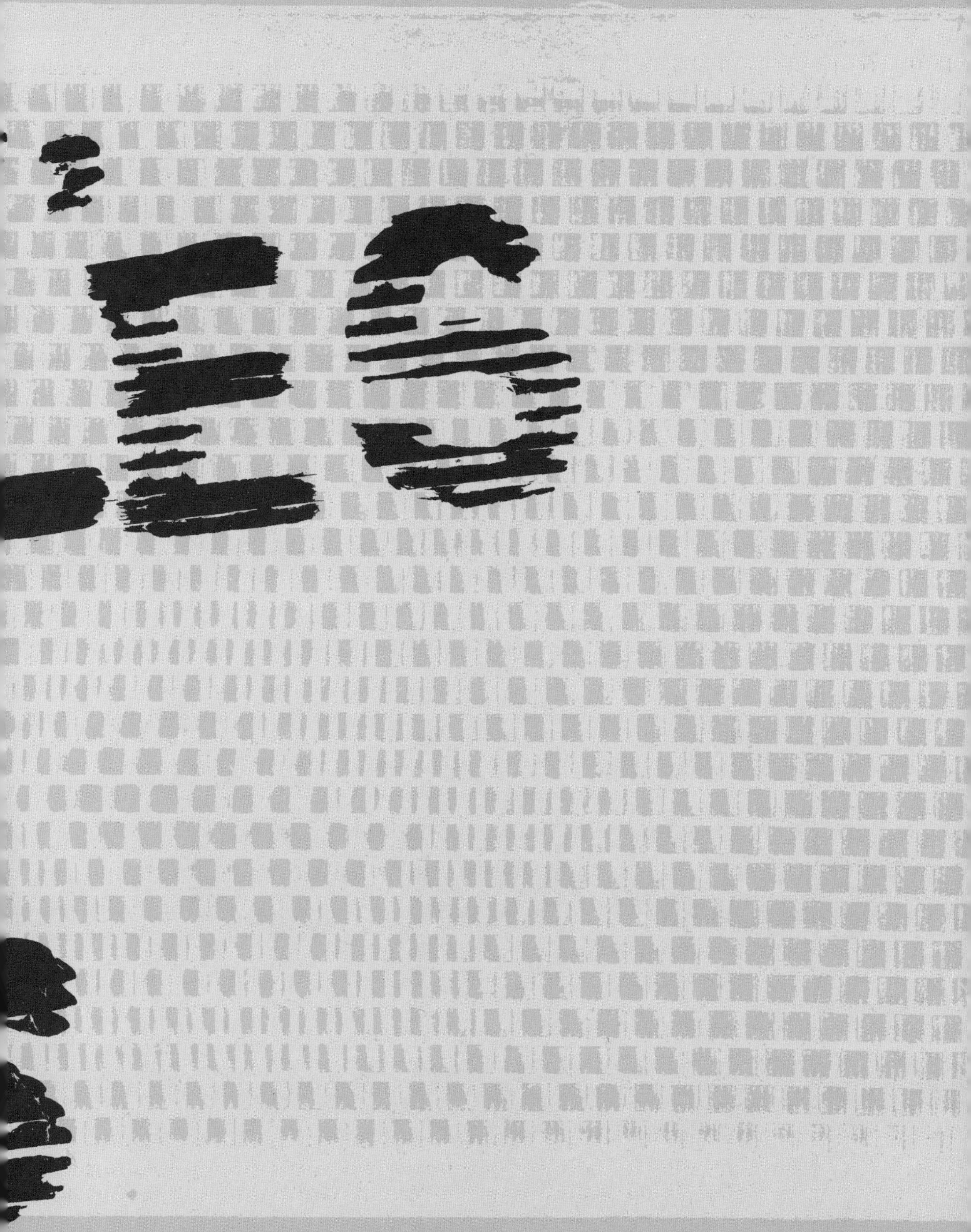

HANG FIRE'S PIT BEANS

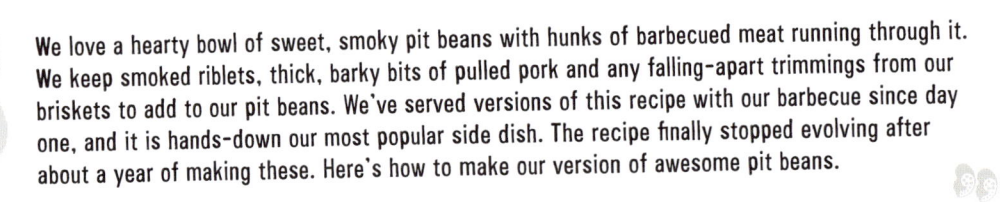

SERVES 6–8, AS A SIDE

We love a hearty bowl of sweet, smoky pit beans with hunks of barbecued meat running through it. We keep smoked riblets, thick, barky bits of pulled pork and any falling-apart trimmings from our briskets to add to our pit beans. We've served versions of this recipe with our barbecue since day one, and it is hands-down our most popular side dish. The recipe finally stopped evolving after about a year of making these. Here's how to make our version of awesome pit beans.

1 tbsp groundnut oil
1 large onion, diced
2 garlic cloves, very finely chopped
1 small red bell pepper, deseeded and diced
5 green jalapeños, deseeded and diced
400g tin or fresh chopped tomatoes
500ml beef stock
200g Hang Fire Smokehouse Barbecue Sauce (page 45), or other barbecue sauce of your choice
400g tin red kidney beans, rinsed and drained well
400g tin pinto beans, rinsed and drained well
400g tin haricot beans, rinsed and drained well
450g smoked barbecue meat of your choice, roughly chopped
small bunch coriander, finely chopped, including stalks

For the Seasoning

1 tbsp smoked paprika
1 tbsp ground cumin
1 tbsp dried oregano
1 tsp chilli powder
1 tsp garlic powder
1 tsp ground cinnamon
1 tsp cracked black pepper
1 tsp fine sea salt

We usually slip a pan of these beans into the grill or smoker when we're cooking other meats. We are going to start the beans off in a large pan and then transfer them to a casserole dish (or cast-iron pan) to cook through. Have your dish or pan to hand to put in the smoker or oven.

First, combine the seasoning ingredients in a bowl and add 4–5 tablespoons of water, just enough to make a paste. Set aside.

If using your grill or smoker, set it up for indirect heat and regulate to 120°C/250°F. If using an oven, preheat it to 160°C/320°F/gas mark 3.

Heat the oil in a large pan and add the onion. Cook over medium heat for 10 minutes, until softened, then add the garlic, bell pepper and jalapeños, and sauté for a further 5 minutes. Add your seasoning paste, stir through to combine for 1–2 minutes. Now add your chopped tomatoes, beef stock and barbecue sauce, then stir well. Lastly, add the drained beans, chopped barbecue meat and coriander. Stir for about 3 minutes, just to warm through. Transfer the beans to your casserole dish or cast-iron pan.

Set in your grill or smoker and cook for 6–8 hours, uncovered, until caramelised and golden on top. If using your oven, bake for around 4 hours. If the beans look like they're drying out, add a little water to loosen them.

SIDES, PICKLES & BUNS

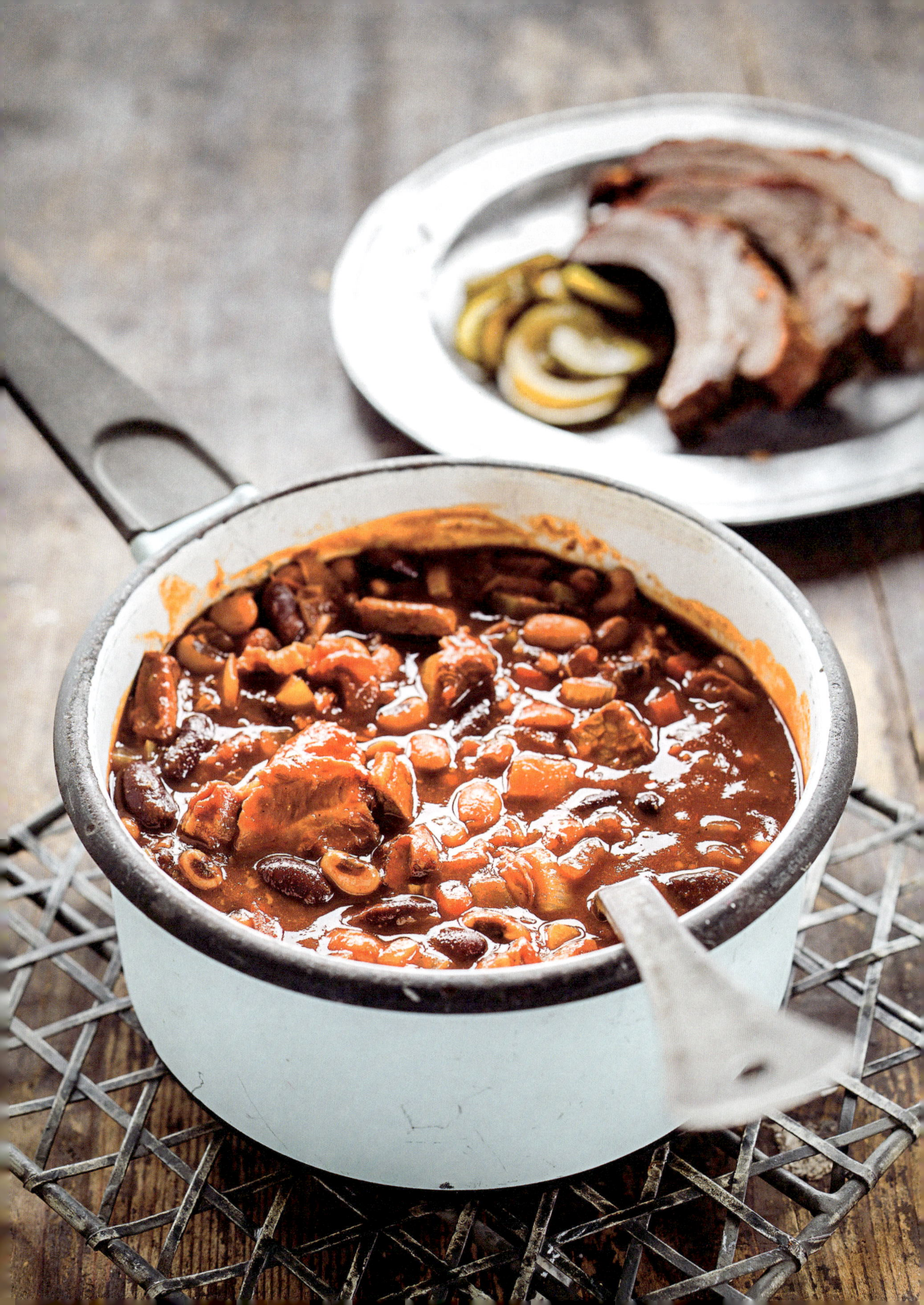

1

2

3

4

SERVES 6-8, AS A SIDE

IT'S ALL ABOUT THE 'SLAWS

The word 'coleslaw' comes from the Dutch word, 'koolsla', 'kool' meaning cabbage and 'sla', salad. As legend goes, the word entered the English language from the Dutch settlers in New York in the late 1700s and travelled south to the Bible Belt. It soon became the side dish staple that goes with barbecue the way strawberries go with cream. For us, the key to a good coleslaw is to not have the vegetables overly dressed with mayo, sugar or sharp vinegars but to find that perfect balance of flavours.

SERBIAN 'SLAW (SALATA OD KUPUSA)

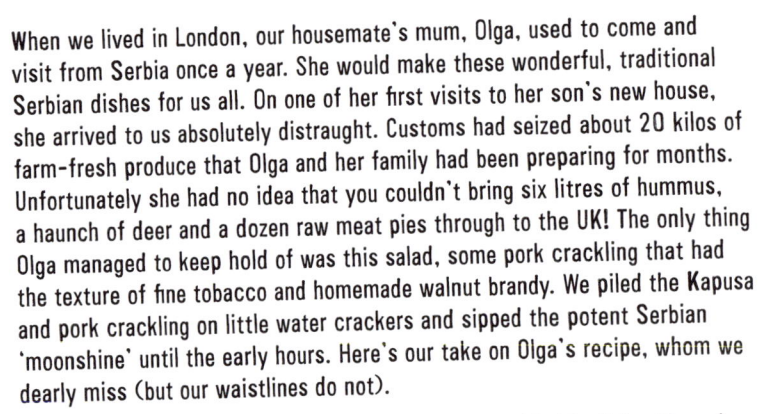

When we lived in London, our housemate's mum, Olga, used to come and visit from Serbia once a year. She would make these wonderful, traditional Serbian dishes for us all. On one of her first visits to her son's new house, she arrived to us absolutely distraught. Customs had seized about 20 kilos of farm-fresh produce that Olga and her family had been preparing for months. Unfortunately she had no idea that you couldn't bring six litres of hummus, a haunch of deer and a dozen raw meat pies through to the UK! The only thing Olga managed to keep hold of was this salad, some pork crackling that had the texture of fine tobacco and homemade walnut brandy. We piled the Kapusa and pork crackling on little water crackers and sipped the potent Serbian 'moonshine' until the early hours. Here's our take on Olga's recipe, whom we dearly miss (but our waistlines do not).

Try this with everything and anything. Have it as a cold side dish with pork barbecue, treat it like a relish in a sandwich, or if you're like us, you'll eat it straight out of the jar.

350g white cabbage
1 garlic clove, very finely chopped
4 tbsp toasted sesame seeds
1 tbsp olive oil
2 tsp fine sea salt
½ tsp chilli flakes
1 tbsp finely chopped curly parsley
½ tsp freshly ground black pepper

Core and shred the cabbage as finely as you can, or use the slicer blade if you have a food processor. Mix the cabbage and garlic in a bowl and put in a vegetable steamer until almost tender, it'll take around 7–10 minutes.

Heat the oil in a large frying pan over medium-low heat. Add the steamed cabbage and garlic along with the remaining ingredients. Stir-fry for about 10 minutes. You can either eat warm, or pack the cabbage mix tightly into a clean jar and transfer to the fridge where it will keep for 1 week.

SIDES, PICKLES & BUNS

MAKES ABOUT 370G

SURE FIRE 'SLAW

This version seems to hit just the right notes with our customers when served alongside our barbecue. In fact, people who are usually 'slaw haters end up being converted after having a taste of our sure fire 'slaw.

2

1kg white cabbage, finely sliced

3 carrots, grated

1 medium white onion, halved and finely sliced

½ red bell pepper, deseeded and finely diced

½ yellow bell pepper, deseeded and finely diced

4 spring onions, finely sliced

3 tbsp finely chopped coriander

3 tbsp finely chopped flat-leaf parsley leaves

For the 'Slaw Cure

juice of 1 lemon

1 tsp fine sea salt

1 tsp white sugar

For the Dressing

50g mayonnaise

3 tbsp buttermilk, or soured cream

3 tbsp South Carolina Mustard Sauce (page 38) or American mustard

1 tsp soft light brown sugar

½ tsp fine sea salt

¼ tsp freshly ground black pepper

Combine the cabbage, carrots and white onion in a bowl, add the ingredients for the 'slaw cure and mix well. Cover and let osmosis do its thing in your fridge for 2–3 hours, or even overnight (the longer you give it, the less 'cabbagey' it will taste). When you're ready, drain the vegetables, discarding any excess liquid.

Whisk up your dressing in a bowl, taste, and adjust seasoning as you like it.

Add the bell peppers and spring onions to your cured veg, and mix well. Now pour in the dressing. Throw in your chopped coriander and parsley, keeping a sprinkling back, mix once again and refrigerate for 1 hour. Some of the dressing will settle at the bottom, so mix well before serving. Garnish with a little of the reserved chopped herbs.

LEXINGTON-STYLE RED 'SLAW WITH BEETS

SERVES 4-6, AS AS SIDE

This is a great mayo-free 'slaw, which has a sweet vinegar dressing. It looks vibrant and tastes delicious and refreshing. With roots in South Carolina, the vinegary notes in this 'slaw complement the vinegar mop sauce used to dress their pork barbecue.

- 1kg red cabbage, cored, finely shredded
- 1 medium red onion, finely sliced
- 3 carrots, grated
- 2 cooked beetroot, grated

For the 'Slaw Cure
- juice of 1 lemon
- 2 tsp fine sea salt

For the Dressing
- 50ml olive oil
- 1 tsp Hang Fire's Almost All-purpose Rub (page 26)
- 50ml cider vinegar
- 3 tbsp ketchup
- 1 tsp caster sugar
- ½ tsp freshly cracked black pepper
- ½ tsp fine sea salt

Combine the shredded cabbage and onion in a large bowl. Add the ingredients for the 'slaw cure, and mix well. Cover and let osmosis do its thing in your fridge for 2–3 hours.

When you're ready to make your 'slaw, pour off any liquid from the onion and cabbage, then stir through the carrot and beetroot.

In a food processor or blender, add all the dressing ingredients except the oil, and with the blade running at medium speed, add the oil very slowly, drop by drop, until the dressing emulsifies and thickens. Pour over the vegetables and toss through, making sure they are all fully coated. Cover the bowl with cling film and allow to sit in the fridge for an hour (to help the flavours come together) before serving.

SIDES, PICKLES & BUNS

SERVES 4, AS A SIDE

FENNEL, PEAR & APPLE 'SLAW
WITH BUTTERMILK DRESSING

The is the type of 'slaw to make when you want something a little different. It is light and zesty and pairs really well with pork, poultry or fish dishes. We prefer to slice the vegetables for this 'slaw with a mandoline set to the largest blade (around 3mm).

- 1 green apple (preferably a sharp Granny Smith)
- 1 slightly under-ripe pear
- 1 fennel bulb, finely sliced
- 150g white cabbage, finely sliced
- 1 tbsp fresh lemon juice
- small bunch chives
- 2 fresh dill sprigs, stalks discarded and leaves chopped
- sea salt and freshly cracked black pepper, to taste

For the Dressing

- 2 tbsp mayonnaise
- 1 tbsp buttermilk
- 1 tsp white sugar
- 1 tsp finely grated lemon zest

Peel and core the apple and pear, slice lengthways (use a mandoline if you have one) and cut into fine matchsticks. Put in a bowl with the fennel and cabbage and mix. Add the lemon juice and mix through (this will stop the fruit oxidising and going brown).

In a small bowl, mix the ingredients for the dressing and add to the vegetables. Scatter over your chopped dill and snip the chives in and season. Stir, then chill in the fridge for 15 minutes to allow the flavours to come together.

'SLAW SAVER

The dressed 'slaws will keep for a day or so before going too soggy. If you want to get a couple more days from your 'slaws, keep the dressing and 'slaw veg separate and mix together as and when you need it. This way you can keep the veg for about three days. Though we would suggest adding a little citrus juice to the undressed veg to keep them from discolouring while they wait patiently to be consumed.

SIDES, PICKLES & BUNS

SERVES 6, AS A SIDE

CLASSIC ASIAN 'SLAW

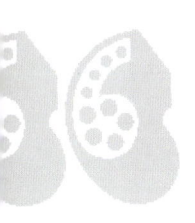

This recipe is loosely based on a salad we ate on an island in Thailand. We'll admit, this 'slaw might seem like it has a million ingredients, but it really is a standout side dish and your family or guests will be sure to appreciate the effort. This is the perfect summer salad to accompany our Mai-Thai Thighs (page 124).

½ Chinese cabbage, finely sliced

½ small red cabbage, finely sliced

2 carrots, finely sliced into long thin strips (use a julienne cutter if you have one)

3 spring onions, sliced lengthways into long, thin strips

100g mangetout, sliced lengthways

100g beansprouts

1 tsp fine sea salt

1 tbsp caster sugar

juice of 1 lime

1 red chilli, deseeded and finely chopped

medium bunch coriander, finely chopped

small bunch mint leaves, finely chopped

small bunch Thai basil leaves, finely chopped

1 tbsp toasted sesame seeds

50g toasted unsalted peanuts, crushed

For the Dressing

1 garlic clove, very finely chopped

1 tsp grated fresh ginger

1 tbsp honey

50ml rice vinegar

50ml olive oil

1 tbsp soy sauce

1 tsp sesame oil

1 tbsp sweet chilli sauce

sea salt and freshly ground black pepper, to taste

Add your prepared vegetables to a bowl. Sprinkle with the salt, sugar and lime juice and toss through.

Put the bowl in the fridge while you prepare the dressing.

Whisk the dressing ingredients vigorously in a bowl. Taste to check the seasoning. Pour the dressing over the chilled vegetables and mix well. Now add the chilli, chopped herbs and sesame seeds and toss through. Allow the flavours to come together in the fridge for 1 hour. Just before serving, sprinkle over the toasted crushed peanuts.

SIDES, PICKLES & BUNS

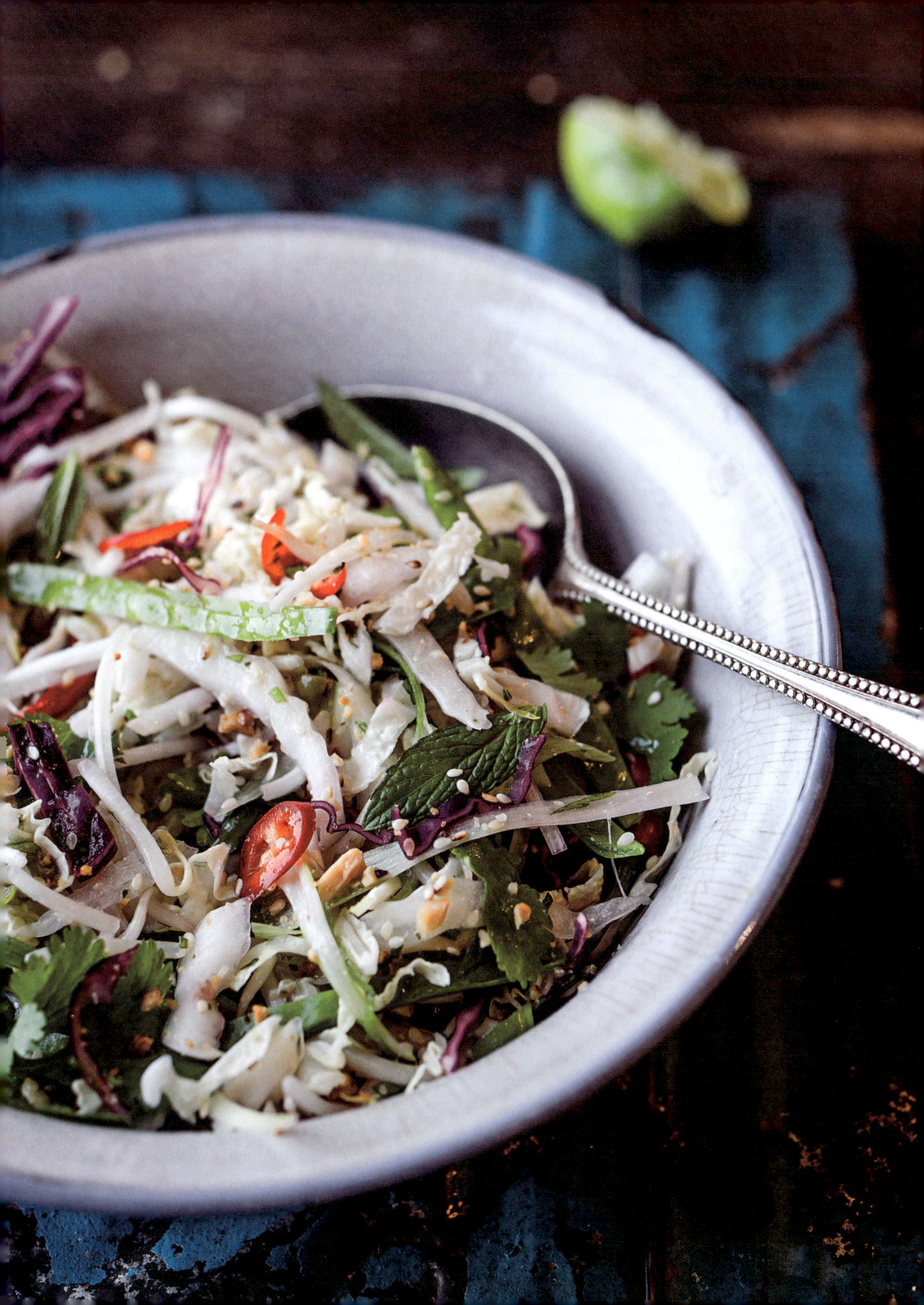

SERVES 4-6, AS A SIDE

SOUTHERN-STYLE POTATO SALAD

Just like 'slaw, in the States, you'll find pints of potato salad sold in pretty much every barbecue joint you come across. Some vary from sweet, mashed potato style, to fancier ones with the European influence of vinaigrette and bacon. This down-home recipe was given to us by our friend's mum who lives in Boston, not traditionally a barbecue State, but her whole family adores this recipe and we do too. It's a traditional Southern-style potato salad with boiled egg. Granted, not an ingredient you immediately think to add, however, it really adds a creamy, luxurious taste to the dish.

6 large potatoes, cubed

100g mayonnaise

50ml soured cream

2 medium, whole sweet dill pickles (page 182), finely diced

3 tbsp South Carolina Mustard Sauce (page 38) or American mustard

1 tsp caster sugar

1 tsp celery seeds

1 celery stick, finely diced

1 small white onion, diced

3 hard-boiled eggs, sliced

handful of snipped chives

sea salt flakes and freshly cracked black pepper, to taste

pinch of smoked paprika, to serve

Cook the potatoes in a pan of boiling water for about 15 minutes, or until they're a whisker away from being fully soft, you want them a little al dente so they don't break apart in the mix. Drain and allow to completely cool.

In bowl, mix the mayo, soured cream, pickles, South Carolina Mustard Sauce, sugar, celery seeds and set aside for 5 minutes to let those flavours come together. In a bowl, add all the other ingredients, tossing gently so they're fully combined. Now add your mayo mix, combine, and add seasoning to your taste. Refrigerate for about 1 hour and sprinkle with a little paprika before serving.

SIDES, PICKLES & BUNS

SERVES 4-6

GERMAN-STYLE POTATO SALAD
WITH OREGANO DRESSING

To be honest, making potato salad is not our strong point. So we've come up with this foolproof potato salad recipe that even we can't mess up. This one is particularly popular when we make it for cook-outs (maybe the clarified bacon fat has something to do with it?), and a sure-fire hit with those who aren't usually fans of gloopy, mayo-esque salads.

1kg red skin potatoes, cubed

8 Down-home Smoked Bacon rashers (page 80–81) or good-quality streaky bacon

2 celery sticks, finely chopped

small bunch spring onions, finely chopped

handful of pitted green and black olives, sliced

2 tbsp finely chopped flat-leaf parsley

For the Oregano Dressing

2 tbsp white wine vinegar

1 tsp white sugar

½ tsp fine sea salt

½ tsp freshly ground black pepper

1 tsp dried oregano

1 tbsp fresh lemon juice

50ml light olive oil

Put the potatoes in a large pan, cover with cold water and bring to the boil over high heat. Reduce to a simmer and cook for about 15 minutes, until just tender, and drain.

While the potatoes are cooking, fry the bacon on medium-high heat, until very crisp. Pour the fat through a fine-mesh sieve, into a bowl. Rest the crisp bacon on kitchen towel, allow to cool then cut into small pieces.

At this stage, decide if you want the skin on or off the potatoes. If you want to remove the skins, peel them using a paring knife while still hot but cool enough to handle. Put the potatoes in a bowl and toss with 2 tablespoons of the sieved bacon fat. Set aside to cool.

Make the dressing by whisking the ingredients, slowly incorporating the oil in a steady stream, until combined.

When the potatoes have completely cooled, mix in the celery, spring onions, bacon bits, olives and parsley. Add the oregano dressing and toss until everything is well combined. Cover and chill in the fridge for 1 hour.

HASSELBACK POTATOES
WITH BROWN BUTTER

SERVES 4 AS A SIDE

Brown butter (also called beurre noisette) is one of those magical secret ingredients that just seems to enhance the flavour of just about anything – sweet or savoury. It has a rich nutty taste and the aroma is out of this world. Here, this savoury, nutty butter and the soured cream transform the humble potato into one decadent side dish.

4 large sweet potatoes, or 4 baking potatoes
olive oil, for brushing
1 tsp sea salt flakes
½ tsp freshly cracked black pepper
4 tbsp unsalted butter
4 tsp soured cream
1 tbsp chopped flat-leaf parsley
smoked paprika, to sprinkle

Preheat your oven to 190°C/375°F. Wash the sweet potatoes and cut off a small sliver on the bottom of the potato to give it a stable surface. Make cuts along the sweet potato into roughly 3mm-thick slices, but leaving about 3mm intact at the bottom. (You can do this by feel, or place chopsticks on either side of the potato and slicing until you hit the chopsticks.) Place the potatoes in a roasting tray.

Brush the potatoes with a little olive oil then sprinkle with the salt and pepper.

Roast in the oven for 45 minutes to 1 hour, until the sweet potatoes are soft in the middle and easily pierced with a paring knife.

About 10 minutes before the potatoes are ready, start making the brown butter. Melt the butter in a small saucepan over medium-low heat. Swirl the pan occasionally, to ensure the butter cooks evenly, and cook gently for about 4 minutes, until browned and nutty in aroma. Don't worry about the froth, this will settle to the bottom of the pan. Be careful not to burn the butter – it's a fine line, so keep an eye on it. Take the pan off the heat when it is done and transfer the browned butter into a heatproof bowl to cool.

To serve, transfer the potatoes to a plate, spoon on a tablespoon of the browned butter, followed by a teaspoon of soured cream, then finish with a sprinkling of parsley and smoked paprika. Serve immediately.

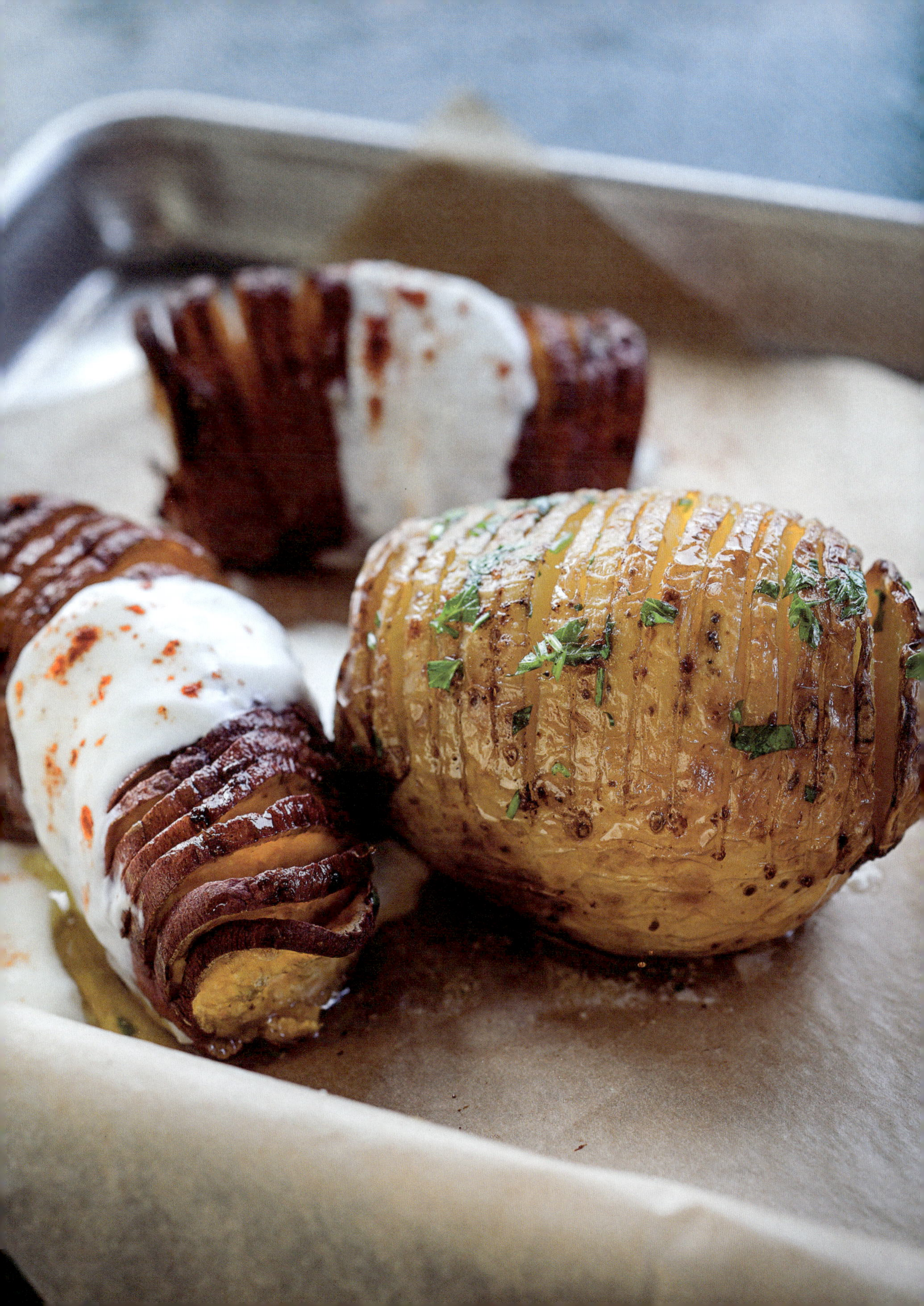

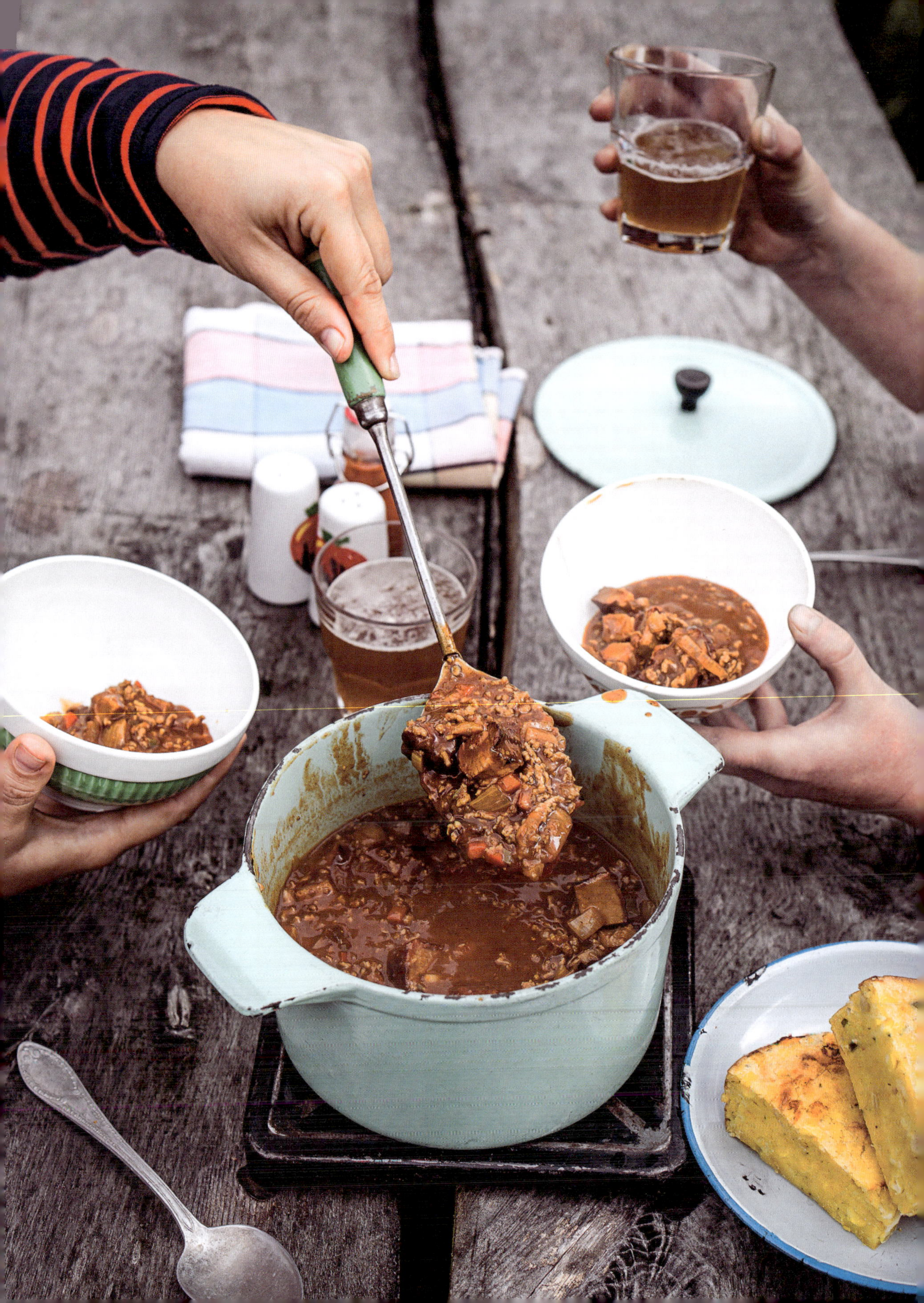

SERVES 4–5, AS A SIDE

BRISKET CHILLI

This is our favourite chilli recipe, and it's one we get a lot of requests for. It's a great way to use up any leftover brisket (if there is such a thing?), or if your brisket smoke hasn't gone according to plan (hey, it happens to the best of us in the beginning) this recipe will be your saving grace.

- 250g coarsely minced chuck steak
- 3 tbsp plain flour
- 1.25 litres beef stock
- 2 tbsp balsamic vinegar
- 50g tomato purée
- 1 large onion, diced
- 3 garlic cloves, finely chopped
- 1 red bell pepper, deseeded and diced
- 2 fresh green jalapeños, deseeded and finely chopped
- 300g smoked brisket, chopped
- 3 tbsp finely chopped coriander

For the Chilli Seasoning

- 2 tsp chilli powder (adjust to level of spiciness desired)
- 3 tsp dried oregano
- 2 tsp smoked paprika
- 1 tsp chilli flakes
- 2 tsp ground cumin
- 1 tsp ground cinnamon
- 1 tsp onion powder
- ½ tsp sea salt flakes
- ½ tsp freshly ground black pepper

In a small bowl, combine all the seasoning ingredients and set aside. Next, in your favourite frying pan, cook the minced chuck over medium-high heat for around 10 minutes, making sure the meat is cooked through. Put the browned minced chuck in a colander set inside a bowl to reserve any fat and leave to drain.

In a saucepan, add 4 tablespoons of the strained beef fat and add the flour. Whisk up into a roux, over medium heat, stirring constantly for about 5 minutes. Gradually add the beef stock, a ladle at a time. Stir in the balsamic vinegar and tomato purée, making sure both are fully mixed. Turn the heat down to low, and simmer for 15 minutes, stirring frequently.

Back to the pan you cooked your minced beef in. Put the pan over medium-high heat, add 2 tablespoons of the reserved beef fat and fry your onion for a few minutes, then add the garlic, bell pepper and jalapeños. Cook until softened, around 5 minutes. Turn the heat down to medium-low and add your seasoning mixture, stir well for a minute or so, then stir in the browned mince. Pour in your roux and let it simmer over low heat for about 40 minutes, stirring frequently to make sure it doesn't stick to the bottom of the pan.

At this stage, take about a quarter of the mixture out and put in a blender or food processor. Purée for 3–4 minutes, until smooth, then return to the pan. This gives a really thick, delicious consistency to your chilli. If your chilli mix needs more liquid, add a splash of water to loosen.

Finally, add in your smoked brisket and coriander and simmer over low heat for 15 minutes before serving. Adjust the seasoning to your taste. Serve with a large slice of warm, buttered Cheddar Jalapeño Cornbread (page 189).

A HEARTY MEAL

If opting to use only raw beef, just up the total weight to 500g. Chuck and brisket are a flavourful combination, and if you want a super-beefy chilli throw in 100g lean minced beef hearts. Trust us, it works.

SIDES, PICKLES & BUNS

HUSH PUPPIES

SERVES 4–5

Originally from Georgia, the story goes that when people made cornbread in the pan, any crusty bits that were left were thrown to the hungry, whining dogs – hush that puppy!

We have been making variations of these tasty, savoury donuts as a side dish at our kitchen takeovers ever since we ate them at our first South Carolina barbecue experience. We serve these with a little Louisiana-style Remoulade (page 45). You can make all sorts of versions of hush puppies, see below for suggestions.

- 250g fine polenta or fine cornmeal
- 150g self-raising flour
- ½ tsp bicarbonate of soda
- ½ tsp fine sea salt
- 2 tsp onion powder
- 2 tsp garlic powder
- 1 tsp freshly ground black pepper
- 330ml brown beer (or sparkling water)
- 120g frozen sweetcorn kernels
- 3 spring onions, finely sliced
- 120g mature Cheddar cheese, grated
- 1 litre vegetable oil, for deep-frying
- 1 tsp smoked sea salt

In a large bowl, add the polenta or cornmeal, flour and bicarbonate of soda, fine sea salt, onion and garlic powder and black pepper, and mix through using a fork or balloon whisk until well combined. Add half the beer, mix through, then pour in the remaining half, making sure all the flour is combined. Next, add the corn, spring onions, grated cheese and mix well to form a batter. Set aside.

Heat the vegetable oil in a large, deep pan and set over high heat. You want the oil to reach about 175°C/340°F. If you don't have a thermometer, the oil is hot enough when a small amount of batter dropped into the pan turns crisp and golden. Using two tablespoons, scoop the batter into one spoon and use the other to push it into the hot oil. It's worth testing one hush puppy first so you can gauge how big you want them. Fry the hush puppies in small batches, for 3–4 minutes, or until they are bobbing on the surface of the oil, and golden brown. Use a slotted spoon to remove them and drain on a plate lined with kitchen towel (or wire rack with kitchen towel underneath). Sprinkle over a bit of smoked sea salt while hot and serve right away.

BOOZY PUPPY

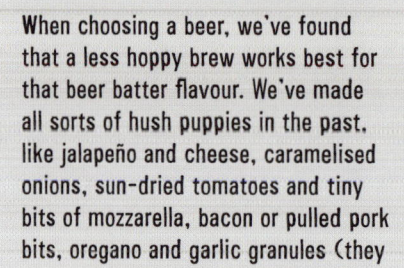

When choosing a beer, we've found that a less hoppy brew works best for that beer batter flavour. We've made all sorts of hush puppies in the past, like jalapeño and cheese, caramelised onions, sun-dried tomatoes and tiny bits of mozzarella, bacon or pulled pork bits, oregano and garlic granules (they are really good), habanero chilli and coriander... and probably half a dozen more. The only thing to beware is falling into the temptation of adding too much cheese; it can go too gooey and prevent the batter from cooking through on the inside.

SIDES, PICKLES & BUNS

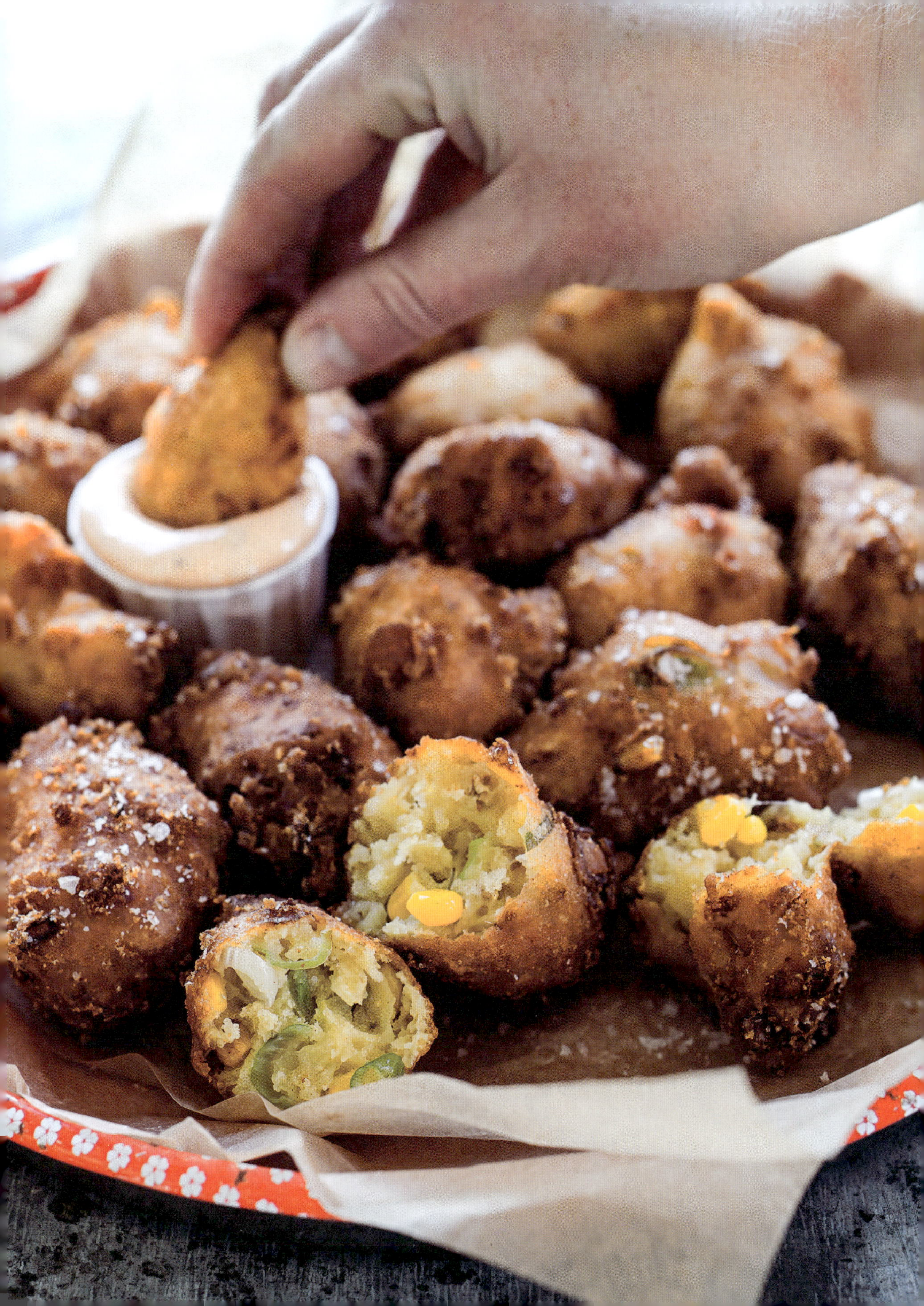

RED BEANS & RICE
WITH TASSO & ANDOUILLE SAUSAGE

SERVES 4

We were in a little café on Decatur Street in New Orleans that served traditional Louisiana dishes. On the menu was a little narrative that said a certain famous Louisiana native used to sign his photos with 'Red beans and ricely, yours, Louis Armstrong'. The name of the dish does not do it justice. It's more of a ham and sausage stew with kidney beans and a pile of rice. This is a truly warming, delicious dish that's fairly straightforward to make. Perhaps play the Jazzin' with Armstrong album to give yourself a little southern swagger as you cook this Creole classic.

- 1 medium onion, diced
- 1 green bell pepper, deseeded and diced
- 1 celery stick, diced
- 1 tbsp unsalted butter
- 2 tbsp Cajun seasoning (page 29)
- 1 tbsp finely chopped garlic
- 3 fresh bay leaves
- 150g Tasso Ham, cubed (page 89)
- 150g Andouille Sausage (pages 76–77), cubed
- 2 x 400g tins red kidney beans, rinsed and drained
- 1 litre chicken stock
- 125g tomato passata
- 1 tbsp finely chopped flat-leaf parsley
- 4 spring onions, thinly sliced
- 250g long-grain rice
- your favourite hot sauce, to serve

In a bowl, mix together your Louisiana 'holy trinity' of diced Creole vegetables: the onion, bell pepper and celery. Melt the butter in a heavy-based pan over medium heat. Add half the 'holy trinity' mix and cook for 10 minutes until softened, then add 1 tablespoon of the Cajun seasoning, the garlic, bay leaves, Tasso, and the Andouille sausage, and turn up the heat to medium-high. Cook for a further 7–10 minutes, stirring. Add the drained kidney beans, pour in the chicken stock and add the remaining 'holy trinity', Cajun seasoning and tomato passata. Bring to the boil over high heat, then reduce to medium-low, cover and simmer for 45 minutes. Add a little more water if the sauce becomes too thick.

Stir in the parsley and half of the spring onions, and cook for a further 5 minutes. Remove from the heat.

While your red beans are simmering, cook your rice. Wash and rinse the rice really well, until the water runs almost clear. Place in a saucepan with enough water to cover the rice by about 4cm, and stir once. Bring to the boil over high heat, then turn the heat all the way down to low and cover the pan tightly with a lid. Cook for 10–15 minutes, until the rice is cooked. Tip into a colander and separate the grains with a fork.

When ready to serve, remove the bay leaves from the beans. Make a little mound of rice on each plate and surround with a generous helping of the red beans. Garnish with the remaining spring onions. Make sure there is a bottle of your favourite hot sauce on the table.

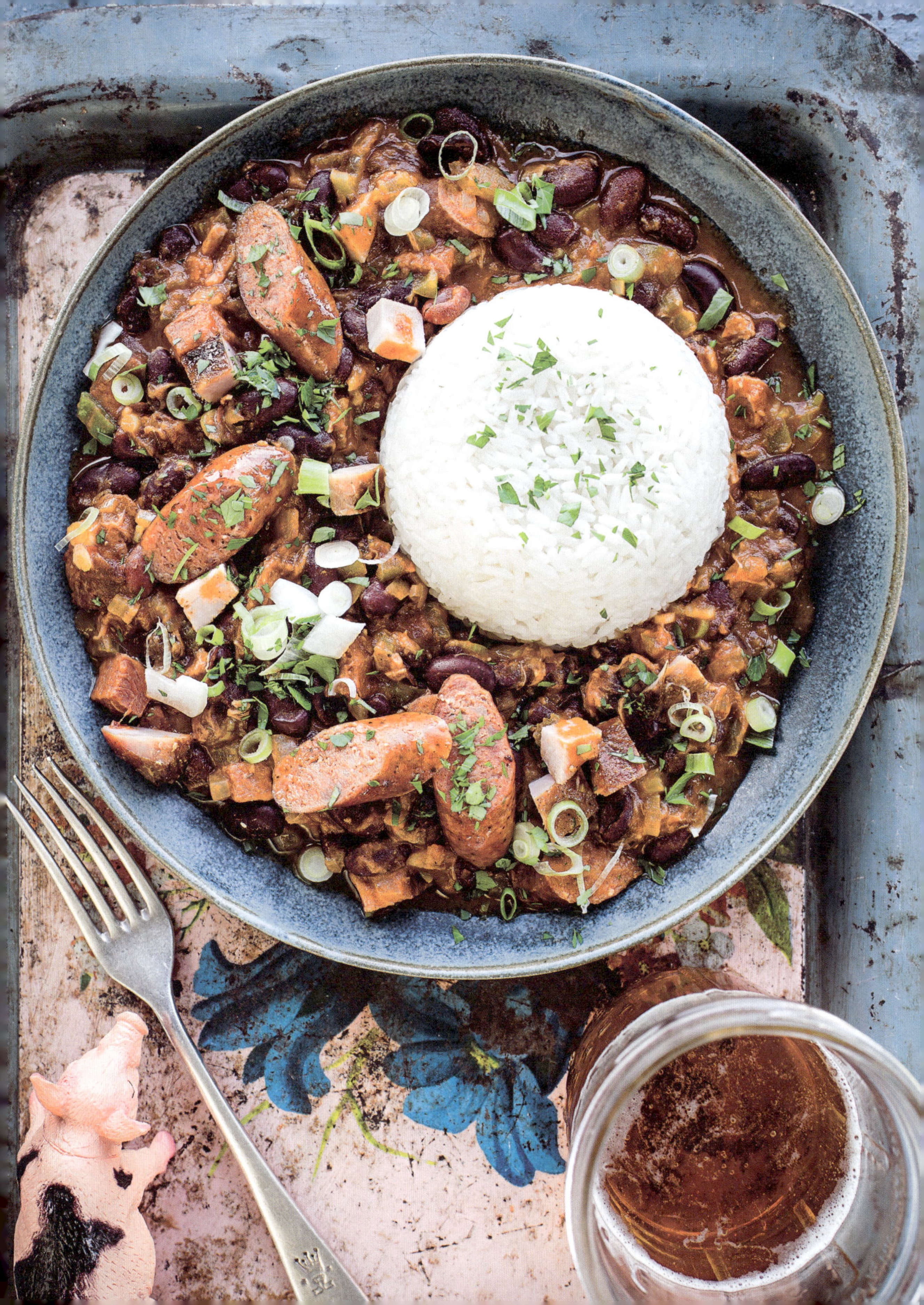

me oh my oh...

oh...Son of

SERVES 4

RED JAMBALAYA
WITH SMOKED CHICKEN, ANDOUILLE & SHRIMP

Jambalaya is a warming, hearty dish loved all over the States. With its Spanish and French influences, it has similarities to paella or blanquette de veau. And in true Cajun style, it takes the best parts of these dishes and brings them together as one. We love to use smoked meats in all our cooking, so if you have a few smoked chicken thighs left over from the yardbird (page 119) and an andouille sausage left over from previous smokes, use them here. If you're all out of smoked meats, use fresh, skinless chicken thighs and chorizo, which will need to be browned and cooked through before adding to the rice. If you feel the need for a little musical inspiration while you cook, listen to Hank Williams' Jambalaya song to get you in the mood!

- 1 tbsp olive oil
- 1 large onion, roughly chopped
- 4 celery sticks, thinly sliced
- 2 small green bell peppers, deseeded and diced
- 3 garlic cloves, peeled and crushed
- 1 tbsp smoked paprika
- ¼ tsp cayenne pepper
- 1 tsp dried thyme
- 1 tsp dried oregano
- 2 bay leaves
- 4 large vine ripened tomatoes, chopped
- 250g smoked chicken, preferably dark meat (page 119), cut into large chunks
- 3 smoked Andouille Sausages (pages 76–77), cut into 1cm slices
- 225g long-grain rice
- 550ml chicken stock
- 1 tsp flaked sea salt
- ½ tsp freshly ground black pepper
- 150g raw jumbo king prawns, shell-on, deheaded (thawed if frozen)
- 6 spring onions, sliced

Start by getting all your ingredients chopped up and ready to go. Heat the olive oil in a deep saucepan over medium-low heat. Add the 'holy trinity' of vegetables: onion, celery and green peppers and cook for 8–10 minutes until softened, stirring occasionally.

Stir the garlic, paprika, cayenne, thyme, oregano and bay leaves, and continue to cook for another minute or so, stirring constantly. Increase the heat to medium-high and add the chopped tomatoes. Cook for another 5 minutes stirring regularly.

Next, add the chicken, sausages and rice and cook, stirring, for about 1 minute. Pour over the chicken stock, season with salt and pepper. Bring to the boil and simmer, covered, for 15–20 minutes or until the rice is just tender and most of the liquid has been absorbed. The jambalaya should be fairly loose, so add a little more stock if it's getting too dry as the rice cooks.

When the rice is tender, stir in the prawns and the spring onions, and cook for about 5 minutes more, or until the prawns are hot and fully pink, stirring regularly. Check for seasoning and adjust as necessary, then serve. We think it's a great side dish to barbecue because it's full of flavour and colour.

SIDES, PICKLES & BUNS

SERVES 4–5 AS A SIDE DISH

ÉTOUFFÉE

Étouffée, pronounced 'eh-TOO-fay', is a dish found in both Cajun and Creole cuisine, typically served with shellfish over rice. Étouffée is most popular in the Acadian area of Southern Louisiana. The dish uses a technique known in Louisiana cuisine as 'smothering', meaning to cook with a small amount of liquid over a long period of time. You can add more shellfish such as clams, mussels, razor clams, cockles, or whatever you fancy to give it that Bayou boogie.

130ml groundnut oil

100g plain flour

1 medium onion, diced

1 green bell pepper, diced

2 celery sticks, diced

3 garlic cloves, very finely chopped

½ tsp freshly ground black pepper, plus extra to taste

½ tsp ground white pepper

¼ tsp cayenne pepper

1 tbsp Cajun seasoning (page 29)

4 spring onions, finely sliced

4 tbsp chopped flat-parsley leaves

2 tsp Louisiana Hot Sauce (page 44), or your favourite hot sauce

400g tin chopped tomatoes

300ml vegetable stock

750g fresh jumbo prawns, head and shell-on

2 tsp filé powder

50g unsalted butter

fine sea salt, to taste

To Serve

500g cooked rice

2 spring onions, chopped

1 tomato, deseeded and diced

1 tbsp chopped flat-leaf parsley

Heat the groundnut oil in a heavy-based pan, or cast-iron casserole, over low heat. Whisk the flour into the oil to form a paste, and cook for about 15–20 minutes, whisking continuously until caramel in colour (this is called a medium roux, see centre illustration below). The roux will be super-hot, so make sure you don't splash yourself, we have had many a speckled roux scar on our hands.

Take the roux off the heat while you add your 'holy trinity' of onion, bell pepper, celery and garlic. Put the pan back on the hob and cook over low heat for 7–8 minutes or so, stirring, until the vegetables have softened. Add the black, white and cayenne peppers, the Cajun seasoning, spring onions, parsley and hot sauce and mix well. Add the tinned tomatoes with their juices followed by the vegetable stock, and stir well. Bring to the boil over medium-high heat, reduce the heat to low and simmer for 35–40 minutes, until reduced and slightly thickened.

When the stew has reduced by a quarter, add the prawns and filé powder. Be careful not to overcook the prawns or they'll be chewy. Cook for 4–5 minutes until the shells turn pink, then immediately remove from the heat, add the butter and stir. Seasoning to taste. Transfer the etouffee to a serving bowl or, if you prefer, individual bowls over some rice. Garnish with the spring onions, tomato and parsley.

THREE STEPS TO ROUX HEAVEN

There are three main colours of roux in Acadian cooking: blonde, medium and dark. The only thing that separates them is time and elbow grease. The darker the roux, the nuttier it will taste and the less it will thicken your dish. The lighter the roux, the thicker (and lighter in colour) your final dish.

SIDES, PICKLES & BUNS

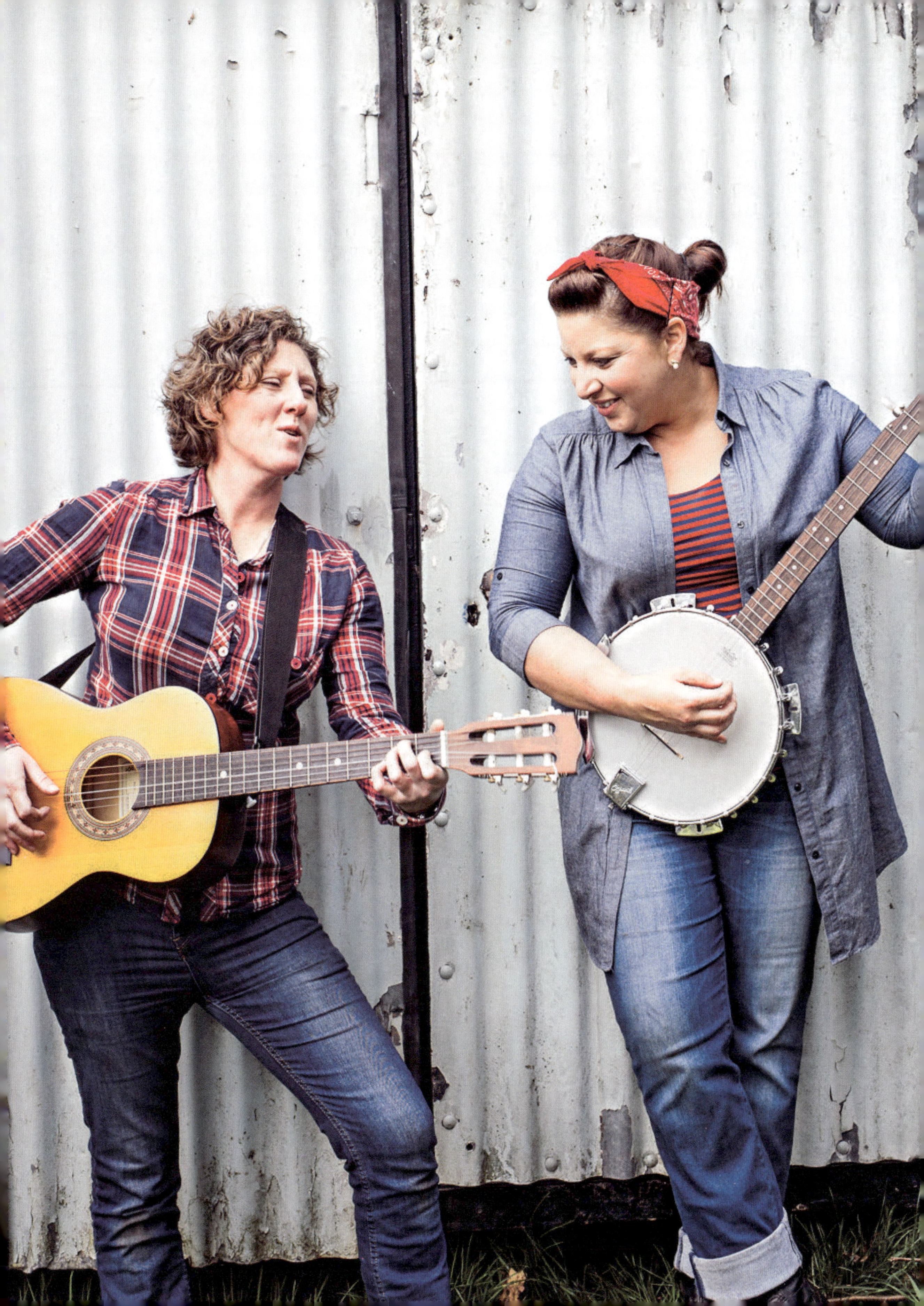

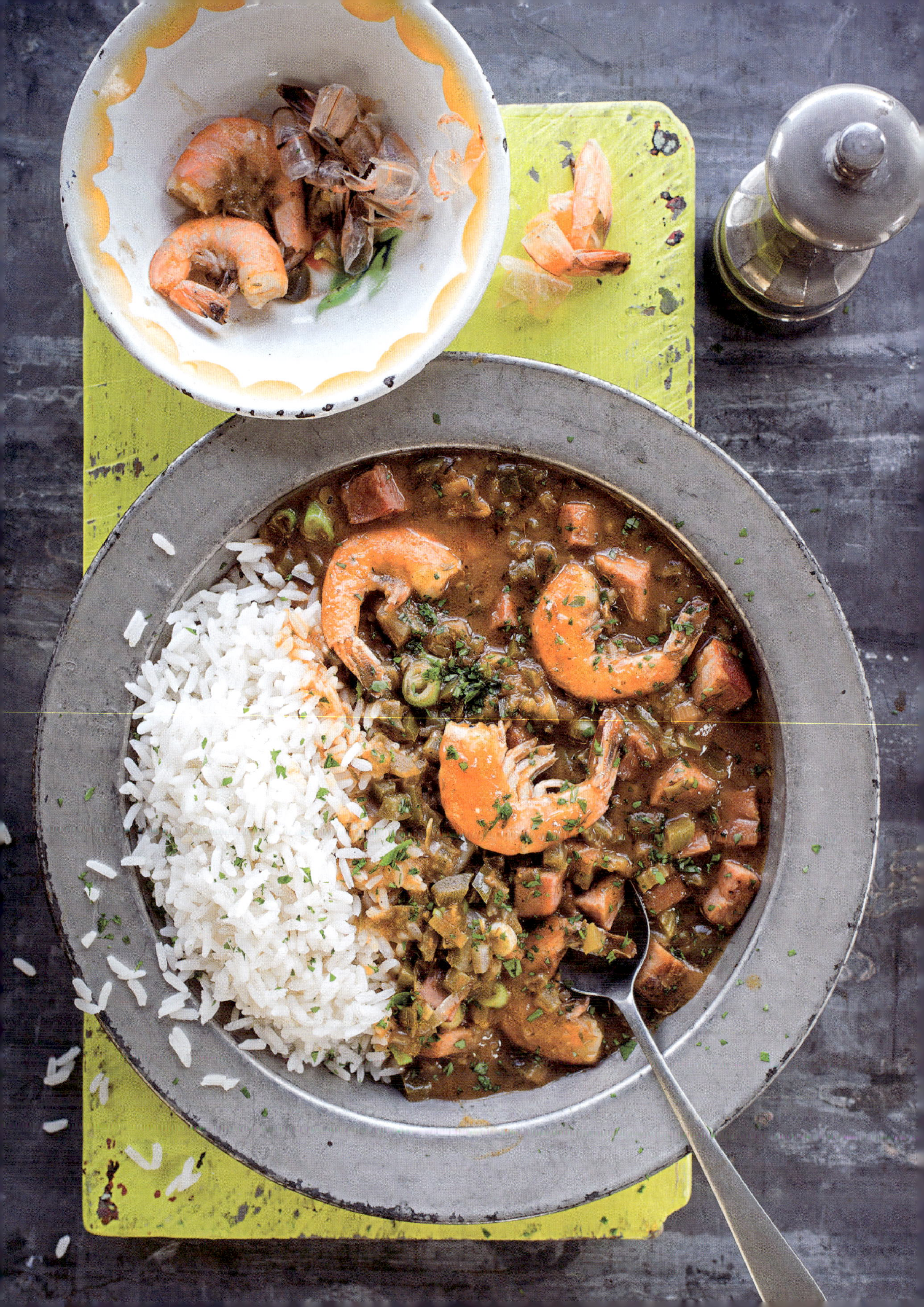

SHRIMP & TASSO FILÉ GUMBO

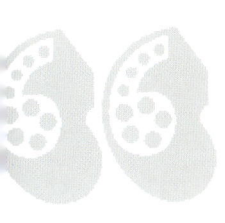

SERVES 4

This is one of the first Cajun dishes we were taught to cook in the States, and really, where our obsession with NOLA cuisine started. Throughout Louisiana, we were always on a mission to try the town's best gumbo. The flavours were so intense and exotic to us that, at the time, we thought that every bowl was good. Essentially, gumbo is a rich thyme-infused stew, full of dark bouillon flavours with hunks of tasty sausage, tasso, chicken and fish.

There's a thrill in the art of perfecting that dark brown roux. Watching it change colour minute by minute, it's mesmerising. You can serve your gumbo over plain rice, a big scoop of Hoppin' John (page 170) or with a hunks of crusty French bread.

- 130ml vegetable oil
- 120g plain flour
- 150g Tasso Ham, diced (page 89)
- 1 medium onion, diced
- 1 green bell pepper, deseeded and diced
- 2 celery sticks, diced
- 3 tbsp Creole seasoning (page 29)
- 2 garlic cloves, finely chopped
- 3 bay leaves
- 1.5 litres cold chicken stock
- 2 tsp dried thyme
- 350g shell-on jumbo prawns, rinsed and heads removed
- 2 tsp filé powder
- 2 tsp Worcestershire sauce
- 2 tbsp finely chopped flat-leaf parsley
- 3 spring onions, finely sliced
- sea salt flakes and fresh cracked pepper, to taste

Heat the vegetable oil in a heavy-based pan, or cast-iron casserole, over medium heat. Add the flour, and use a wooden spoon to mix well. Stir the flour frequently, for 20–25 minutes, until it turns milk chocolate in colour (see our roux colour chart, page 166). Be super-careful it doesn't splash you.

When your roux is ready, add your tasso ham, stir for 1 minute, then throw in your Louisiana 'holy trinity' of vegetables: the onion, bell pepper and celery. Mix through and add 1 tablespoon of the Creole seasoning, the garlic and bay leaves, stirring often for about 10 minutes, until the vegetables have softened. You'll notice the heat of the roux will start cooking the vegetables and ham very quickly.

Next, gradually add the cold chicken stock, a ladle at a time, until fully combined. Stir in the remaining Creole seasoning and thyme. Bring to a rolling boil over high heat, turn the heat down to medium-low, and simmer uncovered for 1 hour. About 10 minutes before the end of the cook time, add your prawns, filé powder, Worcestershire sauce, parsley and spring onions, and season to taste. Cook for 3–5 minutes, until the prawns are fully pink and cooked through. Serve immediately.

HOPPIN' JOHN (RICE & BEANS)

SERVES 4 AS A MAIN MEAL, OR 6–8 AS A SIDE DISH

We first had this tasty little carb-rich dish at a 'mom and pop' gas station diner on our way back from Asheville, NC to Nashville, TN. There wasn't a huge amount to be had on the menu, so we asked for something 'traditional'. We ended up with two bowls of hoppin' John: a hearty blend of pig trotters, rice and black-eyed peas. There are a few theories about how this dish got its name but the one that makes us smile the most is this: 'It was the custom for children to gather in the dining room as the dish was brought forth, and hop around the table before sitting down to eat.' In the absence of trotters, we've made it with ham hocks and it's equally delicious.

- 2 tbsp vegetable oil
- 1 large onion, roughly chopped
- 1 green bell pepper, deseeded and roughly chopped
- 4 garlic cloves, roughly chopped
- 2 tsp chilli flakes
- 3 fresh bay leaves
- 1 litre chicken stock
- 425g tin black-eyed peas, drained and rinsed
- 1 x 400–500g smoked bone-in ham hock (see below)
- 200g long-grain rice
- ¼ tsp fine sea salt
- ¼ tsp freshly ground black pepper
- large bunch spring onions, chopped

Heat the vegetable oil in a large pan, add the onion, bell pepper, garlic, chilli flakes and bay leaves. Cook over medium heat, for 8–10 minutes, until the onion begins to soften.

Add the chicken stock, turn up the heat and bring to the boil. Add the peas, return to the boil and immediately turn the heat down low. Add your ham hock and simmer for 1½ hours until the ham is tender. After this time, remove and discard the bay leaves and use tongs to take out the ham hock. Using a fork, pull the meat from the bone, discard any fat and skin, then return the meat to the pan.

Next, stir in the rice and bring back up to the boil over medium-high heat. Reduce the heat to low and simmer, covered, for about 20 minutes, or until the rice is tender and most of the liquid is absorbed. Season with salt and pepper, and serve with more pepper and the chopped spring onions.

NOTE ON SMOKIN' HOG HOCK

For already cured ham hocks, soak them overnight in the fridge in clean water with a peeled potato in the water, too. The potato will absorb some of the salt. Smoking ham hocks is relatively straightforward. It makes sense to pop a few hocks in while you're smoking other meats. We usually set our grill up for indirect heat at 108°C/225°F and use a bit of our Almost All-purpose Rub (page 26) to get a good bark. Ham hocks that are 300–400g will take 7–8 hours to reach 90°C/196°F.

Look for hocks with plenty of meat on them. If you can't find ham hocks, you can substitute cubes of smoked ham, bacon or leftover pulled pork. Simply fry the bacon off first, and add any of these substitutions right before you add the rice.

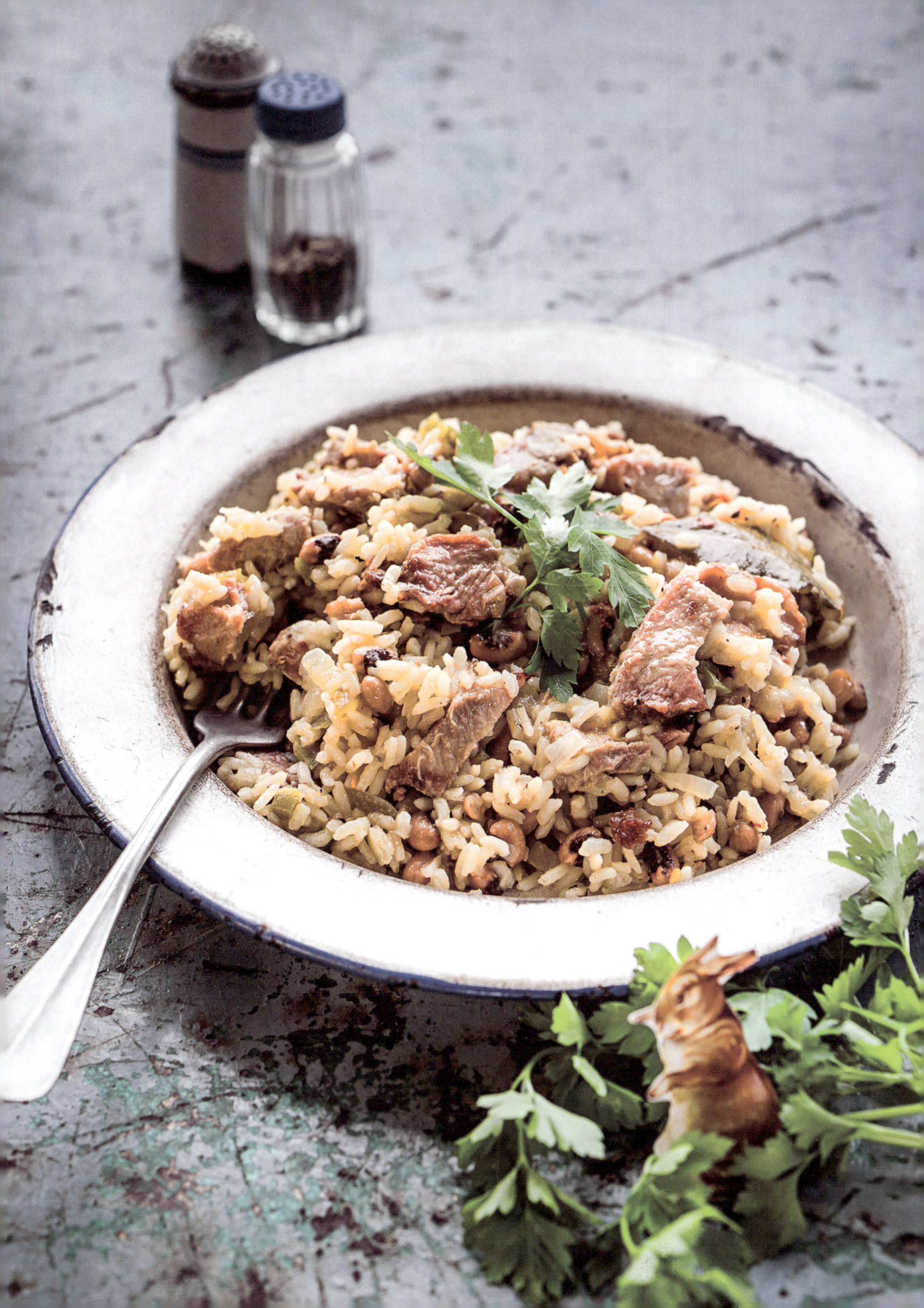

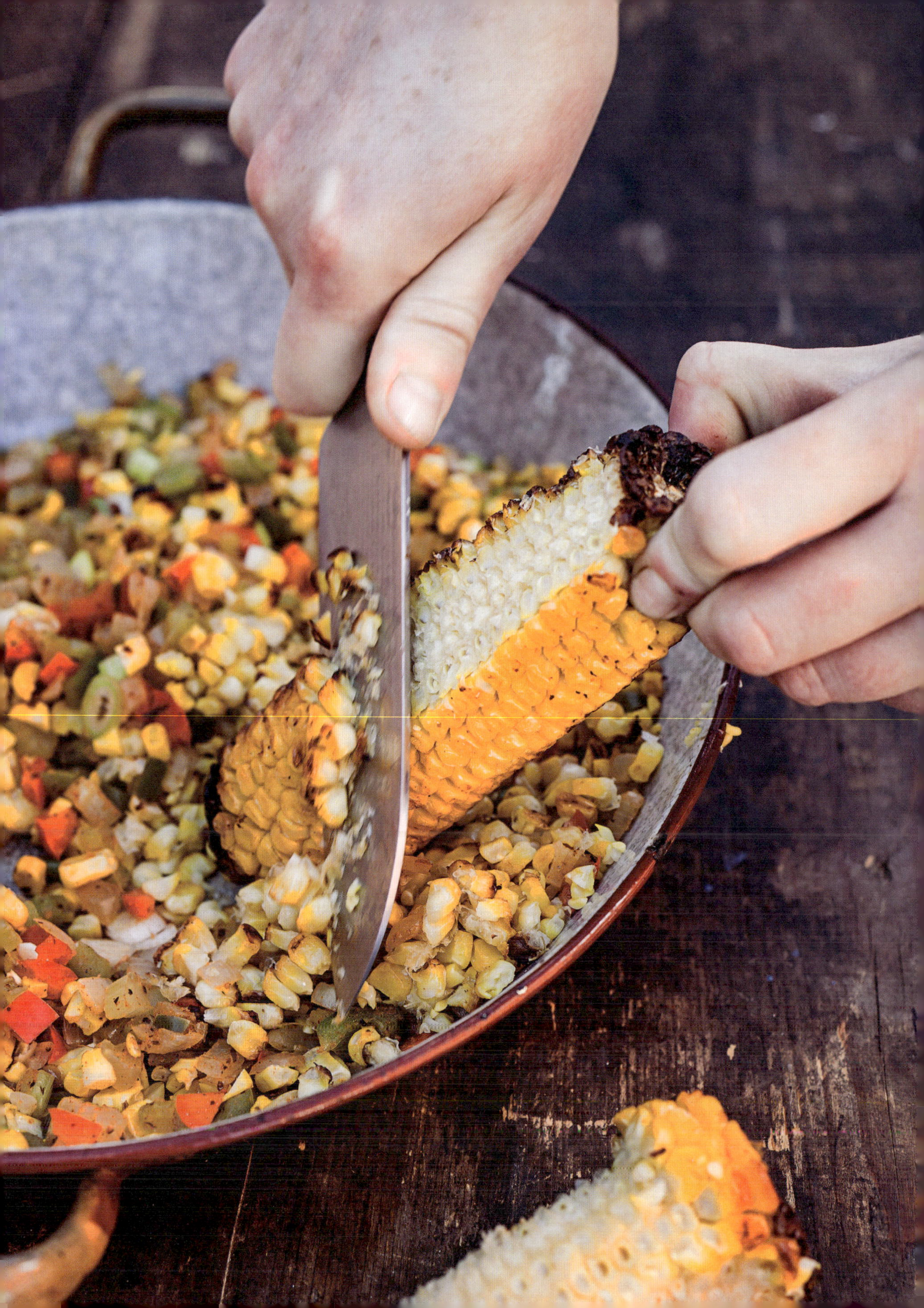

MAQUE CHOUX

SERVES 4

Pronounced 'Mak-shoo', this Louisiana corn dish is, for us, an essential side dish to our barbecue. It's thought to be a marriage of Creole (spices) and Native American influence (the corn). It's vibrant, tasty, sweet, very simple to make and has all those beautiful Creole flavours that go together like horse and carriage. We've served this side dish at our kitchen takeovers from the start and have given this recipe out more times than we have our pulled pork recipe – let's hope that's not saying something about our barbecue!

- 6 fresh corn on the cob, husks removed
- 1 tbsp unsalted butter
- 1 medium onion, diced
- 2 celery sticks, diced
- ½ tsp fresh thyme leaves
- ½ green bell pepper, deseeded and diced
- ½ red bell pepper, deseeded and diced
- 2 tbsp Cajun seasoning (page 29)
- 125ml double cream
- 1 tsp fine sea salt, plus extra to taste
- freshly cracked black pepper to taste
- 3 spring onions, finely chopped
- 2 tbsp finely chopped flat-leaf parsley
- 1 tbsp finely chopped coriander

Start by cooking the corn cobs. We like to grill ours over charcoal, or if they're in their husks you can cook them directly on your barbecue coals. Failing that, you could of course cook them under the grill for 15 minutes, turning frequently, until golden all over.

Melt the butter in a heavy-based pan over medium heat until starting to foam. Add the onion, celery, thyme and bell peppers, and cook over medium-low heat, stirring, for 10 minutes, until soft. Using a sharp knife, slice the corn kernels off the cobs as close to the core as possible, cutting away from you, into the pan. Cook for a further 5 minutes. Now add the Cajun seasoning and stir through. Stir in the cream, salt and pepper, lower the heat and cook for a further 10–15 minutes, stirring, until thickened and reduced. Take a ladleful of the mix and put in a blender or food processor. Blitz until smooth and return to the pan along with the spring onions, parsley and coriander, and cook for a further 5 minutes. Season to taste and serve immediately.

A NOTE ON FROZEN CORN

There's some kind of secret ingredient missing from using frozen sweetcorn in this recipe. Perhaps it's the corn milk that forms like dew as you run the knife down a fresh cob. However, we understand that fresh corn can be tricky to get, so you can substitute the cobs for 400–500g good-quality frozen corn.

SERVES 6

SWANSEA JACK MAC & CHEESE

Macaroni cheese, the greatest, blank canvas, comfort food around. You can pimp it up any way you like, use whatever pasta you have, whatever cheese you can afford. This version is inspired by the great produce found in West Wales. If you want to keep it classic, simply omit the bacon, laver flakes, cockles and laverbread.

500g elbow macaroni

1 tsp olive oil

4 slices thick, good-quality, back bacon (pages 80–81)

1 small leek, halved and finely chopped

150g fresh cockles, washed

2 tbsp toasted laver flakes

60g laverbread (if you can't get fresh, you can order tinned online)

150g Panko breadcrumbs

For the White Sauce

1 litre full-fat milk

150ml single cream

2 fresh thyme sprigs

1 garlic clove, very finely chopped

4 tbsp unsalted butter

3 tbsp plain flour

1 tbsp Dijon mustard

1 tsp English mustard powder

¼ tsp freshly grated nutmeg

½ tsp freshly ground black pepper

1 tsp sea salt flakes

300g Gruyère cheese, grated

200g Monterey Jack cheese, grated

200g mature Cheddar, grated

100g Grana Pedano or Parmesan, grated

Bring a pan of salted water to the boil over high heat. Add the macaroni and cook for 8–9 minutes, until less than al dente. Drain the pasta, stir through the olive oil and mix well to keep it loose, then set aside.

Dry fry the bacon in a small pan over medium heat, until crispy. Remove from the heat, allow to cool and chop the bacon into small pieces. Set aside. In the same pan, fry the leeks in the bacon fat over medium-low heat for 5–10 minutes, until softened. Take off the heat and set aside with the bacon (in Wales, we call leeks fried in bacon fat 'cenyn blydi blasus' which roughly translates as 'very tasty leeks').

Preheat the oven to 200°C/400°F/gas mark 6.

Now, let's make the white sauce. In a small saucepan, heat the milk and cream with the thyme sprigs and garlic cloves over low heat – do not boil, just warm through for 5–7 minutes. Strain the solids and discard, keeping the milk aside.

Meanwhile, melt the butter in a deep, heavy-based saucepan over medium-low heat. Whisk in the flour and cook for about 1 minute or so, stirring constantly, to make a paste. Slowly whisk in the warmed milk to make a roux. Cook for about 10 minutes, whisking constantly, until the mixture is nice and smooth. Stir in the Dijon, mustard powder, nutmeg, pepper and salt until well combined. Stir in the cheeses apart from the Parmesan, and continue to cook for a further 5 minutes and stir until the cheese is melted. Taste for seasoning, bearing in mind the laver flakes, laverbread and bacon will add extra saltiness.

Now, add the cockles, toasted laver bread flakes, bacon bits and finally, the cooked macaroni. Mix well. Pour the macaroni mix into a baking dish, making sure it's at least 5–7cm from the top. Dollop 6–8 teaspoons of laverbread, equally spaced, on the top of the cheese sauce. Sprinkle on the Panko breadcrumbs and the Parmesan and bake for 25 minutes, or until golden brown on top. Serve immediately with your favourite barbecue.

WHO WAS 'SWANSEA JACK'?

Many people believe that this is the name of the famous black dog that apparently rescued people from Swansea docks when they fell in. Others say it was the nickname given to Swansea's sailors, who had a reputation as skilled and dependable mariners. Either way, it's an affectionate term given by the good folks of Swansea and this recipe is dedicated to our West Walian friends and family.

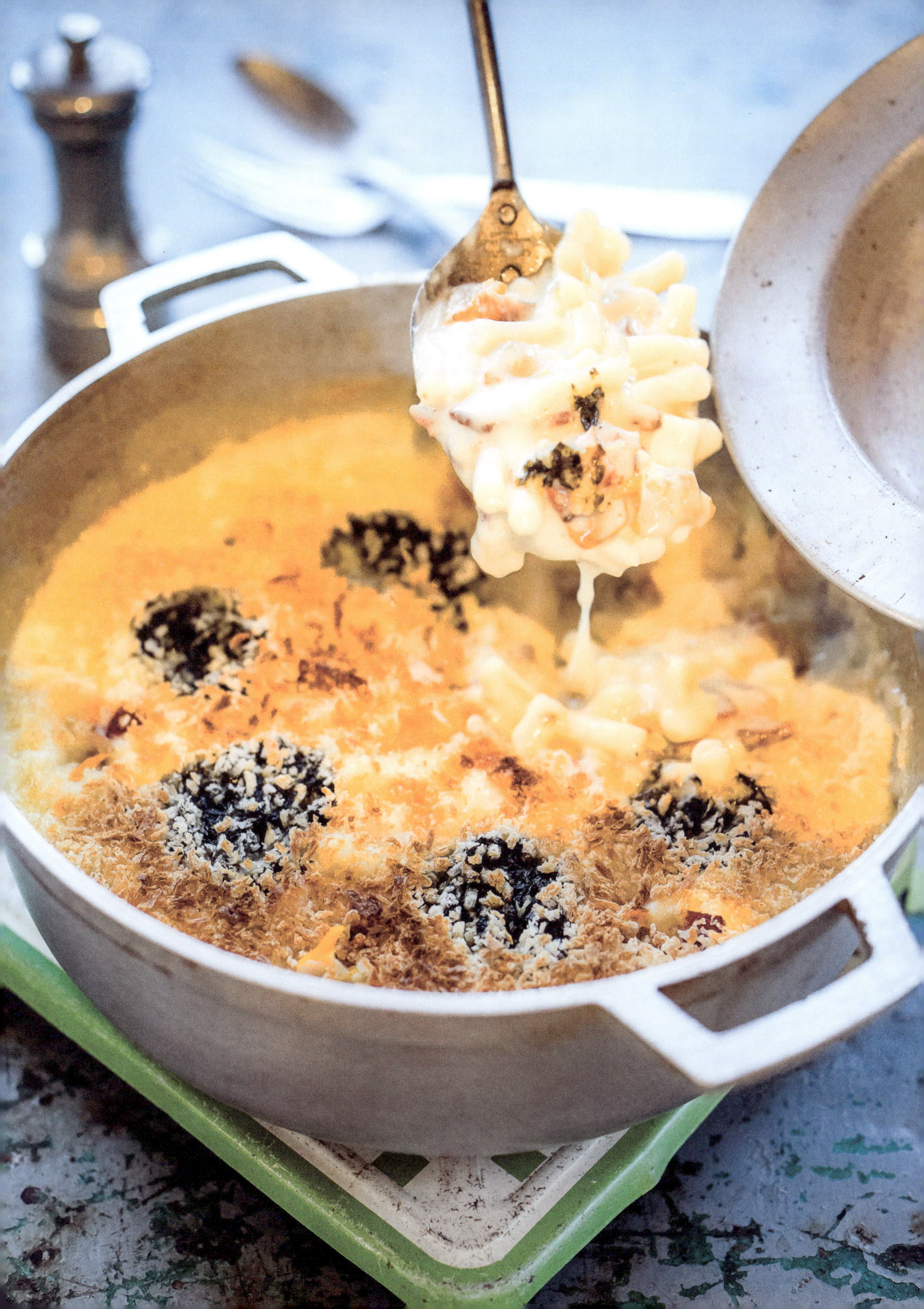

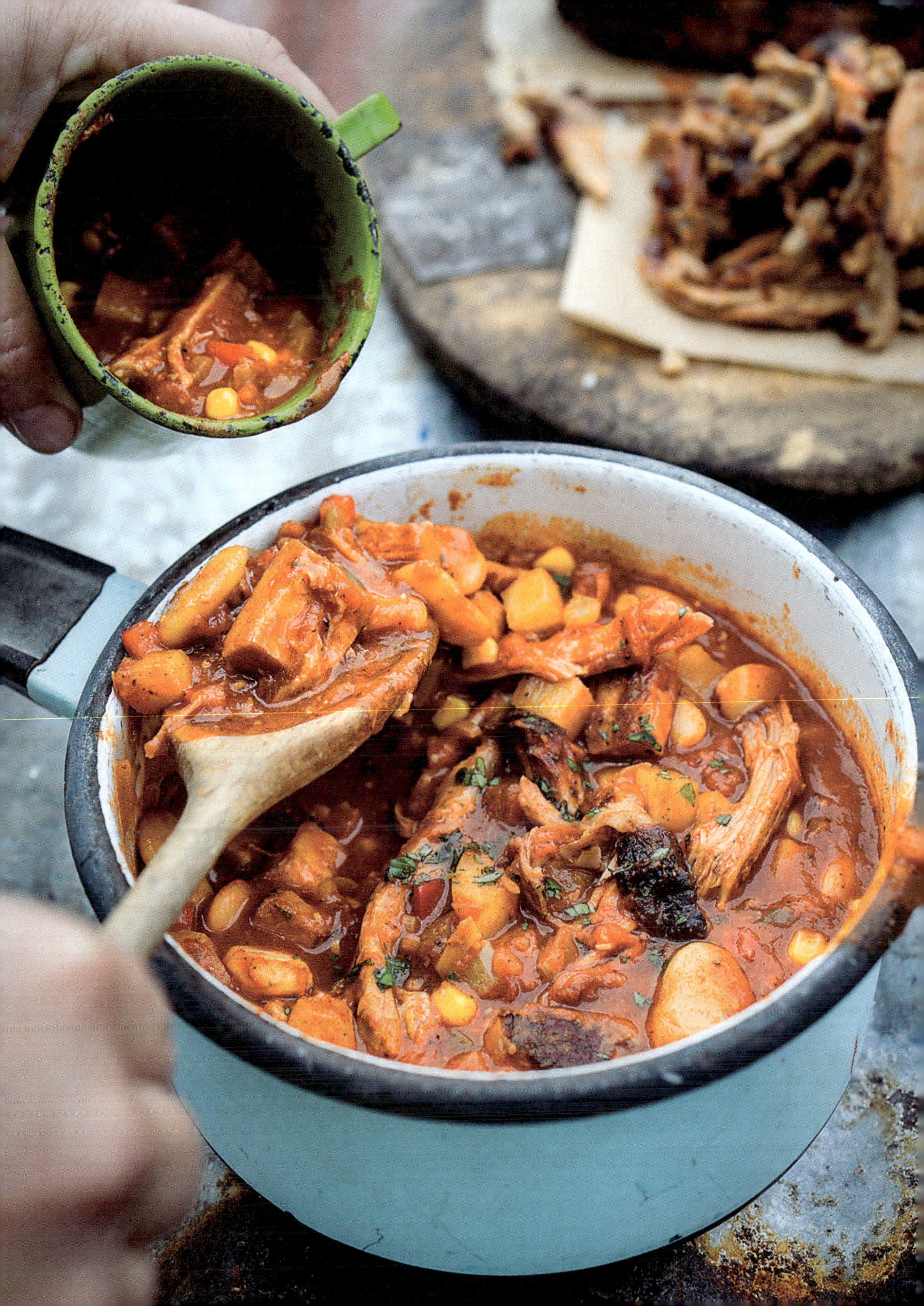

KENTUCKY BURGOO

SERVES 6-10

'If gumbo is the national stew of Cajun country, burgoo is the stew of Kentucky,' Ronni Lundy tells us in her book *Shuck Beans, Stack Cakes, and Honest Fried Chicken*. We ate a fairly questionable bowl of 'local Burgoo' in a desolate cafe just outside Louisville, KY. In true Burgoo style, the meats were a little indistinguishable. But what can you expect from a stew made from ingredients singer Robert Myles describes as 'almost anything that ever walked or flew'? There is talk of it being a derivative of a French ragout, which sounds kinda similar when you say it. We've tried to stay true to the 'wild meat' element and urge you to give it a go!

- 3 tbsp vegetable oil, plus extra if needed
- 1–2 rabbits, cut into large pieces (bone in)
- 900g–1.3kg venison, cut into 8cm chunks
- 3–5 pheasant legs or thighs, bone-in
- 1 large onion, diced
- 2 carrots, diced
- 2 celery sticks, chopped
- 1 green bell pepper, deseeded and diced
- 5 garlic cloves, chopped
- 1 litre chicken stock
- 1 litre beef stock
- 400g tin chopped tomatoes
- 2 large potatoes, cut into small, 1cm cubes
- 60ml Worcestershire sauce, or to taste
- 450g frozen corn kernels
- 450g frozen butterbeans, or tinned black-eyed peas, rinsed and drained
- Cheddar Jalapeño Cornbread (page 189), to serve
- Tabasco or other hot sauce, to serve
- sea salt and freshly ground black pepper

Heat the oil in a large pan and place over medium-high heat. Season the meat with salt and pepper. Working in batches, brown all of the meat, being careful not to overcrowd the pan. Remove to a plate as and when each batch is well browned.

Put the onion, carrots, celery and bell pepper in the pan and turn the heat to high. Cook the vegetables for 7 minutes, until they are well browned – you might need to add a little more oil to the pan if necessary. Add the garlic and fry for 1 minute. Return the browned meat, along with the chicken and beef stocks and the tomatoes. Stir, and season with salt and pepper. Bring to the boil over high heat, cover, then reduce the heat and simmer gently for 2 hours.

After this time, the pheasant and rabbit should be meltingly tender. Fish them out of the pan and use two forks to strip the meat off the bone, and back into the pan. Discard the bones. Remove the venison pieces from the pan and tear into bite-sized pieces. Return to the pan and bring the stew back up to the boil over medium-high heat.

Add the potatoes to the stew, reduce the heat to medium, and simmer until tender. Add the Worcestershire sauce, mix well and adjust the seasoning to taste. Finally, stir in the corn and beans or peas. Cook for a further 20 minutes. Serve with cornbread and a bottle of hot sauce on the side.

SERVES 8 AS A SIDE,
4 AS A MAIN

GREEN CHILLI STEW

Our friend, Elizabeth, first served us this delicious one-pot wonder on a cold November night before we went off to perform in our first open mic night in Tennessee. This thing was bubbling away on the stovetop, filling the house with the amazing scent of coriander. Of course, it's one of those dishes that when we ask what's in it, we're met with a casual 'Oh, whatever is handy'... We often serve this as a side dish as it's fairly light and more like a soup, but you could easily serve it as a main.

- 1½ tbsp plain flour
- 1 tbsp ground coriander
- 1 tbsp ground cumin
- 1 tsp chilli flakes
- 2 tbsp vegetable oil
- 750g lean boneless pork shoulder, cut into 3cm cubes
- 2 tsp fine sea salt
- 1 large onion, diced
- 4 green jalapeños, deseeded and diced
- 1 green bell pepper, deseeded and diced
- 4 garlic cloves, very finely chopped
- 1.25 litres chicken stock
- 400g waxy potatoes, peeled and cubed
- 150g frozen sweetcorn
- large bunch coriander, chopped

Mix together the flour, coriander, cumin and chilli flakes in a bowl and set aside. Heat 1 tablespoon of the vegetable oil in a large flameproof casserole over medium-high heat. Season the pork with the salt. Working in batches, fry the pork, stirring, for 5–7 minutes until browned. Transfer the pork to a plate and pour out all but 1 tablespoon fat from the dish.

Add the remaining tablespoon of vegetable oil to the casserole. Add the onion, jalapeños, bell pepper and garlic and cook, stirring occasionally, for about 10 minutes until softened. Return the pork to the casserole and stir in the flour and spice mix. Cook for a minute over medium-low heat, then gradually add the chicken stock, bit by bit, mixing it well with the ingredients in the casserole until completely incorporated. Cover the casserole and bring to the boil over medium-high heat. Stir the chilli and reduce the heat to medium-low, then simmer, covered, for 1 hour.

After 1 hour, turn up the heat to medium-high and bring the stew to a gentle boil. Add the potatoes and sweetcorn, and check that they are submerged in liquid. If not, pour in a little more water. Simmer for about 30 minutes, stirring occasionally, until the potatoes and pork are tender and the liquid has thickened slightly. Add the fresh coriander and stir through. Serve in soup bowls alongside your favourite barbecue and a few slices of warm Cheddar Jalapeño Cornbread (page 189) for dipping.

SOUTHERN-STYLE BARBECUE GREENS WITH PORK

SERVES 4, AS A SIDE

This dish was presented to us with our first taste of North Carolina pork barbecue. Those delicious green, leathery leaves, coated in homemade stock, were divine. Collards and pork barbecue work so beautifully together, the umami of the green leaves is the Romeo to the sweet Juliet of the smoked pig meat. Unfortunately collard greens are notoriously hard to find here in the UK. We persuaded a friend to grow some for us one year, and they were awesome. However, we've found that any combination of seasonal greens, like spring greens or kale, Swiss chard or mustard greens, all give a very close rendition of that Southern flavour profile we were craving.

You can do a little prep and have this ready to go on your barbecue while you're smoking something else. It'll take a couple of hours, depending on the hardiness of the greens you choose.

225g unsalted butter
1 medium onion, diced
2 garlic cloves, finely chopped
1kg greens of your choice (see above)
300g Smoked Pork Belly (page 86) chopped, or smoked sausages (see pages 76–77, 78), cubed
100ml cider vinegar
1 tbsp sea salt flakes
1 tsp freshly ground black pepper
1 tsp chilli flakes
1 tsp soft light brown sugar
1 tsp Louisiana Hot Sauce (page 44)
1 litre chicken stock

For the Garnish
3 tomatoes, deseeded and diced
small bunch flat-leaf parsley, finely chopped

Melt the butter in a medium-sized frying pan, add the onion and garlic and cook over medium-low heat for 10 minutes, until softened. Roughly chop up your greens, removing the thicker stalks but leaving in the smaller stalks for texture.

Preheat your grill for indirect heat at 120°C/250°F.

In a large roasting tin, add all the ingredients, except the chicken stock, and mix thoroughly. Then, pour in the stock, using a spoon to push the greens so they are submerged in the liquid. Tightly cover the tin with foil and place in your preheated grill. Smoke for 1½–2 hours, until the greens are tender to the bite, but not mushy at all. If they aren't quite there, simply replace the foil tightly and return to the grill until they're cooked to your liking.

To serve, drain any excess liquid, put the greens in a bowl and stir in the tomatoes and parsley.

NO SMOKER? NO PROBLEM

If you want to cook this in the oven or on the stovetop, we find that a flameproof casserole works really well. They'll take about 45 minutes at 180°C/355°F, depending on your variety of greens.

MAKES 2 X 500ML JARS

MISS DAISY'S CHOW-CHOW RELISH

A lovely neighbour from the Fernvale Valley, TN, popped a jar of this over to our log cabin one day and we were instantly hooked on this sweet, savoury relish. We'd been eating a fair few fried green tomatoes at various diners, so we were already fans. This is also a delicious way to use up a green tomato glut. It's even worth growing a few plants of a green tomato variety for your chow-chow or you could just pick unripe ones from regular plants. Miss Daisy's instructions were a little light on detail, as are so many generational southern recipes, however we think this method comes close to her chow-chow.

- 1kg green tomatoes, diced
- 12 green jalapeños, deseeded and chopped
- 3 tbsp fine sea salt
- 300g white sugar
- 2 tsp chilli flakes
- 100g pickling spices
- 1 tsp turmeric
- ½ small white cabbage, chopped
- 3 medium white onions, thinly sliced
- 350ml distilled white vinegar

Place the tomatoes and jalapeños in a bowl, sprinkle over 1 tablespoon salt, cover and leave to sit overnight.

The next day, put the tomatoes and peppers in a colander and rinse well under cold water. Drain.

In a large pan, combine the sugar, chilli flakes, pickling spices, turmeric, 50ml water and remaining 2 tablespoons of salt. Set over medium-high heat and bring the mixture to the boil. Add the drained vegetables, along with the cabbage, white onions and vinegar. Bring to the boil and simmer over medium heat for 30 minutes. (Make sure you have a window open or turn on the extraction hood over your hob if you have one.)

Take the pan off the heat and spoon the mixture into your sterilised jars (page 33) while hot. Place a round of baking parchment on top and close the lid. Store in a cool, dark place for 1 month before eating. This will keep for 3 weeks once opened if stored in the fridge.

MAKES ABOUT 300ML

PINEAPPLE CHOW-CHOW

Not at all like the original Southern State version we have opposite, here is something that we discovered in a little roadside shack in Asia. This vibrant, flavourful, summery relish complements chicken, pork and lamb beautifully. It is delicious when used as a glaze on chicken or pork, or served as a tasty condiment to any barbecue. Feel free to adjust the heat to your liking via the fresh chillies or leave out the cayenne if it has too much poke.

1 medium onion, finely diced
500g fresh ripe pineapple, or tinned, finely diced
150ml pineapple juice
2 red chillies, deseeded and finely chopped
¼ tsp fine sea salt
1 tsp ground cumin
1 tsp ground coriander
¼ tsp ground cloves
¼ tsp ground cinnamon
¼ tsp cayenne pepper
½ tsp ground allspice
½ tsp ground ginger
2 tbsp soft light brown sugar
1 tsp English mustard powder
1 tsp turmeric
2 tsp celery seeds
1 tsp mustard seeds
juice and pared zest of ½ lemon

Combine all the ingredients in a heavy-based saucepan. Place over medium-low heat and simmer for 30 minutes, stirring, until you have a jammy texture. If the consistency looks too wet, simply turn up the heat and simmer, uncovered, for 10 minutes, until the mixture reduces. Keep stirring to prevent sticking.

Remove from the heat, transfer to a sterilised jar (page 33) immediately and let the relish cool completely (preferably, 24 hours) before using. This will keep for 3 weeks once opened if stored in the fridge.

MAKES 2 X 500ML JARS

BREAD & BUTTER PICKLES

Aside from your first successful smoke, there's nothing more satisfying than making your first batch of house pickles. We started making these pickles about eight years ago, as soon as one of us had access to some garden space where we could grow vegetables. We were both terrible gardeners so pickling became a way of using gluts of odd-looking vegetables.

This is the basic recipe for the pickle slices that we eat with just about everything on a daily basis. Feel free to add your own spices and vegetables on your next batch, to create your own signature pickles.

5 cucumbers, sliced about 3–4mm thick

1 large onion, halved and sliced 3–4mm thick

1 tbsp fine sea salt

2 fresh dill sprigs

For the Pickling Brine

250ml cider vinegar

200g soft light brown sugar

1 tbsp yellow mustard seeds

1 tsp black mustard seeds

1 tbsp celery seeds

1 tsp turmeric

½ tsp chilli flakes

5 cloves

1 tbsp fine sea salt

① 24hr Party Pickles (page 184)

② Half-Sour Pickles (page 186)

③ Pickled Fennel & Celery (page 185)

Combine the sliced cucumbers, onion, and salt in a colander set in a large bowl. Refrigerate for 2 hours, or overnight, to drain. The osmosis caused by the salt gives the pickles more crunch.

Drain the vegetables and rinse thoroughly under cold running water. Put back in the colander and allow to drain while you make the pickling brine.

Combine the vinegar and sugar in a non-reactive pan. Set over medium heat for a few minutes, stirring constantly, until the sugar has dissolved. Add the mustard and celery seeds, turmeric, chilli flakes, cloves and salt. Increase the heat to high and bring to the boil, then reduce the heat to low. Add the drained vegetables and stir. Cook for 5 minutes, stirring constantly. Remove from the heat.

Put a sprig of dill in each sterilised jar (page 33), then using tongs, fill your jars with the vegetables. Slowly pour the hot brine over the vegetables in each jar, leaving 5cm space at the top. Poke the vegetables around with the handle of a wooden spoon, to dislodge any air bubbles.

Wipe the rims with kitchen towel, seal with the lid and keep in the fridge for 1 month before eating. They will keep for 3 weeks once opened if stored in the fridge.

WHY PICKLES AND BARBECUE ARE THE PERFECT COUPLE

In the South, pickles are almost always served with barbecue. There's something about a sweet, sharp or salty pickle that cleanses the palate and seems to aid digestion. They're also the perfect contrasting flavour to rich, smoked meats. A little like eating that pickled ginger between mouthfuls of sushi. For us, if the only side served with barbecue were pickles, we'd be happy girls.

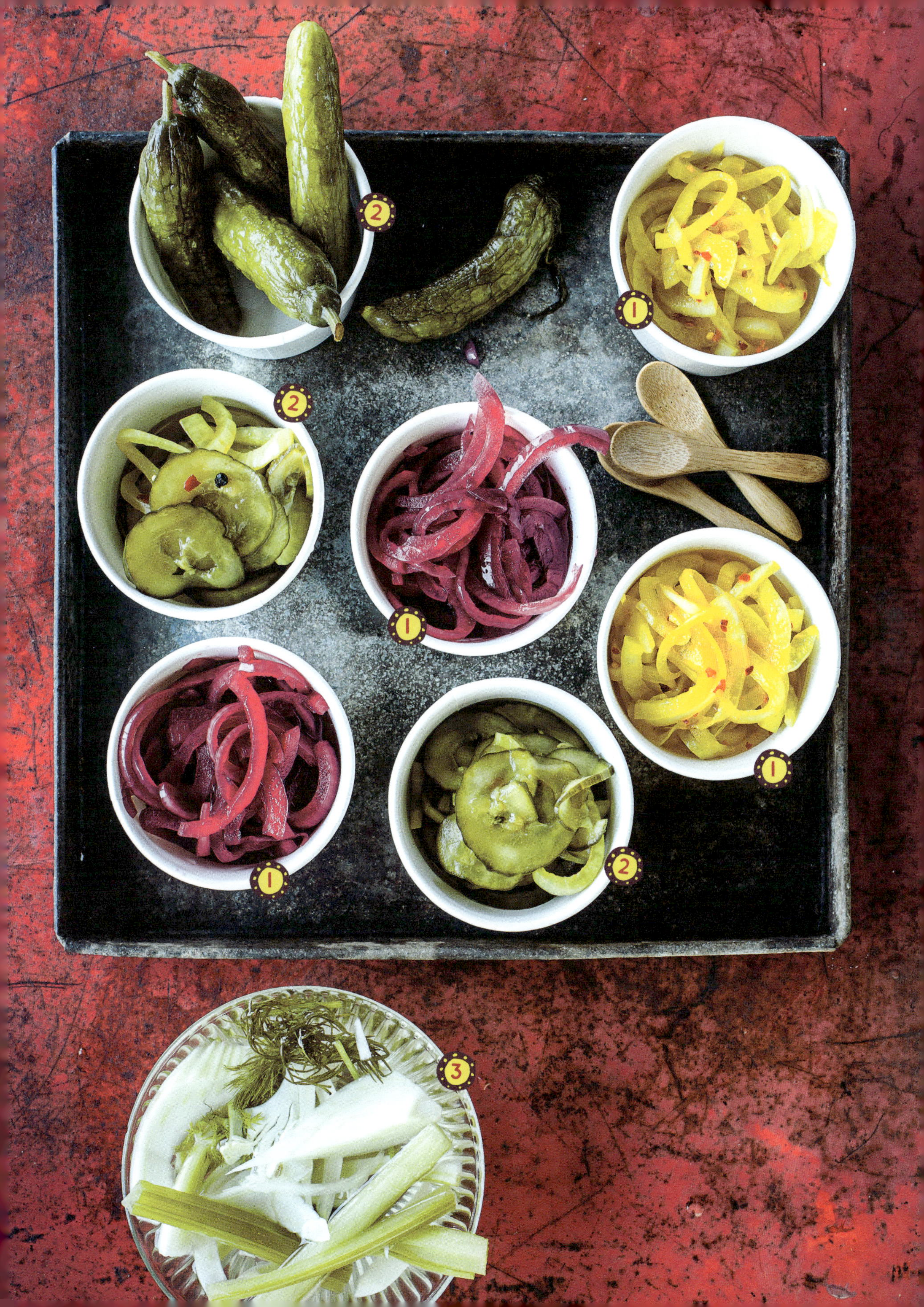
2
1
2
1
1
1
2
3

MAKES 2 X 500ML JARS

TWENTY-FOUR HOUR PARTY PICKLES

These simple bright yellow and red onions pack a punch with barbecue and look vibrant on the side of the plate. They're easy to make and ready in just twenty-four hours. We like to make two jars' worth of pickled onions: the yellow ones spicy, the pink ones sweet. You can also add them to 'slaw for a little sweetness or heat.

For the Spicy Onions

500g white onions, peeled
250ml distilled white vinegar
1 tbsp chilli flakes
1 tbsp Louisiana Hot Sauce (page 44), or your favourite hot sauce
½ tsp turmeric
¼ tsp cayenne pepper
2 tsp fine sea salt

For the Sweet Onions

500g red onions, peeled
250ml distilled white vinegar
100g white sugar
100g soft light brown sugar
2 tsp fine sea salt

Follow the same method for both types of onion. Make in two separate batches, one red, one yellow.

Start by slicing the peeled onions in half down the centre and then into medium slices, about 3mm or so thick.

Mix the remaining ingredients for each type of onion in two separate non-reactive saucepans and bring to the boil over low heat, making sure all the ingredients are well mixed. Add the onions, stir for 2 minutes, then turn off the heat.

Use tongs to add the onions to the sterilised jar (page 33), pushing them down until they're fairly compact. When all the onions have been added, pour over the remaining vinegar solution. With the handle of a wooden spoon, prod the onions to dispel any little air bubbles. Cover the top of the jars with a piece of baking parchment and screw the lid on tightly. Allow to cool completely, then store in the fridge. They will be ready to eat the following day and are best if eaten within 7 days of making. However, they will keep for months in the fridge and will develop in taste.

MAKES 1 X 1 LITRE JAR, OR 2 X 500ML JARS

PICKLED FENNEL & CELERY

Pickled fennel is great with pretty much most meats, especially lamb and chicken. You can use it to add to an extra level of loveliness to 'slaws and salads. We love to have a little arsenal of pickled veg in our storecupboard. It can really make the difference between a great dish and an outstanding one, plus it brings out our inner mad scientist staring at Darwinian-like jars of weird and wonderful pickled vegetable specimens.

- 2 large fennel bulbs, or 3 medium ones, including green fronds
- 6 celery sticks, cut in thirds and sliced lengthways
- 300g white sugar
- 2 tbsp fine sea salt
- 500ml white wine vinegar
- 3 strips pared lemon rind, white pith removed, cut into thin lengths
- 1 fresh dill sprig

Trim the base from the fennel bulbs and remove the tough outer layers. Cut into large chunks or strips, making sure not to make them too thin, otherwise they'll go soft. Reserve the green fronds for later. Cut the celery sticks into long matchsticks.

In a large non-reactive saucepan, bring the sugar, salt and vinegar to a gentle boil over medium heat, turn the heat down to low, stirring until the sugar and salt have completely dissolved. Give it a quick taste, add a little more sugar or salt to your liking. Put in the lemon rind, fennel and celery, then cover and turn off the heat. Allow to steep for 5 minutes.

Wrap the fennel fronds and dill sprig around your fingers to make a nest and put at the bottom of your sterilised jars (page 33). Pack in the fennel and celery pieces on top. Slowly pour over enough vinegar mixture to cover the veg by at least 3–5cm. Give the jar a tap to release any air bubbles – feel free to prod the veg with a clean spoon handle, too. Leave in a cool, dark place to mature for at least 1 week before opening. The pickled veg should keep for 6–12 months. This will keep for 3 weeks once opened if stored in the fridge.

SIDES, PICKLES & BUNS

HALF-SOUR PICKLES

These pickles are extremely popular in delis and a few fancy barbecue joints, and are made with a 3.5 per cent saline solution instead of vinegar, hence the name. The result is a saltier, crunchier pickle that retains a bright green skin. They are a great alternative to the regular sweet and sharp pickles usually served with barbecue.

500g small pickling cucumbers
2 tbsp pickling salt
2 tbsp sea salt flakes
2 tsp fine sea salt
1 tsp chilli flakes
4 garlic cloves, chopped
3 fresh dill sprigs
1 tsp whole black peppercorns

Start by rinsing the cucumbers well under cold running water.

In a heatproof measuring jug, dissolve all the salts in 250ml boiling water, from the kettle. Top up with 250ml cold water, mix in the chilli flakes and set the liquid aside.

Add the garlic to the bottom of a sterilised jar (page 33), then tightly pack the cucumbers in vertically, pushing the sprigs of dill down the sides. Pour the pickling liquid over the cucumbers, to cover completely, leaving 5cm from the rim of the jar. You'll probably have a little liquid left so keep it in the fridge for now. Cover the jar with muslin, or some breathable cloth (we've even used an old but clean pair of tights before!). Secure with a rubber band, or partially screw on the lid. The pickles will start the fermenting process so you need to leave some space for them to breathe.

Put the jar in a cool dark place, like a pantry, and let the pickles ferment for 4 days. During this time, bubbles of carbon dioxide gas will be visible inside the jar as the fermentation process kicks in. Check the pickles each day to make sure they are fully submerged, and if necessary, top up with the reserved pickling liquid. It's fine if the liquid looks a bit cloudy, however, you only need to worry if it looks dark or extremely cloudy – in that case, throw the pickles away and start from scratch.

After 4 days, taste a pickle. It should be crunchy, lightly sour, and salty. The flavour profile will change over time, so try them again over the next few days. When you're happy with the flavour, keep them in the fridge with the lid screwed on tightly; this will slow down the fermentation process and stabilise the flavour. The pickles will keep for up to 1 year in the fridge.

SERVES 4

THREE-PEPPER SALSA

This is a tasty little condiment that we had with some fish tacos in California. We like it served as a salad alongside our lamb and mutton barbecue; the rosemary and capers really cut through the gamey flavour of the meat.

1 small yellow bell pepper
1 small red bell pepper
2 fresh green jalapeños, deseeded and diced
1 celery stick, finely diced
2 tbsp finely chopped flat-leaf parsley
2 tbsp pitted green olives, sliced
1 tbsp capers, rinsed, drained and chopped
sea salt and freshly ground black pepper, to taste

For the Dressing
2 tbsp olive oil
1 tbsp red wine vinegar
1 tsp white sugar
juice of ½ lemon
1 garlic clove, very finely chopped
½ tbsp finely chopped fresh rosemary

If you can access the firebox of your smoker, put the bell peppers directly onto hot coals, turning frequently until charred all over. Alternatively, put the peppers directly on a gas hob over a medium flame, use tongs to turn them, until blackened all over. You could also rub a little oil into the skin of the peppers, and roast them on a baking tray in a preheated oven (200°C/400°F/gas mark 6) for 30–40 minutes, until the skin is blackened. When charred, put the peppers in ziplock bag and set aside for 10 minutes. Rub off all the charred bits. Cut the peppers open, remove the seeds and stalks and chop the flesh into small cubes.

Whisk the ingredients for the dressing, then toss through the peppers and remaining ingredients, and season to taste. Set aside for at least 15 minutes before serving.

SERVES 3–4

PICO DE GALLO

This salad is a perfectly simple and delicious fresh garnish to go with almost anything you make, from smoked to grilled meats and burgers or as a side dish. We can eat tons of this stuff and for our money it's the perfect salsa.

4 ripe tomatoes, deseeded and diced
½ red onion, finely diced
1 tbsp jalapeños from a jar, drained and finely chopped (or 1 fresh green jalapeño, deseeded and finely chopped)
2 garlic cloves, very finely chopped
small bunch coriander, roughly chopped
rind of ½ lime, chopped
juice of 1 lime
1 tbsp olive oil
pinch of caster sugar
sea salt and freshly cracked black pepper, to taste

Stir all the ingredients together in a bowl, cover then put it into the fridge to chill. You could do this the day before. About 20 minutes before you are ready to eat, take the pico de gallo out of the fridge and let it come up to room temperature before serving. Adjust the seasoning to taste, as necessary.

SIDES, PICKLES & BUNS

MAKES 2 X 500ML JARS

CANDIED COWBOY JALAPEÑOS

What's not to love about sweet and heat? These little suckers are addictive, so we recommend making a few jars. You can grow the chillies yourself, or buy locally, mid-summer, and make a big batch. If you use sterilised jars, they'll last for a year, though ours never last more than a few weeks.

1.25kg fresh green jalapeños, rinsed thoroughly
300ml cider vinegar
400g white granulated sugar
½ tsp turmeric
½ tsp celery seeds
4 garlic cloves, sliced
2 tsp black mustard seeds
1 tsp whole black peppercorns

To start, don a pair of disposable gloves – as always when handling chillies. Most people know the reasons why, as the result of going gloveless can later be excruciating! Start by removing the green stalks – they usually just peel off with a little pressure. However, if the jalapeños are very firm, simply trim the stalks off using a sharp paring knife. Cut into 3mm discs and set aside.

Combine the vinegar, sugar and 150ml water in a large, non-reactive pan over medium heat and bring to a simmer. Cook, stirring, for a few minutes until all the sugar has completely dissolved.

NB: Before you proceed, beware; when you add the jalapeños to the hot syrup they will release capsaicin (a.k.a. pepper spray). Please do not hover over the pan, and remember to turn on the overhead fan on your hob, if you have one, or open a window.

Add the jalapeños; the liquid will stop boiling. Bring to the boil again, wait for 30 seconds, then turn off the heat. This will pasteurise the jalapeños. If you wish, leave the jalapeños to boil a bit longer to reduce the overall spiciness. While hot, use a clean slotted spoon to divide the jalapeños between your sterilised jars (page 33). Pack in tightly and pour in the liquid. Poke around with a clean fork to get rid of any air bubbles and make sure the peppers are completely covered in liquid. Screw on the lid and refrigerate for at least 14 days to a month before eating. The longer you leave them, the better they taste. They will keep for 3 weeks once opened if stored in the fridge.

SIDES, PICKLES & BUNS

CHEDDAR JALAPEÑO CORNBREAD

SERVES 4-6

A staple in most Southern barbecue joints. The cornbreads we'd tried on our road trip ranged in texture from sweet, syrupy cake to light, crumbly bread. We like to add a little cheese and onion to ours, and jalapeños to give it a savoury profile and a moist texture. Apparently you should cook your cornbread in a hand-me-down family heirloom skillet, blackened with use and years of baking, imparting a flavour unique to that pan. Lucky you if you have one. If not, like us, use muffin trays or regular springform baking tins to make this recipe.

- 2 tbsp unsalted butter, plus extra for greasing
- 1 large onion, diced
- 2 cooked corn on the cob, husks removed, or 100g frozen corn kernels
- 4 large eggs, beaten
- 200g coarse polenta
- 125g fine cornmeal flour
- 200ml full-fat milk
- 50ml buttermilk
- 1 tsp baking powder
- 75g plain flour
- ½ tsp fine sea salt
- ½ tsp freshly ground black pepper
- 120g freshly grated medium Cheddar cheese
- 2 fresh green jalapeños, deseeded and finely chopped

Preheat your oven to 180°C/355°F/gas mark 4. Grease a 22cm cake tin with butter and line the base with baking parchment.

Melt the butter in a frying pan over medium-low heat and add your diced onion. Fry gently for about 15–20 minutes, until the onion is golden, sticky and caramelised.

Hold one cob upright on a chopping board and carefully run a small knife from the top of the cob to the bottom, cutting all the kernels off. Repeat with the second cob. Add the corn to the pan with the onions and cook for a further 5 minutes. Remove from the heat and set aside to cool for 15 minutes.

In a large bowl, add your eggs, the polenta and cornmeal flour, milk and buttermilk, baking powder, flour, salt and pepper and most of your grated cheese. Beat until well mixed, then stir in your cooled onion and corn mixture and the jalapeños. Pour into the prepared cake tin and bake for 20–25 minutes, until springy to touch.

Remove from the oven and allow the cornbread to cool in the tin for 15 minutes. Turn it out onto a wire rack or serving plate, then flip so the cheesy side is facing up. Cornbread should be served warm – we're not fans of the cold stuff. If you have any left over, it will keep well wrapped in foil for a couple of days. To reheat, put the bread, foil and all, in a medium-hot oven for 10 minutes.

SIDES, PICKLES & BUNS

Pretzel Buns

MAKES 8

We were the first to start selling these delicious buns in Wales at our streetfood events. We've stuffed them with everything from pastrami to Carolina-style pulled pork and buttermilk fried chicken. And in our opinion, a pretzel bun beats a brioche bun when it comes to being stuffed with barbecue any day of the week.

The buns have bite, but are soft, savoury and not too sweet, so they're robust enough to handle as much 'slaw, sauce and filling as you can throw in them. We spent almost two years trying to find a baker to make these the way we wanted. Eventually a French patisserie, based in Cardiff, nailed it for us. This is our recipe that they bake for us.

For the Dough
- 1 × 7g packet dried yeast
- 500g strong white flour, plus extra for dusting
- 2 tsp fine sea salt
- 2 tsp caster sugar
- 40g unsalted butter, melted

For the Poaching
- 30g bicarbonate of soda
- 1 tbsp malt extract

For the Glaze
- 1 egg, beaten
- coarse sea salt, to sprinkle

To make the dough, mix the yeast with 360ml lukewarm water (you want the water at 38°C) in the bowl of a stand mixer. Set aside to rest for 5–10 minutes until it starts to foam.

Now add the flour, salt, sugar and butter, and mix with the dough hook on a slow speed until thoroughly combined. The dough should come together in a smooth and silky ball that easily comes away from the sides of the bowl. (You can also make this dough by hand.)

Cover the bowl with a tea towel and let it rise in a warm place for 1 hour or until doubled in size.

Line two flat baking sheets with a silicone baking mat or baking parchment.

Use your fist to push down on the dough to remove some of the air, then turn out onto a lightly floured surface. Cut

SIDES, PICKLES & BUNS

the dough into eight pieces, each weighing around 130g. To shape, take a piece of dough and start forming a nice round, smooth ball by pulling the sides to the centre and pinching to seal the folds. By doing this, you're creating a smooth skin around the dough ball. Place, pinched side down, on the work surface and lightly cup your hand around the dough ball. Space evenly on the lined baking sheets, pinched seam side down, leaving at least 5cm between each roll.

Cover with a tea towel or lightly with cling film and let the buns rise in a warm place for 30 minutes until doubled in size.

Preheat the oven to 200°C/400°F/gas mark 6 and place your oven racks on the low and middle positions.

Next, we're going to poach the dough. This is what gives the pretzel buns that rich dark colour and helps to crisp up the surface. Fill a large pan with 1.5 litres water and bring to the boil over medium-high heat. Maintaining a gentle boil, slowly add the bicarbonate of soda and the malt extract and stir through. Reduce the heat to a simmer.

Working in batches of 3–4 at a time, carefully lower the rolls into the poaching liquid, seam side down. Poach for 30 seconds, then carefully use a slotted spoon to turn the roll over in the poaching liquid. Poach the other side for 30 seconds, then return to the lined sheets, seam side down. Repeat with the remaining buns, leaving at least 5cm between the buns for baking.

When all your buns are poached, mix together the egg and 2 tablespoons of water. Using a pastry brush, glaze each roll with the egg mixture, making sure to fully coat all sides. Top each roll with a sprinkle of coarse sea salt. With a very sharp straight-edged knife, cut a slash or 'X' (or a 'H' in our case) in the top of each roll. (This allows air to escape and the rolls to expand while baking.)

Bake the rolls for 17–20 minutes, rotating the trays halfway through baking – top to bottom, front to back – for even browning. Pretzel buns are easy to over-bake, so we recommend using an instant-read thermometer – the middle of a bun should read around 95°C/205°F when done.

Remove and transfer to wire racks to cool completely. The buns are best eaten on the day they are baked but they store pretty well in the freezer, tightly wrapped in cling film.

1. The Brioche Burger Bun (page 193)
2. The Kaiser Roll (page 192)
3. Pretzel Buns

MAKES 12 ROLLS

THE KAISER ROLL

The Kaiser roll is the perfect deli roll and one of our favourites to stuff with just about anything. Apparently it's named after Emperor (Kaiser) Franz Joseph I of Austria from the early 1800s. This equally regal Austrian bun made its way over to delis, cafés and restaurants with the European migrants as they settled in the States. It's also the perfect partner for serving with behemoth sandwiches as the firm texture helps you avoid a sloppy mess. Shaping the buns takes a little practice, but with a bit of patience, a gorgeous-looking roll will be your reward.

- 825g strong bread flour, plus extra for greasing
- 2 eggs, plus 1 egg white
- 30g dried yeast
- 2 tbsp vegetable oil, plus extra for greasing
- 2 tbsp malt extract
- 1½ tsp fine sea salt
- 2 tbsp white sugar

CURRIED KAISER

We like to switch up the flavour profile of these rolls from time to time. Try adding in a teaspoon of mild curry powder. The taste won't be too strong, but there will be a lovely aroma and a pretty cool colour from the turmeric, too.

Combine the bread flour with 430ml lukewarm water, 2 whole eggs, yeast, vegetable oil and malt extract in the bowl of a stand mixer fitted with the dough hook. Mix on low speed for about 5 minutes or until blended. Add the salt and sugar, increase the mixer speed to medium, and mix for about 8 minutes, or until the dough begins to pull away from the sides of the bowl, feels elastic and gives some resistance. (You can also make this dough by hand.)

Lightly oil a large bowl and scrape in the dough. Cover the bowl with cling film and set aside somewhere warm to prove for about 1 hour.

Lightly flour a work surface. Uncover the dough and divide it into 12 x 115g balls on the floured surface. Cover with cling film and rest for 15 minutes. Line two flat baking sheets with silicone baking mats or baking parchment.

Uncover the dough and, if necessary, lightly flour the work surface. Press on the dough to release some air and carefully roll each round into a long sausage shape, about 30cm long. Working with one piece at a time, form each length into a loop, crossing the ends with the right end being on the bottom. Pull the right end up and over the centre of the loop and then push it under in the same direction. The left loop should now be pointing right. Take the left end and pull it up and under the central hole and then connect it to the other end. You should now have a roll that is rather like a rosette. Place six rolls, seam side down, onto each of the prepared baking sheets. Cover with cling film and leave to rise for 1 hour.

About an hour before you are ready to bake the rolls, preheat the oven to 190°C/375°F/gas mark 5.

In a small bowl, whisk the egg white with 1 teaspoon cold water for 1–2 minutes, until frothy. Brush the egg mixture on the rolls. Bake for 20–24 minutes, or until the rolls are golden brown and crisp. Remove from the oven and transfer to a wire rack to cool.

The Brioche Burger Bun

MAKES 8 BUNS

This is a pretty ubiquitous burger bun right now and we can see why it's so popular. Not only do they look great with their glazed tops, but the flavour – and density – can take on the most unctuous of fillings. Making brioche is a skill; it combines cake-baking techniques and bread-baking precision. But it's worth it for the buns. They taste better than shop bought (of course), and you can add brioche to your arsenal of awesome cooking skills.

325g strong flour
50g dried milk or dried skimmed milk
2 tbsp unrefined caster sugar
1¼ tsp fine sea salt
1 tablespoon dried yeast
3 large eggs, plus 1 egg separated
3–4 tbsp lukewarm water
10 tbsp unsalted butter

To Sprinkle (optional)
onion seeds
sesame seeds
sea salt flakes

Start by putting all the ingredients for the dough, apart from the 1 egg white, in the bowl of a stand mixer fitted with the dough hook. (It's not recommended that you mix this by hand as you'll be pummelling and kneading away for a solid 30 minutes. If you have a bread maker with a 'dough cycle', then use that, which will save you from all the effort of mixing and scraping the dough on your stand mixer.) Mix on medium speed for about 15 minutes, scraping the dough down the side of the bowl to ensure it's fully incorporated, until the dough is smooth and elastic. Put the dough in a large ziplock bag, and allow the dough to rise for 1 hour. Transfer to the fridge overnight.

The next day, line two flat baking sheets with silicone baking mats or baking parchment. Split the dough into 8 equal amounts (we like to weigh each portion) and roll them into balls. Use your hands to squish each ball flat (or use a rolling pin), about 3cm thick. Transfer the discs to your baking sheets, making sure you leave at least 10cm between each disc. Cover and let the buns rise and prove for a while. On a cold day, this can take 2–3 hours, but on a warm day, about 1 hour. You're looking for them to puff up and start to peel away from the baking sheet a little.

As you wait for the buns to prove, whisk up the reserved egg white with 1 teaspoon of cold water until frothy. When you're ready to bake, brush this solution on the top before baking. Feel free to add any sprinkles like onion seeds, sesame seeds, salt flakes or whatever you fancy.

Preheat your oven to 190°C/375°F/gas mark 5. Put your buns on the middle shelf and bake for 18–20 minutes. To check if they are done, insert a digital thermometer – it should read about 88°C/190°F. It's really easy to over-bake brioche, so keep an eye on them by sight and with your thermometer. When they're cooked, transfer to a wire rack and let them cool completely before making your epic burger with your homemade brioche.

SIDES, PICKLES & BUNS

Road Trip

TEXAS

There's a purity to Texas barbecue. Here, barbecue is revered and protected, and is predominantly beef-centric. From the unwavering loyalty to a preferred wood type, to simplicity of the rub ingredients and dedication to the bovine, Texas produces a very distinctive and delicious type of barbecue. Forget what we thought we knew, this is where the beef barbecue rulebook was written.

Around the mid-19th century, Central Texas was populated by German and Czech settlers who brought with them European-style meat markets selling cuts like brisket, beef shoulder and sausages. These influences and cuts shaped the iconic barbecue joints of Lockhart, Luling and Taylor that produced some of today's most celebrated pit masters.

Austin is the jewel in the Texan crown. This town had everything we were looking for: a thriving streetfood scene, world-class barbecue and live music. Top of our hit list was the revered Franklin Barbecue. Being good students of the school of barbecue, we knew the line at Franklin's would be in full swing by 8 a.m. Up and at 'em on a brisk Texas morning and with coffee in hand, we were in the line by 7.45 a.m. There were 120 people in front of us already. Birthday groups, locals with a day off and tourists a plenty... A while later a woman with a clipboard went down the line asking everyone what they wanted. She put us down for a little of everything: 'Might as well, since you're here, girls.'

We finally reached the front of the line at 1 p.m.; that's over 5 hours waiting for barbecue. There's not a lot to be said about Franklin Barbecue, other than it was definitely, hands down, the most perfect plate of barbecue we've ever eaten. In fact, while we type these words, over two years later, we're still salivating over the most well executed, balanced, moist barbecue we've encountered. The brisket was the show-stopper. So that's what it was supposed to taste like: beefy, thick crust of bark, juiced dripping from the slice and yielding without falling apart.

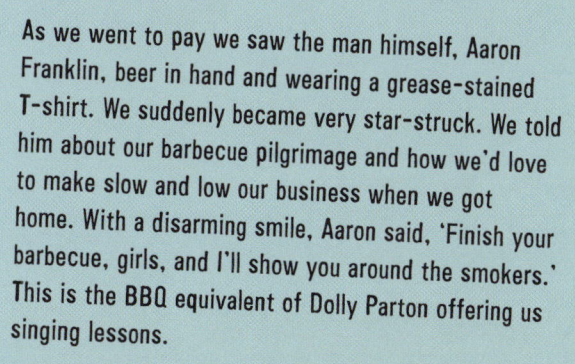

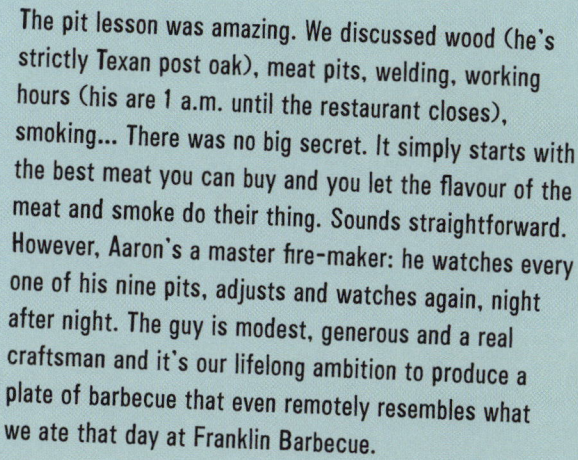

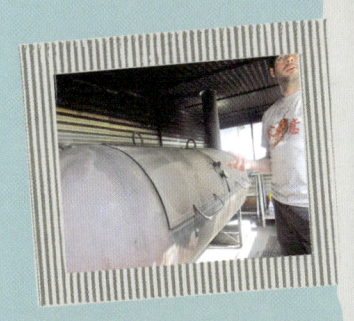

As we went to pay we saw the man himself, Aaron Franklin, beer in hand and wearing a grease-stained T-shirt. We suddenly became very star-struck. We told him about our barbecue pilgrimage and how we'd love to make slow and low our business when we got home. With a disarming smile, Aaron said, 'Finish your barbecue, girls, and I'll show you around the smokers.' This is the BBQ equivalent of Dolly Parton offering us singing lessons.

The pit lesson was amazing. We discussed wood (he's strictly Texan post oak), meat pits, welding, working hours (his are 1 a.m. until the restaurant closes), smoking... There was no big secret. It simply starts with the best meat you can buy and you let the flavour of the meat and smoke do their thing. Sounds straightforward. However, Aaron's a master fire-maker: he watches every one of his nine pits, adjusts and watches again, night after night. The guy is modest, generous and a real craftsman and it's our lifelong ambition to produce a plate of barbecue that even remotely resembles what we ate that day at Franklin Barbecue.

TEXAS
CONTINUED

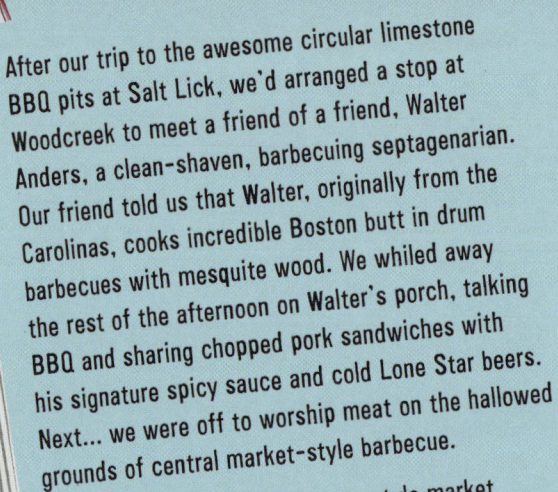

After our trip to the awesome circular limestone BBQ pits at Salt Lick, we'd arranged a stop at Woodcreek to meet a friend of a friend, Walter Anders, a clean-shaven, barbecuing septagenarian. Our friend told us that Walter, originally from the Carolinas, cooks incredible Boston butt in drum barbecues with mesquite wood. We whiled away the rest of the afternoon on Walter's porch, talking BBQ and sharing chopped pork sandwiches with his signature spicy sauce and cold Lone Star beers. Next... we were off to worship meat on the hallowed grounds of central market-style barbecue.

Lockhart is the home of German-style market barbecue. On our list were Kreuz, Smitty and Blacks, three joints that were the result of a Schmidt family 'bar-b-feud' many years ago, so it's no coincidence that they serve practically the same meats from the same-looking pits in the same-looking environment. But just like all barbecue restaurants, customers know the subtle, nuanced differences and declare their loyalty through their palates and wallets. These places are like museums of barbecue, producing vast hunks of meat tantamount to works of art.

In Luling it's all about the City Market, and it was here that we finally had some Texas hot links (spicy beef sausages, essentially) that suited our palates. We'd found most of what we'd had so far gritty and greasy compared to the smooth British banger, with a tendency to spurt hot oil when you bite into it. Here the beef sausage was really good: the meat kept its integrity when we bit in and the casing snapped satisfyingly.

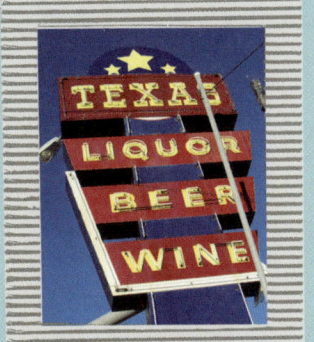

Our next date was in Houston to meet a guy called 'Red Rich'. Rich was organising a big cookout for the annual Houston Livestock Show and Rodeo and suggested we come along. Five foot tall, full of charisma and extensive barbecue knowledge from being part of a competition team called 'Old Dirty Basters', Red asked us to get involved in preparing the hundreds of kilos of brisket that needed to be smoked ready for the Houston Livestock Show and Rodeo. Before we knew it men, women and children were hulking in the 100 USDA briskets, getting them trimmed and rubbed and ready for the smokers. The two smokers were absolutely huge, almost 3 metres by 3 metres. These were a world apart from the static, red brick pits we'd seen in Salt Lick and City Market. They used hickory pellets that were ignited at the back in a firebox, creating pure wood smoke that internal fans would push around the rotisserie grates. They 'hacked' the smokers by adding extra wood chunks into the fireboxes to crank up the flavour. We had such a fun time and to this day it's the most smoked meat we've seen anywhere.

DRUM
AND
DRUM

IKIGO
SCROLL

SERVES 1

STAY PUFT

While sitting around the campfire, it's nice for adults to have a treat alongside the children. The stay puft is a classic flip made with peaty whisky and marshmallows. The peat of the whisky conveys the smokiness of S'mores and cuts through the sweetness of the marshmallow.

- 2 or 3 marshmallows
- 50ml peaty whisky
- 1 generous tbsp Vanilla Gomme Syrup (see below)
- 1 egg yolk
- 2 dashes Angostura bitters
- ice cubes

First, thread your marshmallows onto a cocktail stick and toast until brown and golden.

Next, combine the remaining ingredients, except the ice, in a shaker and shake vigorously for 45 seconds. When you shake without ice, this is called 'dry shaking' and allows the ingredients to gain volume and texture. Then add the ice and shake for an additional 45 seconds. Double strain into a chilled low-ball or cocktail glass and garnish with toasted marshmallows.

BARTENDER'S TIP:

Try putting vanilla pods in a container with the egg/s you will use in the recipe above; the eggs will be infused with vanilla flavour. You can reserve the vanilla-infused egg whites for a drink like a sour or a gin fizz, to minimise wastage.

MAKES 500ML

VANILLA GOMME SYRUP

- 220g granulated sugar
- 500ml water
- 2 drops liquid smoke
- 2 vanilla pods, split lengthways

THERE ARE TWO WAYS TO MAKE GOMME:

If you have a few days' preparation time: Add the ingredients to a glass container. Seal and refrigerate. Give the jar a few good shakes each day for 4 days to help dissolve the sugar. Strain to remove the vanilla pods and keep the gomme in the fridge for up to 2 weeks.

If you are short on time: Heat the ingredients in a saucepan over medium-low heat, and stir for 5 minutes, until the sugar has completely dissolved. Don't let it boil. Take care to check that sugar doesn't burn – this can happen fairly rapidly. Strain to remove the vanilla pods and keep the gomme in the fridge for up to 2 weeks.

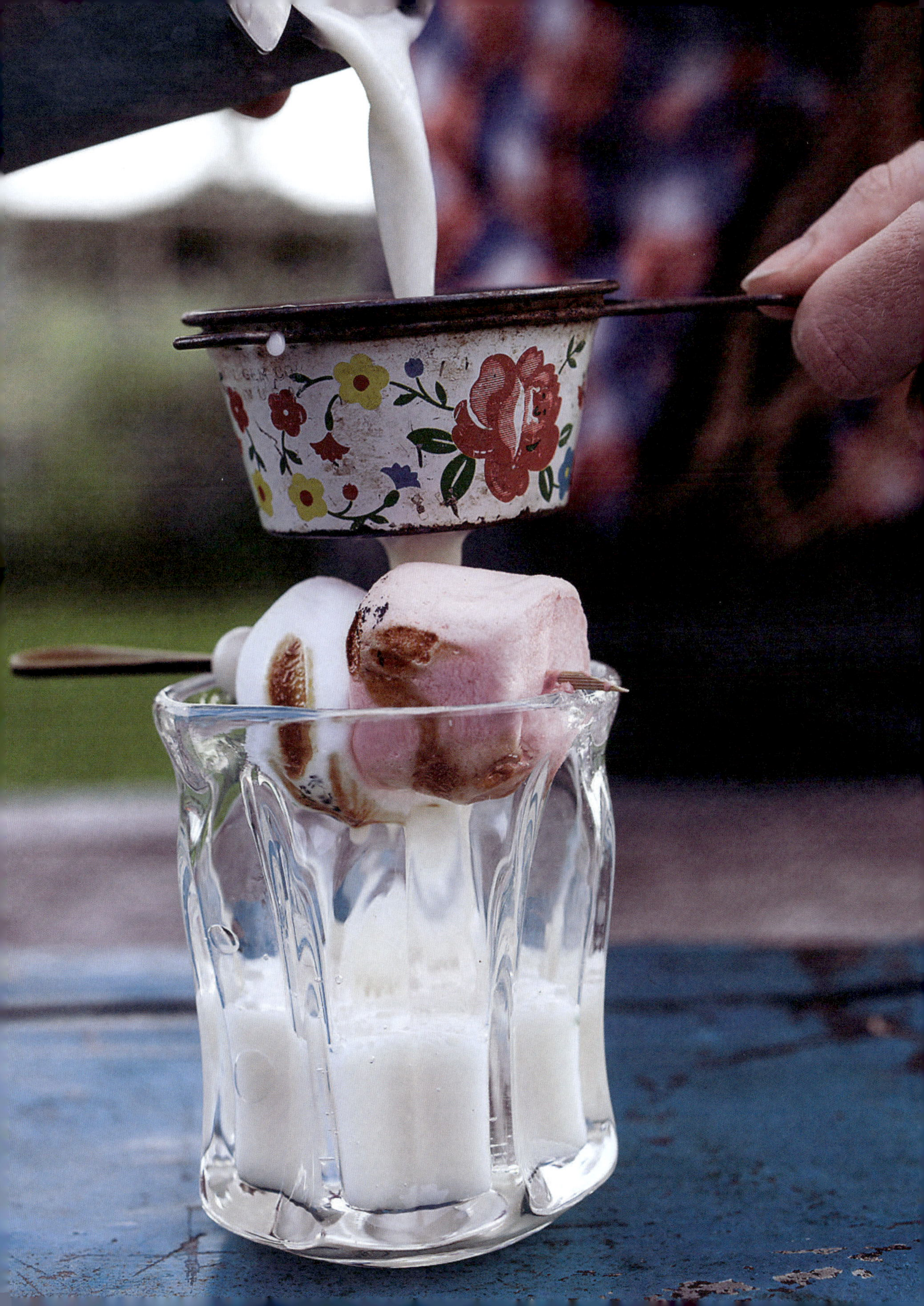

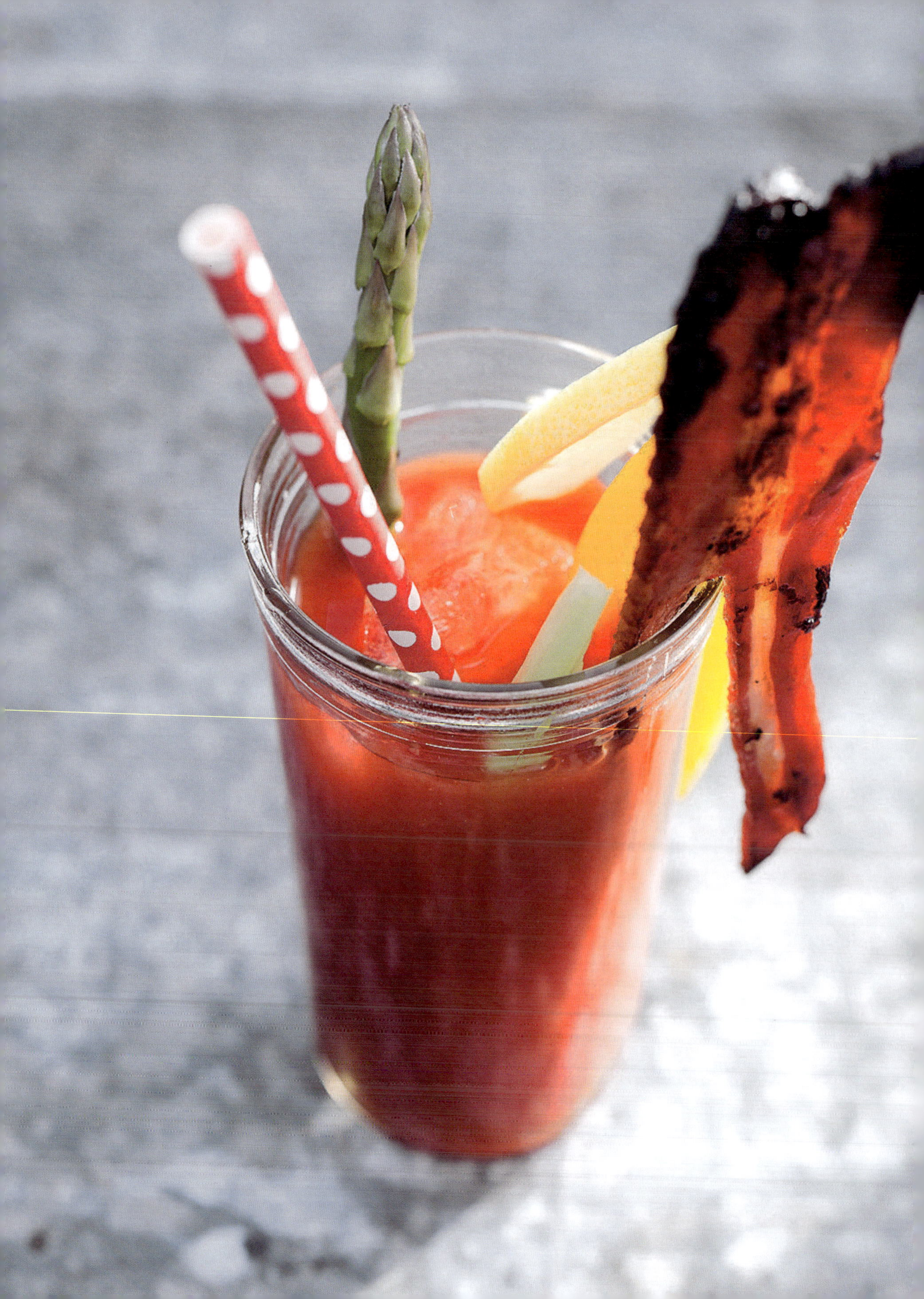

SERVES 1

MEATY BLOODY MARY

To supplement the smoked meat section of this book, we thought it would be fitting to add a meat-infused cocktail. This is a vodka-based Bloody Mary, but you can substitute the vodka for gin if you'd prefer. Infusing the vodka for the cocktail is great way to pack flavour punch. It's good to remember that alcohol is a solvent that strips flavours from anything it's put in contact with; this is best proven with the peppercorns and meat in this recipe. Leftover Bloody Mary-infused vodka can be used as a marinade for meats, base for mussels or clams in a stew or in spaghetti sauce.

fine sea salt, celery salt or smoked salt

ice cubes

50ml Bloody Mary-infused vodka (see below)

125ml fresh tomato juice with a pinch of salt, or shop-bought tomato juice

2 tsp lemon juice, plus extra for rim of the glass (optional)

For the Bloody Mary-infused Vodka (makes 700ml)

700ml vodka

200g fatty cooked meat (bacon works well), chopped

1 tbsp Worcestershire sauce

1 tbsp tabasco

10 whole black peppercorns

1 celery stick, roughly chopped

½ onion, roughly chopped

2 tomatoes, roughly chopped

2 pieces pared lemon rind

For the Garnish (use whatever you have)

lemon wedges

celery stalks

red pepper slices

asparagus spears

green beans

grilled bacon rashers

First, make the infused vodka. Decant your vodka into a 2-litre container and add the remaining ingredients. Allow the mixture to infuse at room temperature for 4–5 hours then put in the freezer for at least 12 hours.

Strain the liquid and discard the solids. You now have spiced bloody Mary-infused vodka.

This is another building cocktail. For an added touch, rub lemon around the rim the glass and dip it in some salt. Put some ice in the glass, pour in the bloody Mary-infused vodka, tomato and lemon juice, and give it a good stir. Finish with the garnishes.

DRINKS & DESSERTS

SERVES 1

Watermelon Sunrise

Watermelon is a staple of the American Deep South. It is healthy, flavoursome and tastes delicious in both sweet and savoury settings. The sweetness of the lime and vanilla oleo complements the smokiness of the mezcal and allows the watermelon to shine. Oleo-saccharum involves extracting the zesty oils from citrus peel and was commonly used in 19th-century bartending to add citrusy flavour and aroma to drinks. Substitute any citrus fruit to the same effect.

For the Lime and Vanilla Oleo-Saccharum (makes 150ml)

5 limes
1 vanilla pod, split in half lengthways
150g white sugar

For Each Cocktail

smoked salt, for the rims of the glasses
lime wedges
ice cubes
75ml watermelon juice
50ml Mezcal (very smoky is best)
25ml lime juice
15ml lime and vanilla oleo-saccharum (see above)
75ml fresh watermelon juice
watermelon wedges, to garnish

First prepare the oleo-saccharum. Use a vegetable peeler to pare the zest from the limes, leaving most of the white pith behind, and put the peels in a ziplock bag along with the vanilla pod and sugar. Set aside the zested limes for your cocktail. Seal the ziplock bag and use a rolling pin to bash the ingredients until the peels begin to release their oils. Leave to macerate for at least 30 minutes, or ideally a few hours. In this time, the sugar will extract the oils from the lime peel to make a fragrant liquid. Strain the peels in a sieve lined with muslin into a bowl. You have your oleo.

This is a building cocktail, which means that you can make it all in one glass, leaving minimal mess.

First, juice your reserved limes and strain using a tea strainer to get rid of all the pips. Sprinkle smoked salt on a saucer and run a lime wedge around the rim of a highball glass before dipping into the salt. Add three ice cubes. Add your ingredients in the order given on the left and stir with a spoon. Garnish with watermelon wedges.

PUNCH BOWL

If making a few cocktails, use a whole watermelon and hollow out the flesh for the juice, then save the husk to use as a punch bowl. Also, watermelon rinds can be pickled so as not to waste.

204 DRINKS & DESSERTS

SERVES 1

MINT JULEP PUNCH

A mint julep is a powerful cocktail that combines fresh mint with bourbon. For a mellowed-out drinking vibe while still enjoying the flavour of a classic cocktail, count the number of imbibers and multiply the below recipe to make a mint julep punch.

fresh mint leaves, plus extra sprig to garnish
ice cubes
50ml bourbon
25ml mint cordial (see below)
100ml brewed mint tea, cooled

For the Mint Cordial (makes about 500ml)

220g white sugar
20g fresh mint leaves

For the mint cordial, combine the sugar with 500ml water in a saucepan. Set over low heat and stir for about 3 or so minutes to dissolve the sugar, taking care not to let it come to the boil. Once the sugar has dissolved, turn off the heat and add the mint leaves. Cover and leave the syrup to infuse at room temperature for 4–5 hours or, ideally, overnight. Strain. Keep the syrup in the fridge for up to 2 weeks. Leftover cordials are great for making non-alcoholic drinks, desserts or sorbets.

This is a building cocktail. Roughly crush the fresh mint leaves in the bottom of a lowball glass. Add a generous amount of ice. Add the bourbon, mint cordial and tea. Give it a good stir with a swizzle stick. Garnish with the fresh mint sprig.

BARTENDER'S TIP:

If you're preparing *a lot* of this punch a day or so ahead of time, put some fresh mint directly in the bourbon bottle.

DRINKS & DESSERTS

LEMON CHESS PIE

SERVES 6-8

This sweet citrus dessert could almost be the American cousin of the French tarte au citron. It's found on the dessert menu of many a Southern smokehouse and a great way to finish your barbecue meal. No one really knows why it's called 'chess pie'; one suggestion is that it is 'chest' pronounced with a drawl, because these pies are baked with so much sugar they could be stored in a pie chest rather than refrigerated! Another story is of the plantation cook who was asked what she was baking that smelled so great – 'Oh, it's Jess' pie' was her answer. The pie can be made a day ahead and served at room temperature.

For the Pastry

225g plain flour, plus extra for dusting
1 tsp fine sea salt
100g cold unsalted butter, diced, plus extra for greasing
3 tbsp buttermilk, chilled

For the Filling

200g white sugar
100g soft light brown sugar
2 tbsp polenta
1 tbsp plain flour
5 large eggs, beaten
150ml buttermilk
50g unsalted butter, melted
3 tbsp fresh lemon juice
grated zest of 1 lemon
1 tsp vanilla extract
pinch of salt

First, make the pastry. Preheat the oven to 200°C/400°F/gas mark 6. Grease a 22cm loose-bottomed tart tin. Tip the flour and salt into a mixing bowl, add the cold butter and toss to coat with the flour. Using your fingertips, rub the butter into the flour, lifting it up as you do so to keep it light and cool. Continue until the mixture resembles breadcrumbs, about 10 minutes. Give the bowl a shake, and any larger lumps of butter will come to the surface. Add the cold buttermilk and mix with a round-edge knife until the mixture starts to come together. Put the dough onto a work surface dusted very lightly with flour. Knead the dough lightly to form a smooth ball. Dust the rolling pin lightly with flour, roll out the dough using short sharp strokes to avoid stretching, and give the dough a quarter turn each time you roll to keep the shape. Roll out to about 5cm larger than the tin. Lift the pastry up, drape over the rolling pin and carefully place on top of the tin. Using your fingers, press the dough into the tin, being careful to patch up any holes. Prick the base then chill for 30 minutes.

Line the pastry case with baking parchment and fill with baking beans. Bake for 18 minutes, then carefully remove the paper and beans. Continue to bake the pastry case for a further 5 minutes, until lightly browned (this is called baking blind). Remove from the oven and, using a small sharp knife, carefully trim off the excess pastry. Allow the pastry case to cool completely.

Meanwhile, preheat the oven to 200°C/400°F/gas mark 6 and make the filling. In a medium bowl, combine the sugars, polenta and flour. In a large bowl, whisk the remaining ingredients; the mix will curdle but that's OK. Slowly add the dry ingredients, mixing well after each addition. Pour the filling into the cooled pastry case and bake for 1 hour–1 hour 15 minutes, until the filling is set around the edges but wobbles slightly in the centre. Allow the pie to cool completely on a wire rack then cover and refrigerate. This is best served at room temperature.

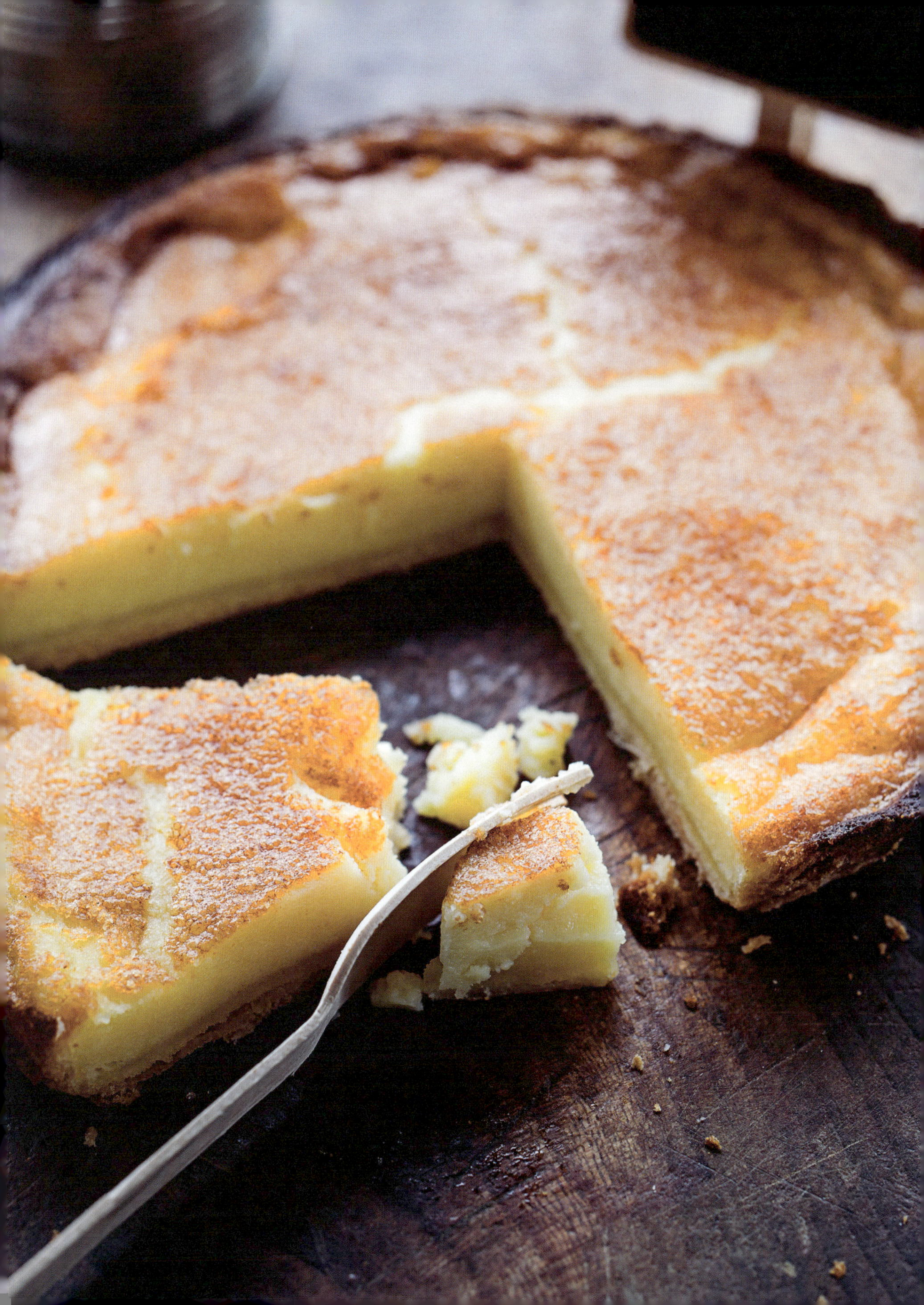

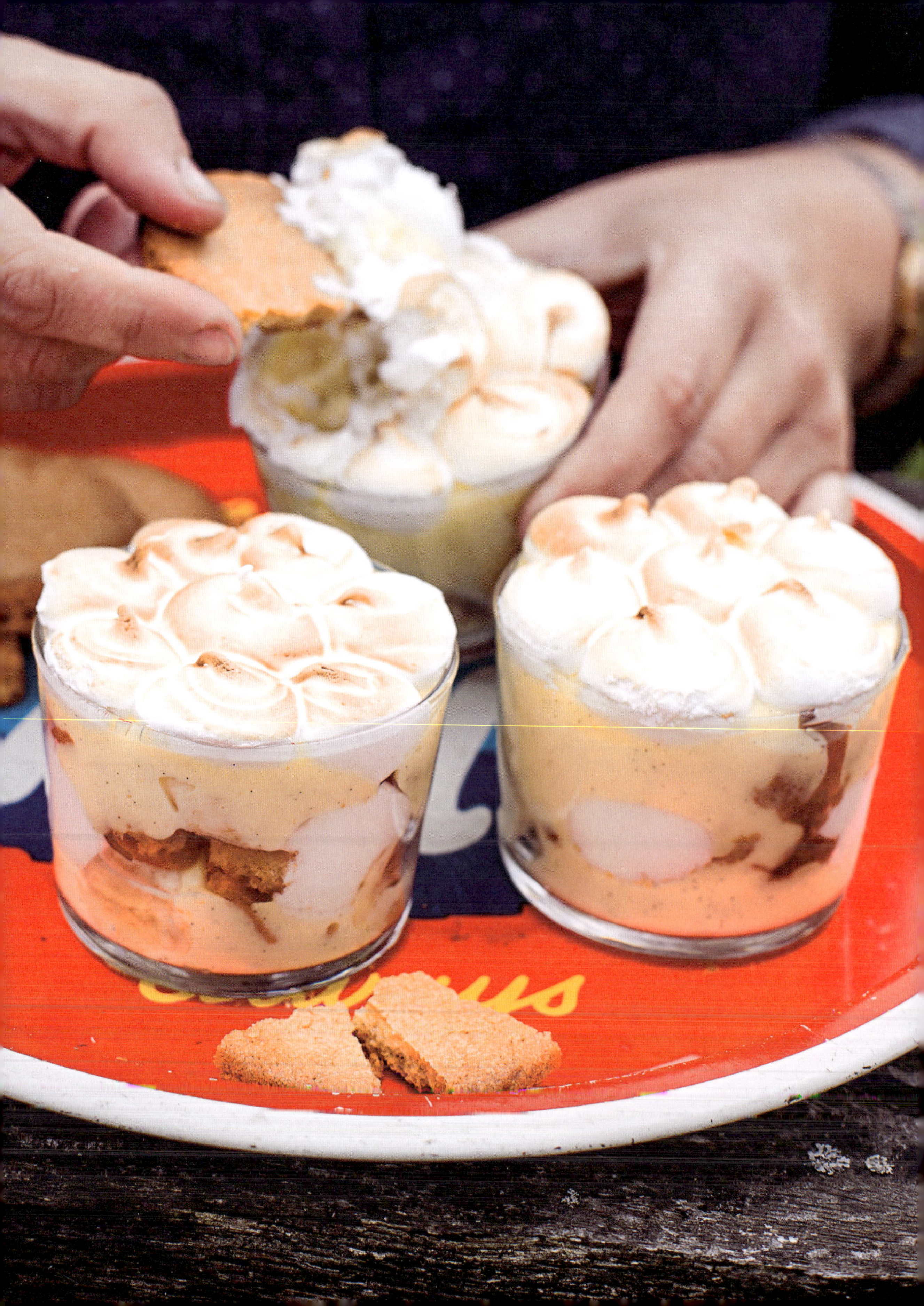

SERVES 6

Banana Pudding

This is one of the most comforting desserts ever invented. It's served in so many barbecue restaurants where, aside from the banana, most of the ingredients come straight out of a packet. That doesn't matter one bit because these creamy custard and banana flavours really work after a meat feast. You can make our version in a big tray batch and set it down in the middle of the table for everyone to dive in.

For the Biscuits

175g softened unsalted butter
200g caster sugar
2 large eggs
1 tsp vanilla extract
400g plain flour, plus extra for dusting
1 tsp baking powder
1 tsp fine sea salt

For the Pudding

50g plain flour
½ tsp fine sea salt
1 litre full-fat milk
1 x 400g tin condensed milk
2 egg yolks, lightly beaten
1 tsp vanilla extract
3 ripe bananas, cut into 3mm slices

For the Meringue

4 egg whites
115g caster sugar
115g icing sugar

First, make the biscuits. Preheat the oven to 180°C/350°F/gas mark 4. Line a baking sheet with baking parchment. Cream the butter and sugar together until pale and creamy, then beat in the eggs, a little at a time, and vanilla extract.

In a separate bowl, combine the flour, baking powder and salt. Gently fold the dry ingredients into the butter and egg mixture. If the mixture feels too sticky to roll out, add a little flour. Halve the dough, form into two fat discs, wrap each disc in cling film and rest in the fridge for 1 hour.

Remove the dough from the fridge and sprinkle a work surface with flour. Place a disc of dough on the surface and sprinkle a little more flour on top. Roll the dough to a thickness of about 5mm. Use a 7cm biscuit cutter to cut the dough into rounds and place them, about 2cm apart, on the prepared baking sheet. Bake for 8–12 minutes, by which time the biscuits should be lightly golden around the edges. Cool on a wire rack.

For the banana pudding, heat the oven to 160°C/320°F/gas mark 3. In a medium saucepan, combine the flour and salt and set over medium heat. Gradually whisk in the milk, condensed milk and egg yolks and cook, stirring constantly, for 8–10 minutes, or until thickened to a custard consistency. Remove from the heat and stir in the vanilla extract. Allow to cool to room temperature.

Next, make the meringue. Use a stand mixer or electric whisk to beat the egg whites until they are foaming. Add the caster sugar, one teaspoon at a time, beating for 2–4 minutes until stiff peaks form and the sugar dissolves. Sift in the icing sugar and using a metal spoon, fold gently into the whisked egg whites.

In a baking dish, pie dish or individual dishes, arrange a third of the banana slices, followed by a third of the pudding mixture and third of the biscuits. Repeat the layers two times, then smooth the meringue over the top. Bake for 15–20 minutes, until the meringue is golden. Cool for 30 minutes then serve.

LAVA CAKES

MAKES 4 CAKES

These lava cakes are a great treat and ever so quick to make, especially if the ingredients are prepared in advance. Cooked on a cranking hot grill, we're sure this sweet treat will satisfy that chocolate craving!

250g softened unsalted butter, plus extra for greasing
115g good-quality dark chocolate (70% cocoa solids)
2 large eggs
50g caster sugar
1 tbsp plain flour

To Serve

icing sugar, for dusting
whipped cream
handful of mixed berries of your choice

First, grease a 4-hole muffin tin with a little butter.

Melt the chocolate and 250g butter in a bowl set over a pan of simmering water, stirring until smooth and well blended. Remove from the heat to allow to cool briefly.

In a large bowl, whisk the eggs and the sugar until pale and fluffy, about 10 minutes. Slowly fold in the warm chocolate and butter into the whisked eggs, until smooth. Add the flour and mix to make sure all the ingredients are well blended. Pour the chocolate mixture into the greased tin. At this stage, you can keep the muffin tin with the mixture in the fridge for a couple of hours if you're not ready to cook the cakes immediately.

Prepare the grill for indirect cooking over medium heat. You'll need to crank up the heat up to about 200°C/400°F to make sure you get a good bake on the cakes. (You could cook them in the oven at this temperature.)

Put the muffin tin in the grill and close the lid for 10–12 minutes (or bake in the oven). If you've taken the tin straight out of the fridge, you might want to give it closer to 15 minutes. You'll know when the lava cakes are ready as the tops should have a little crust, be firm and when the tin is wiggled, the mixture should not move. The centre is supposed to be runny like 'lava' and slightly uncooked. Take out of the grill or oven and let the cakes rest in the tin for about 10 minutes.

When ready to serve, run a small flexible knife around the edge of each cake. Put a plate large enough to cover all the cakes on top, hold the tin and plate firmly and flip over to invert the cakes onto the plate. Tap the bottom of the tin to help loosen the cakes from their holes. Dust the lava cakes with a little icing sugar and transfer them to individual plates. Serve with berries and whipped cream.

KEY LIME PIE

SERVES 6–8

Key lime pie was supposedly born in the early 20th century when refrigeration was scarce, so condensed milk was used a lot in cooking. Legend has it that the famous pie was created with what the Florida sponge fisherman had to hand: a tin of condensed milk, limes and crackers. Today, it's beloved by many and is even the official state pie of Florida.

10 digestive biscuits
120g unsalted butter, melted, plus extra for greasing
2 tbsp runny honey
fine salt

For the Filling
¼ tsp sea salt
1 x 400g tin condensed milk
4 large egg yolks
125ml fresh lime juice (from about 3 limes)
1 tsp finely grated lime zest

For the Topping
500ml double cream
3 tbsp runny honey
finely grated lime zest (optional)

Preheat the oven to 180°C/350°F/gas mark 4. Place the biscuits in a ziplock bag and use a rolling pin to crush them gently. Put the crumbs in a large bowl and stir to combine with the butter, honey and a small pinch of salt. Grease a 23cm round loose-bottomed tin or pie dish with butter. Pour the crumb mixture into the prepared tin and use your fingers to press it down evenly to form a crust on the bottom and the sides. Bake for 15 minutes, then remove from the oven and allow to cool.

Meanwhile, combine the condensed milk, egg yolks, lime juice and zest in a large bowl. Mix well. Pour into the cooled pie crust, then bake for 15 minutes, or until set. The surface should have a 'just set' wobble to it. Remove and cool to room temperature. Chill in the fridge for at least 4 hours, but preferably overnight.

When ready to serve, beat the cream and honey together for the topping until stiff peaks form. Using a spatula, evenly spread the whipped cream on top of the pie and garnish with the additional lime zest, if desired. Slice and serve.

DRINKS & DESSERTS

APPLE & BLUEBERRY SOUTHERN FRIED PIES

MAKES 6-8 PIES

The closest thing we'd eaten in the UK to one of these tasty little creations was a certain, gloopy, apple dessert made by a well-known burger chain. You know, the one that painfully blisters your tongue if eagerly ingested. That being our experience, the thought of eating a molten sugar pie after a meaty plate of barbecue did not appeal. However, with fried pies or 'pocket pies' being such a Southern staple, we had to give a few a go.

1 litre vegetable oil, for deep-frying
icing sugar, for dusting
vanilla ice cream, to serve

For the Pastry

500g plain flour, plus extra for dusting
½ tsp fine sea salt
225g cold unsalted butter, diced

For the Filling

1 sweet apple, peeled, cored and diced
1 tsp grated orange zest
1 tbsp cornflour
1 tbsp soft light brown sugar, or more to taste
½ tsp ground cinnamon
400g blueberries

SCARED TO FRY?

If you're watching those calories or don't fancy standing over hot oil you can bake the pies in the oven. Line a baking sheet with baking parchment, brush the pies with a little egg wash or milk and bake for 15-20 minutes in an oven preheated to 180°C/350°F/gas mark 4.

Start by making the pastry. Sift the flour into a large bowl and add the salt. Add the butter, toss to coat in the flour, and using your fingertips, rub it into the flour until you have fine breadcrumbs. Add 2-3 tablespoons of cold water, just enough for the dough to come together. Wrap the dough in cling film and refrigerate for 1 hour.

To make the filling, put the apple, orange zest, cornflour, sugar, cinnamon and 1 tablespoon of water in a saucepan. Cook over low heat for 10 minutes, stirring occasionally. Now add 300g blueberries and cook for 7-10 minutes, using the back of a spoon to mash up the blueberries as they soften. At this point, the sauce will be thick and chunky. Add the remaining blueberries and continue to cook for 5 minutes over low heat. Take off the heat and let the mixture cool down while you prepare your pie pastry for filling.

Take the dough out of the fridge and place on a lightly floured surface. Use a rolling pin to roll out your dough until it's about 3mm thick. Take a tea plate, or a saucer, that's about 10-12cm in diameter and use this as a cutting guide. Cut your rounds and place them to one side.

In a large, heavy-based pan, heat the oil to 180°C/350°F, and use an instant-read thermometer to keep an eye on this. You may need to adjust the heat source as necessary to keep the oil at a steady temperature.

To assemble the pies, moisten the outer edge of the pastry with water. Place a heaped tablespoon of pie filling in the middle. Fold in half, and, using the back of a fork, press well to seal the edges. When all your pies are made, you are ready to fry them, two at a time. Carefully drop one pie into the hot oil – you'll see the edges start to brown after 30 seconds – flip the pie over for another 20 seconds. Remove the pie and drain on kitchen towel. Repeat with the remaining pies until done. Serve dusted with a little icing sugar alongside vanilla ice cream.

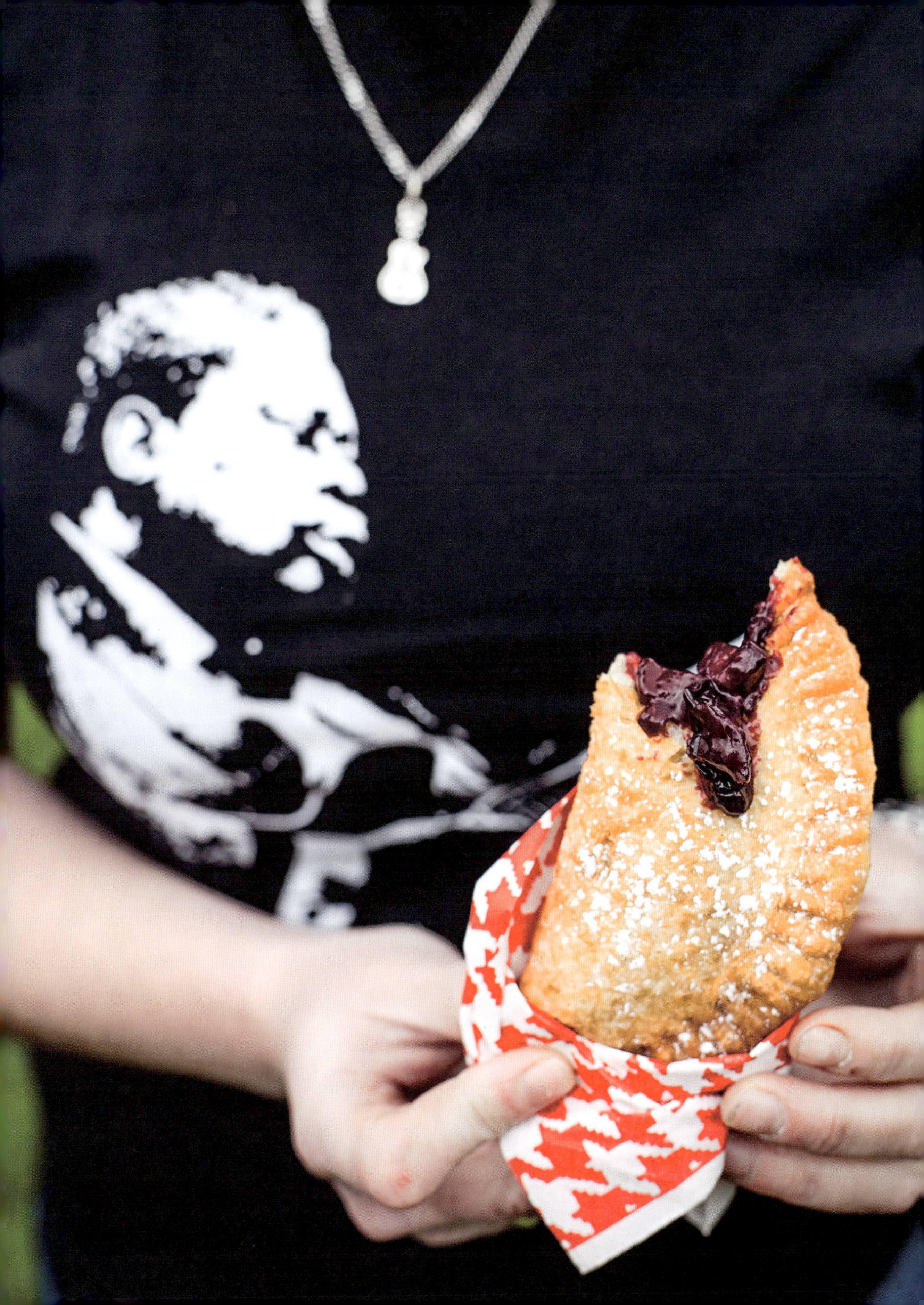

SERVES 6–8

PUMPKIN PIE

Pumpkin pie is a traditional sweet dessert often eaten for Thanksgiving and Christmas in the United States and Canada. Pumpkin is a symbol of harvest time and this pie celebrates that time of year with its spiced, warming notes and creamy filling. In the US and increasingly in the UK, you can buy tins of pre-made pumpkin pie filling, which makes the recipe a doddle.

For the Pastry

- 225g plain flour, plus extra for dusting
- 1 tsp fine sea salt
- 100g cold unsalted butter, diced
- 3 tbsp buttermilk, chilled

For the Filling

- 1 x 400g tin of pumpkin pie filling
- OR
- 750g pumpkin, peeled and cut into 5cm cubes, seeds reserved
- 1 tsp ground nutmeg
- ½ tsp ground ginger
- 2 tsp ground cinnamon
- 3 tbsp caster sugar
- 2 tbsp maple syrup
- 2 large eggs, beaten
- 275ml double cream

First, make the pastry. Preheat the oven to 200°C/400°F/gas mark 6. Grease a 22cm loose-bottomed tart tin.

Tip the flour and salt into a mixing bowl, add the cold butter and toss to coat with the flour. Using your fingertips, rub the butter into the flour, lifting it up as you do so to keep it light and cool. Continue until the mixture resembles breadcrumbs, about 5–10 minutes. Give the bowl a shake, and any larger lumps of butter will come to the surface. Add the cold buttermilk and mix with a round-edge knife until the mixture starts to come together. Gather the dough with your hands, wiping it round the bowl to pick up any stray pieces. Put the dough onto a work surface dusted very lightly with flour. Knead the dough lightly to form a smooth ball. Dust the rolling pin lightly with flour and roll out the dough using short strokes. Roll out to about 5cm larger than the tin and to the thickness of a pound coin. Lift up the pastry, drape over the rolling pin and carefully lay it on top of the tin. You can use a small piece of dough to press it into the tin. Prick the base with a fork then chill for 30 minutes.

Line the pastry case with baking parchment and fill with baking beans to weigh the pastry down. Place the tin on a baking sheet and bake for 15 minutes, then carefully remove the paper and beans. Continue to bake the pastry case for a further 5 minutes, until lightly browned (this is called baking blind). Remove from the oven and, using a small sharp knife, carefully trim off the excess pastry. Allow the pastry case to cool completely.

Once the pastry has cooled, make the filling if not using tinned. Reduce the oven to 180°C/350°F/gas mark 4.

DRINKS & DESSERTS

Arrange the pumpkin cubes in a shallow roasting tray in a single layer. Sprinkle with the nutmeg, ginger and cinnamon. Cover the tray tightly with a double layer of foil and bake for 45 minutes until soft and caramelised. Remove from the oven and allow the pumpkin to cool.

When the pumpkin has cooled, transfer to the bowl of a food processor. You should have about 600g cooked pumpkin flesh. (Don't forget to scrape out the sticky bits in the tray, too.) Blitz until smooth, then transfer to a bowl. Add 2 tablespoons of the sugar, the maple syrup and eggs. Mix well and stir in the cream. Pour into the cooled pastry case and bake for 45 minutes.

While the pie is baking, rinse the reserved pumpkin seeds in water to remove the stringy bits. Pat dry with kitchen towels and then lay them flat on a baking sheet lined with baking parchment. Sprinkle with the remaining 1 tablespoon caster sugar and bake in the oven with the pie during the final 10 minutes, until the seeds are crispy.

Remove the pie and the seeds from the oven. Leave the pie to cool, then sprinkle with the candied seeds. Serve warm or at room temperature, with cream or ice cream.

DRINKS & DESSERTS

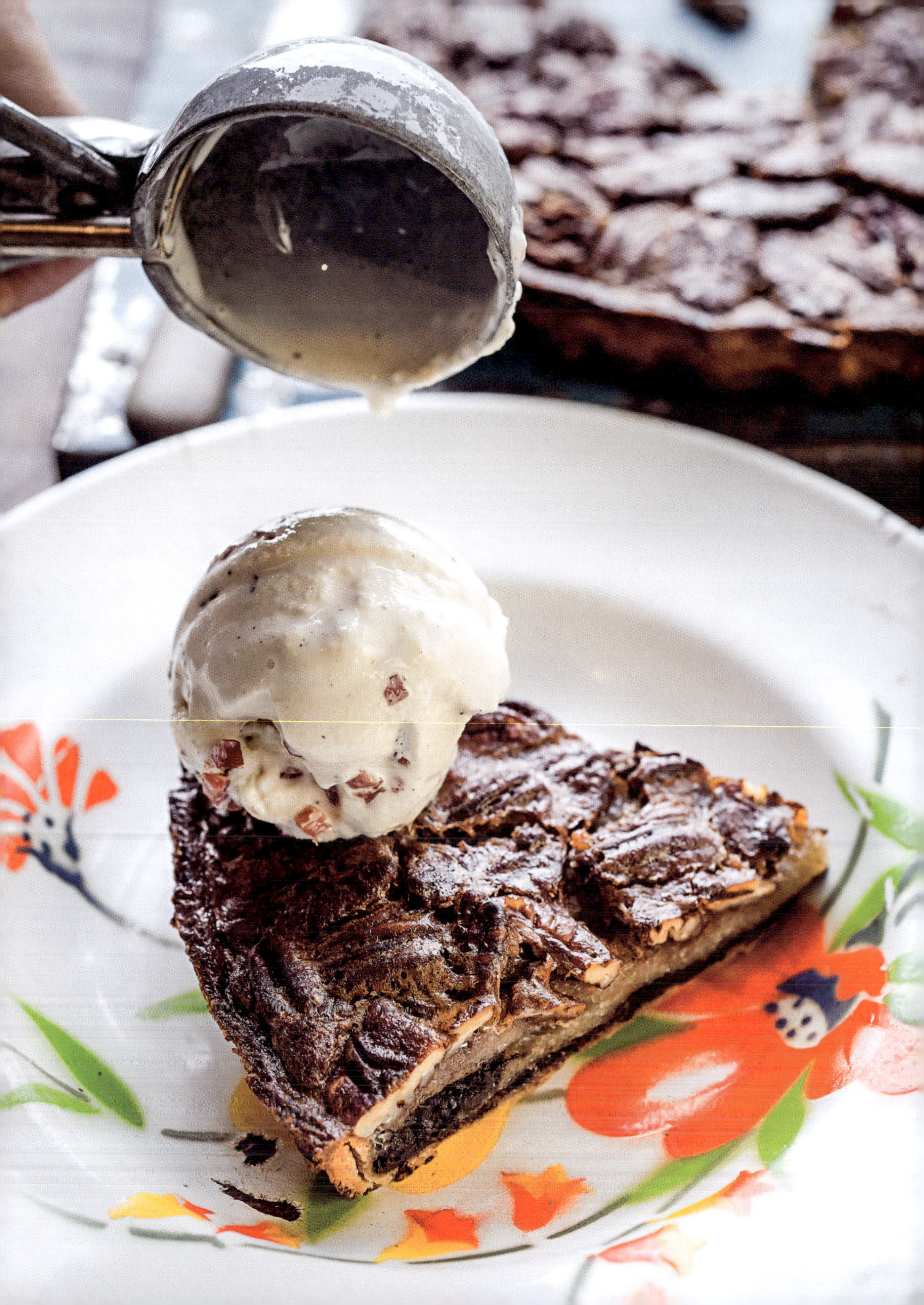

PECAN PIE

SERVES 6-8

What better symbol of the South than a sticky nutty piece of pecan pie? It graces festive spreads from New England to California. We had proper, Southern-style pecan pie at our first Thanksgiving dinner. It was a decadent way to end a decadent meal and we fondly recall hunting for some when we had the munchies later that night after a few glasses of wine!

- 75g softened unsalted butter, plus extra for greasing
- 100g caster sugar
- 175g golden syrup
- 175ml maple syrup
- 3 large eggs, beaten
- ¼ tsp fine sea salt
- ½ tsp vanilla extract
- 400g pecan halves
- 250ml double cream, whipped, to serve

For the Shortcrust Pastry

- 225g plain flour, plus extra for dusting
- 100g cold unsalted butter, diced
- ½ tsp salt

Start by making the pastry. Preheat the oven to 190°C/375°F/gas mark 5. Sift the flour into a large bowl, add the butter and use your fingertips to rub the butter into the flour, until the mixture resembles fine breadcrumbs. Stir in the salt, then add 2–3 tablespoons of cold water, or just enough to form a firm dough. On a floured surface, gently knead the dough for 1–2 minutes, until smooth. Wrap the ball of dough in cling film and chill for 30 minutes.

Grease a 23cm springform tart tin with butter. Roll out the dough on a lightly floured surface to a round that is just a bit larger than 23cm and 3–4mm thick. Drape the pastry over the rolling pin, and carefully transfer to the prepared tart tin. Gently push the pastry into the corners of the tin. Let the pastry hang over the sides a little. Prick the base with a fork and chill for 30 minutes, or until firm.

Line the pastry case with baking parchment, fill with baking beans and bake for 17–20 minutes. Remove the beans and parchment and cook for a further 5–10 minutes, until the pastry is golden. Use a small knife to trim off the overhanging pastry at this stage. Leave to cool for 20–30 minutes while you prepare your pecan filling. Increase the oven temperature to 200°C/400°C fan/gas mark 6.

In a bowl, beat the butter and sugar together with an electric whisk until light and fluffy. With the beaters still going, pour in both of the syrups. Gradually add the beaten eggs, followed by the salt and vanilla extract, and mix until combined. Stir through 200g of the pecans and pour the mixture into the cooled tart case. Use the remaining pecans to make a circular pattern on the surface of the tart, following the shape of the tin.

Bake for 10 minutes, turn the heat down to 160°C/275°F/gas mark 3 and continue to bake the tart for a further 30–35 minutes. The pie should be golden brown but the filling should wobble a little in the middle. Leave to cool in the tin for 15 minutes before serving with whipped cream.

PIMP MY PECAN

There are all sorts of ways to add another flavour dimension to the humble pecan pie. You can add melted chocolate to the pastry base or a shot of bourbon into the mix when you add the syrups, or a few tablespoons of peanut butter to make it double nutty. If you want to get super-decadent, make some bacon ice cream to serve with your pie as we have.

DRINKS & DESSERTS

DARK MOLASSES GINGERBREAD CAKE

SERVES 6-8

This rich, impressive cake was served up to us when we went to a friend's house for dinner in Tennessee. Its pitch black, moist sponge perfectly complements the white, cream cheese frosting.

200g unsalted butter, cut into chunks, plus extra for greasing
350g blackstrap molasses
150g soft light brown sugar
75g white sugar
220g plain flour
2½ tsp bicarbonate of soda
½ tsp fine sea salt
2 tsp ground ginger
½ tsp ground cinnamon
2 tsp espresso coffee powder (optional)
1 tsp vanilla extract
2 large eggs, beaten
375ml full-fat milk

For the Cream Cheese Icing

200g full-fat cream cheese, at room temperature
50g plain flour
225g white sugar
¼ tsp fine sea salt
225ml full-fat milk
1 tsp vanilla extract

Preheat your oven to 180°C/350°F/gas mark 4, or set up your grill for indirect heat (no wood necessary). Lightly butter two 22cm springform cake tins and line them with baking parchment.

Melt the butter in a saucepan set over medium heat. As the butter melts, whisk in the molasses and sugars. When the butter is liquid and the sugar crystals have dissolved, give it a final stir, then set aside to cool. (The molasses will slightly separate from the melted butter – this is fine.)

In a large bowl, use a clean dry whisk to combine the flour, bicarbonate of soda, salt, ginger, cinnamon, and espresso powder if using. Whisk the vanilla, eggs and milk into the pan with the molasses and melted butter, until completely combined. Add to the bowl of dry ingredients and whisk thoroughly to combine, making sure there are no lumps.

Divide the thick batter between the prepared tins and bake (or grill) for 45–50 minutes, or until a cocktail stick poked into the centre of the cakes comes out clean. Let the sponges cool for 20–30 minutes, then carefully remove the cakes from the tins and cool completely on a wire rack.

To make the icing, whip the cream cheese in the bowl of a stand mixer (or use an electric whisk) on high speed for 6–8 minutes, until completely smooth and silky.

Whisk the flour, sugar and salt in a small saucepan. Set over medium heat and slowly add the milk, whisking constantly, until it begins to the boil. It will look lumpy at first but whisk vigorously to create a smooth paste. Simmer for 1 minute – the mixture will thicken rapidly – then scrape the flour and milk paste into a bowl. Beat using your electric whisk or in a stand mixer for 8–10 minutes, until it becomes light and cooled. Slowly add the whipped cream cheese and vanilla extract, beating continuously until well combined, smooth and silky. It is best to let this icing firm up a bit more in the refrigerator but you can use it now to ice a completely cooled cake.

Spread half of the icing on one side of your cooled sponge and top with the other sponge to make a sandwich. Put the rest of the icing in a piping bag and pipe onto the cake in an appealing pattern. You're now ready to slice and serve.

16

INDEX

Page numbers in *italics* indicate illustrations separated from recipe entries

A

apples
   apple & blueberry Southern fried pies 212
   chorizo & apple stuffing 82–3
   crab apple butter 33

B

bacon
   bacon jam 30
   down-home smoked bacon 80–1
banana pudding 209
batter: hush puppies 160
beans
   Hang Fire's pit beans 144
   red beans & rice with tasso & andouille sausages 162
beef
   beef ribs 94
   braised & smoked cheeks 106
   brisket & burnt ends 92–3
   brisket chilli 159
   Hang Fire's AA bacon cheeseburger 114–15
   pastrami 112
   salt beef 111
   smoked feather blade steak 110
   smoked forerib 108–9
   steaks 100–5
   Texas hot links 96–7
   whisky boys' tri-tip 98–9
beer: hush puppies 160
beetroot: Lexington style red slaw with beets 150
black-eyed peas: Hoppin' John 170
blue cheese dip 74
bone marrow butter 47
bourbon: mint julep punch 205
bread *see also* buns
   Cheddar jalapeño cornbread 189
brine 127
briquettes 21
brisket & burnt ends 92–3
brown ale: brisket & burnt ends 92–3
buns
   the brioche burger bun 193
   the Kaiser roll 192
   pretzel buns 190–1
burgers
   Hang Fire's AA bacon cheeseburger 114–15
   perfect pork & halloumi burgers 85
buttermilk dressing *147*, 151
butters
   bone marrow butter 47
   chilli & smoked garlic butter 33
   crab apple butter 33
   hasselback potatoes with brown butter 156

C

cabbage *see* slaws
cakes
   dark molasses gingerbread cake 218
   lava cakes 210
charcoal
   grilling 18–19
   smoking 21, 23
cheese
   blue cheese dip 74
   Cheddar jalapeño cornbread 189
   Hang Fire's AA bacon cheeseburger 114–15
   perfect pork & halloumi burgers 85
   Swansea Jack mac & cheese 174
chicken
   cola hot wings 120
   Hang Fire yardbird 119
   Mai-Thai thighs 124
   red jambalaya with smoked chicken, andalouille & shrimp 165
   smoked chicken lollipops 123
chillies
   brisket chilli 159
   candied cowboy jalapeños 188
   Cheddar jalapeño cornbread 189
   chilli & smoked garlic butter 33
   chilli jam 31
   green chilli stew 178
   Louisiana hot sauce *37*, 41–4
chipotle peppers
   blackberry chipotle barbecue sauce *37*, 39
   sweet chipotle barbecue sauce 36
chorizo & apple stuffing 82–3
cider: country-style pork ribs with West Country cider liquor 63
coffee: mocha rub 28
cola hot wings 120
coleslaw *see* slaws
competitions 68, 116
condiments *see also* jam; sauces
   chermoula 44
   Louisiana-style remoulade 45
   rustic harissa 46
cucumber
   bread & butter pickles 182
   half-sour pickles 186
curing: down-home smoked bacon 80–1

D

desserts
   apple & blueberry Southern fried pies 212
   banana pudding 209

dark molasses gingerbread
     cake 218
key lime pie 211
lava cakes 210
lemon chess pie 206
pecan pie 217
pumpkin pie 214–15
dips
   blue cheese dip 74
   Kentucky-style 136–7
drinks
   meaty Bloody Mary 203
   mint julep punch 205
   stay puft 200
   watermelon sunrise 204
dry shake: Memphis dry
   shake 29
duckstrami 128

E
equipment 10–11

F
fennel
   fennel pear & apple slaw with
     buttermilk dressing
     147, 151
   pickled fennel & celery 185
flavour profiles 81

G
gomme syrup, vanilla 200
greens: Southern style barbecue
   greens with pork 179
grilling 18–19
gumbo: shrimp & tasso file
   gumbo 169

H
ham
   Cuban mojo ham hock 73
   shrimp & tasso file
     gumbo 169
   tasso ham 89
harissa, rustic 46
herbs *see* rubs; seasonings

J
jalapeños *see* chillies

jam
   bacon jam 30
   chilli jam 31
jambalaya: red jambalaya with
   smoked chicken, andalouille
   & shrimp 165

K
kebabs: aloha boyo grilled lamb
   kebabs 138

L
lamb
   aloha boyo grilled lamb
     kebabs 138
   grilled butterflied lamb leg
     with Kentucky mop
     sauce 136–7
   smoked lamb shoulder 133
lava cakes 210
laverbread: Swansea Jack mac
   & cheese 174
lemon chess pie 206
limes: key lime pie 211

M
macaroni: Swansea Jack mac &
   cheese 174
'meat stall' 65
money muscle 70
mustard: South Carolina
   Mustard sauce *37*, 38

O
onions
   bread & butter pickles 182
   twenty-four hour party
     pickles 184

P
pancetta: maple bourbon
   barbecue sauce *37*, 40
pecan pie 217
peppers *see also* chillies
   maque choux 173
   three-pepper salsa 187
pesto: chimichurri 32
pickles
   bread & butter pickles 182
   half-sour pickles 186

pickled fennel & celery 185
twenty-four hour party
   pickles 184
pies *see* desserts
pineapple chow-chow 181
pork *see also* bacon; ham; ribs;
   sausages
   braised & smoked
     cheeks 106
   competition pulled
     pork 68–70
   green chilli stew 178
   hot pig wings 74
   maple bacon weaved pork
     tenderloin with chorizo
     & apple stuffing 82–3
   North Carolina-style pulled
     pork 64–5
   perfect pork & halloumi
     burgers 85
   smoked pork belly 86
   smoked pork chops with West
     Indian style salsa
     verde 72
   Southern style barbecue
     greens with pork 179
potatoes
   German-style potato salad
     with oregano
     dressing 155
   hasselback potatoes with
     brown butter 156
   Southern-style potato
     salad 154
Prague Powder #1: 77
prawns
   étouffée 166
   shrimp & tasso file
     gumbo 169
pumpkin pie 214–15

R
rabbit: Kentucky burgoo 177
relishes
   Miss Daisy's chow-chow relish
     180
   pineapple chow-chow 181
remoulade, Louisiana-style 45
ribs, beef 94
ribs, pork
   baby back ribs 61
   country-style pork ribs with

West Country cider liquor 63
king ribs 86
St Louis-style spare ribs 57–8
rice
　Hoppin' John (rice & beans) 170
　red beans & rice with tasso & andouille sausages 162
　red jambalaya with smoked chicken, andalouille & shrimp 165
road trips 8–9
　Kansas 116–17
　Kentucky 130–1
　Louisiana 140–1
　Tennessee & the Carolinas 48–51
　Texas 194–7
roux 166
rubs
　competition rub 68–70
　garden rub 28
　Hang Fire almost all-purpose rub 26
　mocha rub 28
　overnight lamb rub 133
　Texas Grindhouse rub 26
　yardbird rub 28

S

salads *see also* slaws
　German-style potato salad with oregano dressing 155
　Southern-style potato salad 154
salsa
　pico de gallo 187
　salsa verde 72
　three-pepper salsa 187
sauces
　Alabama white barbecue sauce *37*, 38
　blackberry chipotle barbecue sauce *37*, 39
　burger sauce 114–15
　chermoula 44
　cola barbecue sauce 120
　Hang Fire's homestyle ketchup 35
　Hang Fire smokehouse barbecue sauce 45
　Kentucky mop sauce 136–7
　Louisiana hot sauce 41–4
　maple bourbon barbecue sauce *37*, 40
　South Carolina Mustard sauce *37*, 38
　sweet chipotle barbecue sauce 36
sausages 77
　andouille sausage 76–7
　chaurice sausages 78
　red beans & rice with tasso & andouille sausages 162
　Texas hot links 96–7
seasonings
　Louisiana seasonings 29
　Memphis dry shake 29
slaws
　classic Asian slaw 152
　fennel pear & apple slaw with buttermilk dressing *147*, 151
　Lexington style red slaw with beets *147*, 150
　Serbian slaw *146*, 148
　sure fire slaw *146*, 149
smoke rings 23
smokers 12–17
　building 12–16
　care of 17
　types of 13
smokestacks 13, 14, 16, 23
smoking 20–3
spices *see* rubs; seasonings
steaks
　cooking 104–5
　toppings for 105
　types of 100–3
stew
　étouffée 166
　green chilli stew 178
　Kentucky burgoo 177
stick burning 20
stuffing, chorizo & apple 82–3
sweetcorn
　Cheddar jalapeño cornbread 189
　hush puppies 160
　maque choux 173
syrup: vanilla gomme syrup 200

T

tasso ham *see* ham
tomatoes
　Hang Fire's homestyle ketchup 35
　meaty Bloody Mary 203
　Miss Daisy's chow-chow relish 180
　pico de gallo 187
turkey crown & whole turkey 126

V

venison: Kentucky burgoo 177
vodka: meaty Bloody Mary 203

W

watermelon sunrise 204
whisky
　stay puft 200
　whisky boys' tri-tip 98–9
wood 20–2
　types of 22

We'd like to thank a bunch of people for helping us on our journey so far. It may be a cliché but it's true, we couldn't have done it without you:

Both our amazing families; the Guinns and the Evanses and our close friends for their unwavering belief and support. Cath and Pete for giving us our first chance at The Canadian. All the pubs and bars in Cardiff that gave us residencies; Binki, Cerys, Tom & Gwyn at The Lansdown, Dan & Dave at Porters, Steve Bines & The Full Moon crew, Nat at BrewDog and Sean & Serge at The Pilot. Smudge Mark, our best pal and Hang Fire Smokehouse employee of the month (every month). Sign maker, guitar player, photo taker and generally awesome friend, Matthew 'Cookie' Cook. Our streetfood crew and kitchen takeover team; Rhi-Rhi Gill, Haybales, Cotton Eye Chlo, Darren & Emma Croquewich, Mo, Rhian 'Dance with me' Jones, Dave Moll and Jamie the lumbersexual plus Jo 'TOAST' Chittenden, Cath 'Pink' Kerry and Little Andy Williams, our gay artist in residence.

Consistently superb produce from the Farmers Pantry in Llantwit with great service from Dawie, Paul (pig wings?), Len and Simon. Special 'Diolch yn fawr' to Gaynor and Rhodri from Rosedew Farm for all their support and the loan of their barn (we smoked the mice out!). Laurian Veaudour at Cocoricco Patisserie in Cardiff, a MOF in the making if ever there was and his amazing team of patisserie perfectionists. Lynsey Maguire and the team at McGowans for printing us lovely stuff. Phil Chappell for landing us in Llantwit (it's all your fault). Turner & George for incredible British meats and top notch service. Our lovely Matt Fresh for delivering our fruit and veg with a laugh and a smile – we've still got your Grandmaster Flash CD! Erica Duffy, the UK's finest mixologist and world's most interesting person, that is a fact, thank you for all your hard work and willingness to do pretty much anything we need! Ivan and Toni for always bailing us out when we've over committed and their unwavering and constant support (and tequila nights!).

Gareth 'Boardy' for teaching us all how to weld and giving up so much free time to help us.

Eira for all her amazing homemade goodies. Sue 'the brew' Hayward (Waen Brewery) for our 3 fantastic beers and hopefully all our future beer colabs. Donna & Sonia, and the butcher boys of Bridgend; Dean & Andrew, we love your enthusiasm and support! The Penylan Pantry girls – Mel & Jo, you're both bonkers and we love you! Jack and his lovely family at Elephant & Bun Deli for their support. David ap John Williams & Business Wales. Rolant Tomos & Cywain.

The kilos and kilos of beautiful smoking wood and A-grade hardwood lumpwood from Marvellous Matt at Oxford Charcoal Co. Our meat would remain raw and unsold without you!

Macs BBQ for all their fantastic products, Ian McKend in particular, for always being on hand to support us whatever crazy gig we're doing and with what we need. You're a star, mate.

Pedro Donavan for being THE Hang Fire champion and heading up our fan club (currently with one member). Kath for hilarious life affirming nights in the Welcome Chest. Tech pal, Lisa for always looking at ways we streamline our business with her code writing sorcery. P.Dilly because everyone needs a ginger princess to chew a beef bone with.

Our pals Debby, Lily Pie, Evan, Carol and of course, Brian (we love and miss you), Ben, Lisa and the kiddy winks. Our loyal vegetarians, vegan and flexitarians: Julian, Roaul, Tamsin, Alex, Cath, Tom, Fran, Rani and Shane. Ellie (who Makes Music with Laura, Joni & Nick) and the James Family; 'Hey' Jude. Pops and Brother Ben. Julie Catflaps, Marty McFly and Charlie.

All the good people of Llantwit Major who have been amazingly supportive (and inquisitive) and welcomed us to their beautiful town. Big shout out to everyone at our second home, The Old Swan Inn, that have welcomed us, bruised, battered and thirsty from gigs, listened to our business woes and helped us on our quest for consistent alcoholism!

Team Cowshed for always having our back and getting this book deal-a-rollin' and Sarah Lavelle and everyone at Quadrille Publishing for spotting our potential very early on and helping us share our story. Anita Mangan, one of the most creative and inspirational designers we've worked with, who never travels without a felt parrot on a stick in her pocket (you never know, right?).

The BBC Food Programme and the Food & Farming Awards 'Hello, I'm' Sheila Dillon, Paula McIntryre, Giorgio Locatelli, Dan Saladino, Claire Salisbury & Radio Anna. This book wouldn't have been possible without your very wise and correct judgement!

The people that helped us in our journey across the States: Our wonderful friend Kevin 'Kevlar' Redman. Elizabeth Anderson, Steve 'Daddy' Turner, Pat and Harvey, Bill Kenner, Gerry and Debby, Vivi and family, Daisy and Tony, The Blankenships and Nanananana and all of our good friends in the Fernvale Hollar including Elliot, a great pit boss! The Whisky Row boys, Jennifer, Piers and Daniel, The Carolina Bitches A.K.A Mandy and Eva. Countess Vicy, lovely Dayna & Teo. Melissa B our Austinian. Thank you for the music Mark, Shannon, Henry and Scrappy aka The Cheeksters. All the pit masters that let us ask questions and hang out and explained why they do what they do. In particular Aaron Franklin who was hugely generous with his time (and smoked beer).

The bloggers that have written about us regularly, eloquently, factually correct and with decent grammar: Gourmet Gorro, Plate Licked Clean, Grill & Barrell, Kitchen Klonc.

The Welsh press in particular, Wales Online, who always have our backs and are great champions of independent businesses in Wales.

The Pickle Belly Newts (may they rest in peace...for now).

Dolly Parton, Gillian Welch, Alison Krauss, Big Mama Thornton and The Carter Family for soundtracking our lives.

....

Publishing Director **Sarah Lavelle**
Creative Director **Helen Lewis**
Project Editor **Laura Herring**
Art Director & Designer **Anita Mangan**
Cover Design **Gemma Hayden**
Photographer **Paul Winch-Furness**
Design Assistant **Ewa Lefmann**
Food Stylists **Samantha Evans, Shauna Guinn, Rukmini Iyer**
Prop Stylist **Rachel Jukes**
Production **Steve McCabe**, **Vincent Smith**

This edition first published in 2019 by Quadrille, an imprint of Hardie Grant Publishing

Quadrille
52–54 Southwark Street
London SE1 1UN
quadrille.com

Text © Samantha Evans and Shauna Guinn 2016
Photography © Paul Winch-Furness 2016
Additional road trip photography © Samantha Evans and Shauna Guinn 2016
Illustrations © Anita Mangan 2016
Design and layout © Quadrille Publishing 2016

The rights of the author have been asserted. All rights reserved. No part of this book shall be reproduced, stored in a retrieval system, or transmitted by any means – electronic, mechanical, photocopying, recording, or otherwise – without written permission from the publisher.

Cataloguing in Publication Data: a catalogue record for this book is available from the British Library.

ISBN: 978 178713 425 6

Printed in China

Additional photography:
P2–3 Huw John Photography
P6 (pic of burger) Biscuit Pictures
P12 ALS Photography
P14–15 Biscuit Pictures
P17 ALS Photography
P40 Huw John Photography
P97 (pic of Shauna) Huw John Photography
P107 Huw John Photography
P115 (pic of Sam) Huw John Photography
P191 Matthew Horwood